BACCHANALIA
REVISITED

To Dad,

on the occasion of

Christmas, Nineteen hundred
and Eighty-two.

Happy holidays and don't
drink too much! Ha. Ha!

Love,

Jess

BACCHANALIA REVISITED

WESTERN CANADA'S BOOZY SKID TO SOCIAL DISASTER

JAMES H. GRAY

Western Producer Prairie Books
Saskatoon, Saskatchewan

Copyright © 1982 by James H. Gray
Western Producer Prairie Books
Saskatoon, Saskatchewan

Printed and bound in Canada by
Modern Press
Saskatoon, Saskatchewan

Cover design by John Luckhurst/GDL

Western Producer Prairie Books publications are produced and manufactured in the middle of Western Canada by a unique publishing venture owned by a group of prairie farmers who are members of Saskatchewan Wheat Pool. From the first book published in 1954, a reprint of a serial originally carried in the weekly newspaper, *The Western Producer,* to the book before you now, the tradition of providing enjoyable and informative reading for all Canadians is continued.

Canadian Cataloguing in Publication Data

Gray, James H., 1906-
    Bacchanalia revisited

    Includes index.
    ISBN 0-88833-093-6

    1. Liquor problem - Prairie Provinces.
2. Temperance. I. Title.
HV5306.G69   362.2'92'09712   C82-091236-0

Vice is a monster of so frightful mien
as to be hated needs but to be seen;
Yet seen too oft, familiar with her face,
We first endure, then pity, then embrace.

Alexander Pope, "Essay on Man".

CONTENTS

PREFACE   ix

Chapter One
EVERYBODY KNOWS THE TROUBLE WE SEE   1

Chapter Two
PROHIBITION: THE FACTS AND THE MYTHOLOGY   14

Chapter Three
BACK TO THE BOTTLE, RELUCTANTLY   30

Chapper Four
MANITOBA BOOTLEGGERS CAME WITH REPEAL   46

Chapter Five
THE THIRSTY THIRTIES BROUGHT CHEAP BOOZE   59

Chapter Six
FIGHTING THE WAR ON THE LIQUOR PERMIT FRONT   76

Chapter Seven
FORGET THE FACTS, LET'S GET BACK TO THE BARS   93

Chapter Eight
WHERE THE SOLUTION IS THE PROBLEM   116

Chapter Nine
ALCOHOLICS ANONYMOUS, A PRAIRIE GROWTH INDUSTRY   137

Chapter Ten
IF IT WERE A NEW DRUG, NO GOVERNMENT WOULD ALLOW IT   156

Chapter Eleven
SO WHAT DO YOU SUGGEST?   176

NOTES   197
INDEX   201

PREFACE

There is a Shakespearean quotation I would like to adapt to illuminate the presentation of this work. The quotation is: Some men are born to greatness, some achieve greatness, and some have greatness thrust upon them. This is a book about alcohol and alcoholism. I was born to an awareness of alcoholism; I achieved an awareness of alcoholism; and I have had an awareness of alcoholism thrust upon me.

I was *born* into an alcoholic home for my father was an alcoholic before I remember him. He was, indeed, an alcoholic before alcoholics were invented and in his day would have been known as a "pay-day drunk" or a "periodic drunkard." He was utterly incapable of holding a steady job so I learned all there was to learn very early in life about the pauperizing influence of alcohol upon the working class. By the time I was eight I knew, when the bailiffs came to evict us and seize our furniture for non-payment of rent, that they had to leave us a table, some chairs, some dishes and at least one bed; which, if they were kindly bailiffs, they would stack on the verandah while we searched for alternative accommodation. If they were not they would pile it on the sidewalk. By the time I was nine I knew all there was to know about the aberrant behavior of alcohol abusers; and I was on familiar terms with the interiors of the bars from foraying into them in search of my father on paydays.

I therefore know all it is necessary to know about the great Prohibition crusade of 1915-1916. Like so many thousands of other drunks, my father was a fervent Prohibitionist because he believed if the bars were shut he and others like him would be rescued from temptation and able to get home with his pay on payday. So I belonged to the Loyal Temperance Legion, stood with my parents on street corners handing out temperance tracts, and delivered hand-bills into mailboxes advertising temperance rallies. Once I even got taken to such a rally where there were lots of singing and petition signing and impassioned speeches that made my mother cry.

My father had been dead right about the bars. When the bars were closed in 1916 he got a steady job, kept it, and brought his pay home every week. The early Prohibition years from 1916 to 1920 were the best years of our lives. But they came to a clattering halt after the 1920 hiatus, when my father discovered the bootlegging hotels. So did my formal education and after a couple of grocery delivery jobs I got a job in the Winnipeg Grain Exchange as an office boy.

There I *achieved* an awareness of the operation of the bootleg aspect of alcohol consumption. Some of the vessel brokers in 1923 had vaults stacked ceiling high with whiskey. Some relied on the daily supply from bootleggers. Some patronized the Grange Hotel across the street. When my boss was busy on the trading floor he would instruct me to phone one of his bootleggers to bring around a bottle and hand me a ten-dollar bill with which to pay for it when it arrived at the office.

My young friends who worked in the option brokers' offices frequently managed to do a fast shuffle with order forms and divert some of their customers' profits into their own pockets. When they did we would go off to a St. Boniface bagnio for fun and games. They made it a point of having me along because I did not drink and hence could keep track of their change and keep them from getting "rolled" by their hosts or hostesses.

Years later, as a working journalist I had alcoholism *thrust upon* me from all sides, from drunken police court reporters, drunken police magistrates, even drunken Queen's Bench judges; from drunken Ottawa Press Gallery correspondents and drunken members of parliament.

All this is to explain why, in the chapters on the Prohibition era, I have chosen not to resort to other authorities for documentation. I was there when it happened and I am my own authority, though I have of course gone back to the written record to reinforce memory.

Incidentally, I have noticed many aspects of beverage alcohol use and abuse in several of my previous books — *The Boy from Winnipeg, The Roar of the Twenties,* and *Booze* in particular. Readers of those books may find familiar some of the material herein. Others may wish to consult those works for more extensive treatment of themes mentioned only in passing here.

When the narrative moves beyond the Prohibition era I have

documented the references where required. The material on the evolution of the liquor commissions derives from the annual reports of these boards and from Statistics Canada. Indian Affairs supplied a great deal of valuable factual material as did the individual provincial Alcoholism Foundations.

I gratefully acknowledge permission to quote excerpts from publications: to the author and the *American Journal of Orthopsychiatry* for material from Ann P. Streissguth, "Maternal Drinking and the Outcome of Pregnancy: Implications for Child Mental Health," *AJO* 47, no. 3 (July 1977); to the Canadian Medical Association and The Addiction Research Foundation for material from John R. Seeley, "Death by liver cirrhosis and the price of beverage alcohol," *CMA Journal* 83 (24 Dec. 1960); to the author and the Canadian Medical Association for material from Sumner J. Yaffe, "A clinical look at the problem of drugs in pregnancy and their effect on the fetus," *CMA Journal* 122 (22 March 1975); to the author and the *Journal of Studies on Alcohol* for material from Dr. N. S. Cotton, "Familial Incidence of Alcoholism," *Journal of Studies on Alcohol* 40, no. 1 (Jan. 1979):89-116. Copyright by Journal of Studies on Alcohol, Inc., New Brunswick, N.J. 08903.

I am particularly indebted to the librarians of the land, to the public librarians who went hunting through the backroom stacks of long forgotten material in search of obscure factual material for me; to the staff of the University of Calgary Medical College Library who led me by the hand through their maze of stacks and reference material. And without the assistance of the librarians at the Addiction Research Foundation of Ontario I would never have found the key to the maze in the first place.

In my research I had the enthusiastic co-operation of the directors and the staff of the provincial alcoholism foundations and, of course, of members of Alcoholics Anonymous. I am also especially indebted to Chief Brian Sawyer of the Calgary Police Department and to the police departments of the other prairie cities who were all wholeheartedly supportive and co-operative. Senior officers of the Royal Canadian Mounted Police across the west were also helpful with information and advice. Several of my doctor friends, and particularly Dr. Morley Tuttle of Calgary, went to a great deal of trouble to keep me out of trouble wrestling with scientific terminology. To them all, I express my deepest thanks, along with special thanks to Lois Gregor who, for about the fifth time, wrestled my hopelessly untidy drafts into a presentable manuscript.

CHAPTER ONE
EVERYBODY KNOWS
THE TROUBLE WE SEE

Bacchanal (bae kanal) (ad. L. Bacchanalis)
A. adj. 1. Of or pertaining to Bacchus or his
worship. 2. riotously drunken, roistering.
B. 1. a devotee of Bacchus, a Bacchant or Bacchante.
2. A drunken reveller. 3. A festival in honour of
Bacchus. 4. An orgy. 5. A dance or song in
honour of Bacchus. 6. A sense of revelry painted
or sculpted. *Bacchanalia* 1. The festival held in
honour of Bacchus. 2. Drunken revelry, an orgy.
Bacchus. The god of wine, hence wine.
The Oxford Universal Dictionary (abridged)

To equate, as does this book's title, the ethos of Prairie Canada at
the onset of the 1980s with that of ancient Rome of 200 B.C. may
appear to resort to a particularly fanciful hyperbole. Roman history
buffs will be quick to observe that the Bacchanalian rites were a
religious observation undertaken to propitiate the god of the Roman
vineyards and agriculture. The suppression of the Bacchanalia by
Cato's senate in 186 B.C. had strong overtones of anti-Greek
religious prejudice as well as impatience with the worship of the god
of wine that had gone berserk. There are no such religious aspects to
the orgies that are coming to be more and more a featured part of the
summer-time drinking scene on the Canadian prairies.

In the beginning the Roman Bacchanal was a simple cult with
membership limited strictly to women. To celebrate a successful
grape harvest the women drank copiously from double-sized goblets,
cavorted in dance, and sang to the glory of Bacchus. Then men were
admitted, sex was added to boozing and the secret meetings spilled

1

out onto the streets and, in the words of one historian, shocked the not too squeamish public.[1] By 186 B.C. the Bacchanals had become such a threat to the peace, order and good government of Rome, and indeed to the whole republic, that the Senate ordered their suppression. Thereafter men caught participating were subject to public execution. Before the suppression of the cult was completed five years later, several thousand were executed. Women were turned over to their families for punishment, public execution of women being illegal.

Where there is a parallel between Cato's Rome and the western prairies is in the threat which Bacchanalia-type orgies pose to the peace, order, and good government of the area. It is not yet the kind of threat that would require the Draconian measures of the Roman Senate, but the votaries of Bacchus have brought boisterous defiance of the law to a pitch unimaginable fifty years ago.

In Calgary, for example, the Rome of the modern analogy, the police department in 1981 added a water cannon to its law enforcement equipment. The decision to purchase the cannon was rooted in the frustrating experience in 1980 of trying to bring public boozing on the streets under control. The most prominent example of defiant youth running wild occurred on a quiet residential area in early October. As the *Calgary Herald* reported:

> A weekend party that involved 200 drunken young people and required 50 policemen and fire hoses to cool things off had residents of a southwest Calgary neighborhood cowering in their homes. Thirteen young people were to appear in provincial court today on charges relating to the party which spilled from a house on 24th Avenue S.W. onto several city blocks.

The riot started after the police, responding to calls from irate neighbors, visited the party site to order the suppression of the noise. It was only one of fifty such calls the department got that night from all over Calgary. By the time the police reached the scene the party had already spilled out of the house onto the lawn. Greeted with a barrage of beer bottles, rocks, and shouted obscenities, the police retreated out of range until reinforcements could be summoned.

In the ensuing hiatus the drinkers amused themselves by throwing bottles through neighboring windows, climbing trees to urinate on those below, and bellowing obscenities at sober citizens. When the police reserves arrived the drinkers renewed the beer bottle barrage and still would not leave, did not do so in fact until the police called on the fire department to help. The fire hoses were hooked up, turned on, and the crowd not taken into custody was dispersed. The episode naturally raised questions of the wisdom of having the fire department doubling as a riot control agency. But it did demonstrate the efficacy of a fire hose as a crowd disperser so the City of Calgary bought the water cannon.

The out-of-control party season on the Prairies now begins with the 24th of May weekend, coupled with the high-school graduation dances, and runs roughly through until freeze-up. But it does not necessarily confine itself to the Prairies. In 1981 it spread over the border to Kalispell, Montana, a resort community 80 miles south of the Alberta-British Columbia border.

The Kalispell merchants had conducted a sales promotion campaign to attract border Canadians to their town for the first long weekend of the year on Victoria Day. They attracted several thousand "young adults" and before the weekend wound down 285 of them were in police custody for "disorderly conduct, disturbing the peace, carrying open liquor containers on the streets, traffic offenses, and urinating in public."

Such occurrences are by no means confined to the cities. Indeed the most riotously out-of control wassails take place in the rural areas. On the same 1981 Victoria Day weekend, Moose Mountain National Park in south eastern Saskatchewan was completely taken over by gangs of rowdies. Assistant RCMP Commissioner Robert Mills described Moose Mountain as where gangs of rowdies go on weekends to get drunk and make the place uninhabitable for other people. The Victoria Day weekend was, he said, a disaster.

In Manitoba, where similar disturbances occurred in the national and regional parks in 1980, the authorities at the Clear Lake National Park took action at least to defuse the long weekends. On Victoria Day, Dominion Day, Civic Holiday, and Labor Day they ban the bringing of booze into the park at all. The odd group that circumvents the searching at the park gates and becomes objection- able can be evicted and black-listed by the national parks system for a year. The ban applies even to the Rocky Mountain ski resorts.

The problem in city and country alike is numbers. A couple of policemen, or park wardens, have no difficulty restoring order where one or a handful of drinkers is concerned. Where things get out of hand is when a couple of policemen are confronted by 50 or

100 drinkers. Then the possibility of the police resorting to force to get compliance with the law is considerably reduced, a fact recognized by both sides. Buoyed up as they are by booze courage, frequently compounded by marijuana highs, the partiers become belligerent, mischievous, loose mouthed, and easily provoked to action. In late May 1981, in Yorkton, Saskatchewan, the police were called to a trailer court where a party was out of control. There, between drinks, the participants had taken to hot-rodding the adjacent streets in their cars. The police were met by a barrage of flying bottles and glass. It took police reinforcements from 1:00 A.M. to 4:00 A.M. to break up the party and arrest a dozen of the drinkers.

In Regina two policemen were trying to assist paramedics to load a man injured in a drunken brawl into an ambulance for transport to the hospital. They were set upon and roughed up by at least thirty party-goers before they could complete the job. Ultimately after a struggle they were successful in arresting two of the ringleaders.

In Alberta in 1981 the police were working on a new system of dealing with the rural weekend debaucheries. Instead of moving in, in force, when the king-sized country parties erupt into drunken brawls, they "mousetrap" the revelers. They learn where the big outdoors bashes are to be held, block the access roads, and search the ingoing cars for booze and drugs. In doing so they never have to confront more than a handful at a time and that handful is usually sober. Sometimes enough booze is confiscated to keep the party from over-consuming. Where parties get under way without the knowledge of the police, after-party road blocks for booze searches along the existing routes of the celebrants at least diminishes the outflow of drunken drivers onto the streets and highways.

The problem is with numbers, but it is not *only* with numbers or, perhaps, even *mostly* with numbers. It may even be primarily a problem of age and morals. In a society where moral value is defined by reward and punishment, people submit to rules and authority to avoid punishment and to obtain rewards, or to avoid rejection or dislike by others. What makes such a moral system work is certainty of the consequences; the rewards must flow automatically from compliance and penalties be imposed automatically for violation. Always, it has been accepted that behavior modifying rules were essential for the peaceful co-existence of people in communities. Unhappily a new generation has matured since the war, in an affluent and increasingly permissive society, which refuses to recognize the worth of any such system, or abide by its rules.

As it was in ancient Rome, the Prairie Bacchanals are mainly confined to the young, to the fifteen to twenty-nine year olds. It is a group whose defiant behavior has escalated since the drinking age was reduced to eighteen years from twenty-one. By common consent, that change in 1972 reduced the de facto minimum drinking age to fifteen or sixteen. Saskatchewan, the lightest drinking of the Prairie Provinces, recognized that and raised its minimum to nineteen years. Yet even in Saskatchewan the leakage from the nineteen year-olds down to the sixteen year-olds is apparent from a recent survey. It revealed that seventy-four percent of the nineteen and under people interviewed were classed as light to moderate drinkers. In the twenty to twenty-nine year group, the percentage of drinkers reached eighty-six percent and only fourteen percent were abstainers.

On a mid-September weekend in Calgary, it seemed to the police that a large group of drinking teenagers participating in an out of control house party were waiting for the police to arrive to start a riot. When the cruiser car pulled up on a quiet, middle class street in answer to complaints from neighbors it was greeted by a shower of rocks and bottles. Then a mob estimated between 150 and 200 surged around the car with rocks, bottles and clubs, smashed the windows of the car, and forced the policemen to flee from the scene. In their absence the mob vandalized the inside of the car, smashing everything that would break. Reinforcements were called and a dozen policemen were eventually able to scatter the mob and put eight of the drunken rioters under arrest. Of the eight, only two were over the 18-year-old minimum legal drinking age, the others were 16 and 17 year olds. How does it happen that 150 to 200 teenagers turn up for such parties? One reason is they advertise them openly on high school bulletin boards and mark the streets with direction signs.

In Winnipeg, the teenage drinking party problem has not developed to the extent it has in Alberta, perhaps because law enforcement against such parties has been much more severe from the beginning. But there are indications that Winnipeg nonetheless has an alcoholic problem with the sub-teens just as serious as anything elsewhere in the country. In September 1981 the Provincial Government announced that it had purchased the old Canadian National Institute for the Blind headquarters and dormitories on Portage Avenue, its purpose to provide treatment facilities for junior high school alcoholics.

The CNIB establishment — a three-storey office building, a two-storey dormitory, and two single-family houses — will also serve as the headquarters for the Alcoholism Foundation of Manitoba. Hon. L. R. Sherman, the minister of health, described the purchase of the $1,700,000 property as a milestone in the growth of the foundation because it recognized the severity of the alcoholic problem with the younger generation, a problem that was bound to get worse. He described the pressure he expected to encounter over the next decade as "overwhelming".

The chairman of the foundation said because in Winnipeg the young people established their drinking and drug habit between the ages of 12 and 14 years, there was widespread public pressure to establish a teenage drug center. The government proposed to spend $600,000 refurbishing the old buildings to make them habitable for the teenagers.

It is the under thirty group that is causing most of the drunken driving and other traffic charges. It is within the bottom level of this group, the sixteen to twenty-five year olds, that the disrespect for and lack of fear of the law is concentrated. It is an attitude reinforced by the realization that defiance of the law is likely, and by long odds, to go unpunished.

When it comes to mass drunks, it is a demonstrable fact that there is safety in numbers. In any police action more than one reveler in ten is seldom arrested and it is almost unheard of for any first offender to receive a jail sentence. For youngsters earning $100 to $200 a week, a $25 to $50 fine for disturbing the peace is no penalty at all. Even where higher penalties are imposed for more serious offenses, the payment of the fine out of earnings can usually be negotiated. Clearly, the psychology of soldiers going into battle has become part of the mass-drinking, law-defying scene: "If we keep up this bottle throwing, property damaging, and police baiting somebody is going to get arrested. But it will be somebody else, not me!" It is a believable philosophy, based on the fact that it has been seen to work — again, again, and again.

Only in the most heinous criminal cases does a first offender face the possibility of being sent to jail. Even in the cases of rapists and child molesters, defense attorneys plead for suspended sentences on the grounds their clients were drinking at the time of the offenses. Curiously enough, many judges still accept that excuse as an ameliorating circumstance. Thus in 1979 four young Estevan drunks embarked on a gang rape of a young woman friend. They were unable to complete the assault, despite the inflicting of severe physical abuse. They got off with a year in jail because they had been drinking.

In Winnipeg in August 1980 a thirty-five year old baby sitter who confessed to criminally assaulting a four-year-old entrusted to his care was sentenced to three years in prison. His lawyer had pleaded for a suspended sentence so that the accused could get treatment for his drinking and sexual problems.

Were these the kind of things that went on in Rome during the Bacchanals? Unhappily the history texts are vague as to details. Mostly references to the Bacchanals are dismissed with a paragraph or two referring to drunken orgies of varying degrees of profligacy.

The Canadian historian on the other hand can resort to statistics on developments on the Canadian Prairies in the last fifty years. For example, in the first twenty years of the cocktail bar era, roughly from 1958 to 1978, liquor consumption across the Prairies increased five-fold. Violations of the law fully kept pace with increased consumption of alcohol, and in some cases the increases were more than ten-fold, as the following table shows:*

	1958	1978
Sexual offenses all types	184	2,231
Rape and seduction	51	476
Assault	504	21,807
Homicide	17	154
Assault on Police	—	1,080
Obstructing Police	(316)	1,181

* from Statistics Canada data

To attribute the entire increases to the ingestion of alcohol and ignore such other influences as unemployment, social unrest, etc., would not be logical, of course. But that there is a relationship between the ingestion of alcohol and the commission of crimes of violence and anti-social behavior is beyond question. Several police chiefs are on record that if it were not for booze they could cut staff by 50%. The Royal Alexandria Hospital in Edmonton, the city's largest, reported that 90% of the weekend emergency admissions to the institution were liquor related. In the Canadian Government's Special Report on Alcohol Statistics 1978 its committee of experts estimated that between 30% and 51% of the 149,524 crimes of violence committed across Canada that year were alcohol related. Fifty percent of the divorces granted on grounds of physical and mental cruelty were considered alcohol related. A third of the battered children were suspected of being victims of alcohol related child abuse. The 342,596 violations of provincial liquor acts constituted 84% of all offenses involving provincial statutes.

Rape has skyrocketted in the Prairie cities since mass consumption of alcoholic beverages became a fact of life. That there is a definite relationship between drinking and rape has been demonstrated by a study of police records undertaken by three Prairie sociologists, Stuart D. Johnson, Lorne Gibson, and Rick Linden.[2] The records they examined were 344 cases of rape and attempted rape reported to the Winnipeg Police Department from 1966 to 1975 inclusive. To maintain compatibility with comparable research done in American cities, this study excluded the attempted cases and concentrated on 244 cases classified by the police department as "founded" complaints. Alcohol was a factor in 72.4% of the cases: present in both parties in 38.4%; in the offender only in 24.4%; and present in the victim only in 9.2% of the cases. The study concluded that there was greater likelihood of force and injury to the victim when alcohol was present. Of the cases where at least one party had been drinking, 85% of the rape victims were injured. The likelihood of injury was greatest where both the victim and offender had been drinking; of the 93 such cases, 48 recorded injury to the victim.

What was there about alcohol consumption that triggered increased aggression on the part of the offenders? Does alcohol per se increase aggression physiologically? Or is the aggression caused primarily by social factors, by the circumstances of the drinking? It is not yet possible to provide conclusive answers but the research goes on.

Unfortunately for the researchers, complicating factors have begun to intrude which may make it difficult to arrive at any crystal clear answers. Since the mid 1970s there has been a penchant developing on the part of young drinkers in particular to mix other substances, particularly marijuana, with their booze. This may stem from an urge to double the impact of the alcohol or the marijuana. Or it may be no more than unthinking puffing on pot while working on a case of beer. But for those drinkers whose aggressive personalities are activated by alcohol, marijuana seems to have a synergistic effect that triggers psychotic behavior, towards others or towards themselves.

Police officers in Calgary say they are noticing the presence of marijuana at the scene of automobile accidents where alcohol is involved. In 1980, it began turning up in criminal prosecutions for such offenses as rape and murder, and in cases where rape led to murder. Two cases of the tragic consequences of combining the drugs surfaced in Alberta within a six-month period. The first ended in murder. The second involved a thirty-year-old man torturing a fourteen-year-old girl to perform repeated obscene acts and then beating her into unconsciousness. Defense attorneys, accustomed to pleading for leniency because their clients had been drinking, make the plea even stronger when their clients have been on booze-pot trips. Seemingly judges listen, for the sentence in the latter case was three years in prison.

Because the newspaper headlines and the political pronouncements stress the youthful aspects of the Prairie Bacchanals it might be easy to assume that out-of-control boozing was a monopoly of the young. That is far from the case. All the urban police departments know that as darkness falls on Friday evenings their phones will start ringing with complaints from the citizenry about boisterously out-of-control neighbors. Answering such complaints becomes the first order of business for the police for the rest of the weekend. As like as not the noisemakers will include a full quota of fathers-in-law, mothers-in-law, and grandparents. And as the leaders of Alcoholics Anonymous group therapy sessions will affirm, most of those appearing for the first time on their doorsteps are still the middle-aged drunks.

The difference between the over-forties and the under-twenty-fives is in attitude rather than in fundamental behavior. The former tend to drink in smaller groups and to stay under cover. The youngsters carry gregariousness to infinity and overflow the premises even when they start indoors.

Equally conclusive proof of the ill effect of increased alcohol consumption on Prairie society are convictions for drunken driving: in Alberta alone more than 25,000 motorists lose their licenses annually for the offense. Over the three provinces in 1978 almost 50,000 arrests — an increase of 50 percent in four years — were made for liquor-related driving offenses.

Socially the deleterious impact of excessive drinking is rising at about the same rate. In Manitoba a study of the relationship between alcohol and welfare costs indicated that half the people on welfare rolls were there because of alcohol. In Alberta authorities estimated that 70% of the children in the care of the Province were the victims of excessive drinking by their parents. And in all the major cities something new was added to social welfare response in the 1970s — the establishment of refuges for battered and beaten wives. In almost every case the women seeking shelter have been beaten by drunken husbands. In every city the demand on the services of the refuges quickly filled them to capacity.

Saskatchewan with a population of 961,000 reported in 1980 that out of its 495,000 drinkers over the age of 15 it had 45,000 problem drinkers. On the accepted basis that alcoholism affects five other people in addition to the alcoholic himself, an estimated 270,000 people, or 28% of the population of Saskatchewan, are affected by alcoholism directly or indirectly. Extending those ratios to the other two provinces would put the number of alcoholics on the Prairies at close to 200,000, and the number affected by alcohol directly and indirectly at more than 1,200,000 out of a population of 4,500,000. The startling fact is that the alcoholic population is increasing at a much greater rate than the population itself.

Almost matching that growth rate, are the discoveries coming thick and fast from the medical researchers on health impairing, death advancing effects of alcohol addiction; discoveries of facts undreamed of even twenty years ago. The scientific community then was divided over whether the cirrhosis of the liver of advanced alcoholics was caused by alcohol or was the result of malnutrition. All doubt on that score has been dispelled: *it is the ingestion of excessive quantities of beverage alcohol.* Once it was the exclusive disease of the elderly, something that developed only after years of heavy drinking. Now it is being encountered more and more frequently in men and women in their early thirties, the inevitable result of consuming large volumes of alcohol over extended periods. The length of the time it takes to develop is dictated by the amount consumed. And it is being diagnosed everywhere at such rates of increase that it is being described as one of the country's most pressing public health problems.

The liver is only one of the vital organs vulnerable to damage from alcohol. Under certain circumstances it can and does damage the heart. That it attacks the central nervous system has, of course, been accepted for many years, as has the fact that serious brain damage can result from over-exposure to the substance.

It is not only the adult population that is affected. Alcoholic mothers can give birth to babies with all the signs of alcohol addiction; alcohol retards fetal growth and leads to the birth of retarded children. The connection between the rapid increase across the country of retarded children and mothers drinking during pregnancy is being investigated. Other researchers have even discovered a genetic factor in alcoholism: sons of alcoholic fathers are more prone to alcoholism than sons of normal fathers.

Researching the effects of alcohol on body organs, tissues, and functions has developed into a world-scale growth industry, supported by innumerable foundations and government agencies. Research papers are pouring out of the research facilities into the journals of the medical specialists. One of the best and most active agencies in the field of scientific research is the Ontario Addiction Research Foundation — the ARF — whose scientists have received world recognition for their work and whose papers regularly appear in the journals of two continents. On the Prairies too the governments have alcohol and drug addiction agencies in business, all continually expanding their operations as the need increases to serve the army of alcoholics that grows bigger almost by the hour. On the Prairies, however, the focus is on care and treatment not on scientific research.

In the Prairies, it is vital to understand, nevertheless, we have a view of Canada and the world in microcosm. The problems afflicting the Prairies are the problems afflicting British Columbia, to an even greater degree, and Ontario, Quebec, and the Maritimes. The Canadian Special Report notes that British Columbia and Quebec have the highest rates of deaths from cirrhosis of the liver among males. Ontario has the highest rate among females. Alcoholism is highest among males in Alberta and among females in British Columbia. Alcoholic psychosis is highest in Nova Scotia. Traffic fatalities are highest in Prince Edward Island, New Brunswick, and Nova Scotia; injuries highest in Ontario, Saskatchewan, and Alberta; property damage highest in Alberta, Saskatchewan, and Ontario. The heaviest drinking populations in the thirty years and over group is in Ontario, Quebec, and British Columbia for men and in Ontario and the Prairies for women. In the under twenty-nine years group the heaviest drinking men are on the Prairies and the women in Quebec and Atlantic provinces. All across Canada the sharpest increase in usage is in the lower and upper teens with the current rise of the females being greater than that of the males. The highest rate of teenaged drinking is in the Atlantic provinces.

Obviously there is a great deal that is relevant for the rest of

Canada, and for the rest of the world for that matter, in the experiences of the Prairie Provinces. Before an attempt is made to consider solutions for the present problems, elementary common sense would seem to dictate that we get things into a historical perspective. The Prairies have gone through a sixty-year cycle of annually increasing alcohol consumption, and alcoholism has become a problem. Was there a time, then, perhaps when this climb started, when alcoholism was not a problem?

Indeed there was, and it was the Prohibition era on the Prairies between 1916 and 1923. It was a time when one could walk down any street in any city at any time of the day or night and seldom, if ever, encounter anyone the worse for drink; it was an era in which a student nurse in Regina could complete her hospital training course and never encounter a single case of delirium tremens; when the great Winnipeg strike could run its entire six weeks' course without a serious drunken disturbance being reported; when alcohol consumption per adult male dropped to a fraction of a bottle a year; when drunkenness convictions dropped eighty-five percent below the 1914 peak and stayed at that level.

There were, of course, other important contributing causes to these changes in social mores. The First World War drained off the large surplus of single men whose steady patronage kept many of the bars in business. Criminal activities deriving from poverty were minimized by the banishment of unemployment. And while those with unslakeable thirsts still managed access to slaking material it was the banishment of the bars with the enactment of nationwide Prohibition that contributed most to the change.

How then did Prairie society get from there to here? From an almost arid Temperance Valhalla to a Bacchanalia that out-Romans the Romans? It got here by sheer, unadulterated drifting before the gently changing winds of public opinion, but a public opinion that became ever more strongly established the farther it got from the Prohibition era.

The Bacchanalian orgies are the end product of that drift, but the Bacchanalia, the violence and nose-thumbing disrespect for law, order, and common decency, are only the surface manifestations of a much deeper and infinitely more serious social malaise. To the law enforcement agencies the symptoms of that malaise are the slaughter on the highways and physically violent reactions. Social scientists focus on family disintegration, divorce, wife beating, and child abuse. Medicare administrators attend to the impossible strain imposed on their facilities. Administrators of the criminal justice system concentrate on the impossible burden being imposed on their facilities. But most important of all, the practitioners of the medical specialties, singularly and collectively, now see the malaise as a health destructive, life shortening threat to our society.

That's what this book is all about — the tracing of that drift and the measuring of those winds so that all these diverse concerns can be brought into single focus on the imperative need to alter course to avoid the social maelstrom into which we are drifting.

CHAPTER TWO
PROHIBITION: THE FACTS AND THE MYTHOLOGY

The onset of Prohibition in 1916 ushered in an era of social tranquillity without precedent in Prairie history. With the closing of the bars that had proliferated around the urban railway stations went the single most pauperizing influence on the working class. Husbands stopped beating their wives and battering their children, and children no longer went hungry and bootless to school. The commission of crime dropped so sharply that urban police forces could reduce their staffs and close neighborhood precincts. Manitoba and Saskatchewan even closed three provincial jails because of a shortage of incarcerants. And for good reason: crimes of all kinds in the three Prairie provinces dropped from 51,000 in 1914 to 22,000 in 1917. Arrests for drunken and disorderly behavior declined from 14,000 during 1914 to 2,400 in 1917.[1]

All these facts, of course, fly in the face of the almost universal perception of our Prohibition era on the Prairies. Canadians generally believe that Prohibition was something that was foisted upon a reluctant populace by a bunch of fat old ladies while the bulk of the male population was off fighting the First World War. When the soldiers returned, so the story goes, and discovered what had been done in their absence they reacted instantly with demands for a new plebiscite and ended Prohibition once and for all. But not before, it was alleged, it had spawned a new breed of gangsters and racketeers; fatally impaired public respect for law and order; led to wholesale bootlegging; and vastly increased public consumption of booze of all kinds, particularly bath-tub gin and rot-gut moonshine. In short, a public disaster unmitigated by any trace of social gain or even amelioration of conditions it sought to eradicate.

None of these articles of faith has any validity within a Prairie context. That they have become basics of a Canadian credo is indicative only of our overwhelming passion for grafting Canadian conclusions onto American premises, confusing Canadian reality with American mythology. In Stephen Leacock's fetching phrase we have been gathering moonbeams from a larger lunacy.

In point of fact, few of these beliefs have much validity in an American context either. The word "bootlegging" itself goes back to the American colonial era when the whiskey traders carried their booze in their boots. Illicit production of alcoholic beverages in home-made stills was a thriving American cottage industry in the days of George Washington. Between 1880 and 1920, when American Prohibition began, Federal revenue agents averaged between 1,500 and 2,500 seizures a year of illicit stills. As for Prohibition spawning gangsterism and racketeering, organized crime has been a hallmark of American cities since the American Civil War. What Prohibition did in New York, Detroit, Chicago, and New Orleans was provide already well-organized gangs with lucrative new fields in which to operate.[2] With the concurrent arrival on the American scene of the automobile and motion pictures, it also provided the myth-makers and lily-gilders with new areas of operation.

The social gains on the Canadian Prairies during the Prohibition era exceeded those of any other similar period of our history, as is clear in the historical record. For one thing, it modified drinking patterns that had lasted for generations. Yet it was an era that lasted only seven years. It came in like the power and the glory with the social reformers ecstatically convinced that they achieved a victory that would last for all time. Complacently they rode off in search of other dragons. As well they might have, when they contemplated the magnitude of their victory — 203,000 dry votes against only 88,000 wets in the three provinces. Later, as a result of a Federal edict in 1919, which forced the people back to the polls again in October 1920, the majority for Prohibition was still substantial, 209,000 to 145,000 despite the fact that the soldiers were all back from the war. The returned soldiers, nevertheless, were the drys' undoing. Their increased agitation, fueled with brewery slush funds after 1920, forced still other plebiscites in 1923 and 1924 which ended Prohibition by 100,000 votes. Not, it should be emphasized, because the people loved control of public boozing less but because they loved the money governments could make from booze monopolies more. So deep seated was public revulsion against the pre-Prohibition bars that it would be thirty years after government monopolies replaced Prohibition before public opinion would be prepared to tolerate the ingestion of anything stronger than beer in public places.

Sixty years after the onset of Prohibition, history on the Prairies has come full circle. There are not enough jail cells to accommodate the drunks, so the police have stopped bothering with only the moderately disorderly. Alcoholism has become the number one public health problem of the region and the nation, bloodying the highways and byways, filling the hospitals and wrecking cars, welfare budgets, and family lives.

The statistics tell the story, starting from 1925 by when the provincial governments all had their provincial liquor monopolies in place. During the next fifty years, the combined populations of Manitoba and Saskatchewan increased by fifty percent; in the same period their combined liquor sales increased by 3,500 percent. In Alberta the population increased by two hundred percent; liquor sales by 3,800 percent and profits by the same proportion.

In swinging from unrestricted boozing to control and back to the bottle, Prairie Canadians were only making a short run around a circle mankind had been traveling since he emerged from the caves. Jess Carr, in his book *The Second Oldest Profession*, has traced the consumption of wine or malt beer back to 6,000 B.C. The Greeks, who learned the art of beer making from the Egyptians, added the use of hops and passed the recipe along to the Romans and Spaniards.

The widespread use of the distillation process came much later to western Europe than it did to the Levant and the eastern civilizations. The Chinese were distilling sautchoo from rice and millet as early as 500 B.C. The Caucasians were producing arika from mare's milk and the Japanese were making rice whiskey about the same time. But it was 500 A.D. before the early Britons were distilling mead from honey, 1,000 A.D. when the Italians began making brandy from grapes, and 100 years later still when the Irish began converting their barley malt beer into usquebaugh.

From earliest times, however, the social consequences of unrestrained boozing were being viewed with alarm by social thinkers. The consequences of Noah's battles with the bottle are detailed in the Old Testament, and there are injunctions, pro and con alcohol, in the New Testament. The prophet Mohammed too wrestled with the problem, Islam at first prepared to live with booze. When that didn't work the codifiers of the Koran decided on total prohibition, and they did not mean maybe, either then or 800 years later, when getting caught with a bottle of whiskey was a criminal offense punishable by instant jailing, or worse. The Moslem experience points up a fact about alcohol that has continued to surface over the last five thousand years: when booze becomes plentiful it tends to become severely over-used, at which time the community tends to opt for some kind of control.

So long as northern Europeans confined their drinking to beer and wine, consumption of alcohol did not seem to pose much of a threat to public order. But all that changed when distilled spirits began to make their appearance. By the seventeenth century excessive drunkenness was becoming a problem in all the American colonies as well as in northern Europe.

In its American colonies[3] the British Government seemed more interested in expanding and maintaining its colonial markets for spirits than concerned about debauching the Indians. Even the storied *Mayflower* carried a cargo of ale and brandy, along with its pious Pilgrim Fathers, on its historic voyage to Plymouth Rock in 1620. And, until the American Revolution, the British Government was involved in endless skirmishing with the colonists in order to exact the maximum financial benefit from the colonial thirst.

In Europe, gin, developed first in a medical laboratory in Holland, became so popular that the Dutch were soon exporting millions of gallons a year. British soldiers, returning from wars or the continent, introduced it into England where the London populace, consuming it undiluted, by the tankard full, as they once had drunk British ale, set off London's massive gin binge of 1720 to 1750. Trevelyan[4] has noted that at the height of this grand drunk twice as many burials as Christenings were being conducted in the churches. Out of the gin debauch was born the first prohibition law in western Europe. In 1751 the British Government imposed almost prohibitive import duties and excise taxes on gin, and forbade the distillers and shop-keepers to sell the stuff.

In the colonies, faced with such leaders as Washington, Jefferson, and Adams all taking public pride in their distilling skills, the temperance advocates seem to have been voices crying in the wilderness. Nevertheless, as the Temperance movement slowly gathered steam in the United Kingdom and in the Scandinavian countries, it became a force to be reckoned with in the United States as well. The Massachusetts Society for the Suppression of Intemperance was founded in 1808 and 20 years later there were 6,000 local societies with more than 1,000,000 members in the United States.

In French Canada, drinking problems reached crisis proportions in the earliest days of settlement.[5] The problem was such by 1657 that Louis XIV issued an edict against the sale of brandy to the Indians, with a fine of 300 livre for the first offense. When that failed to halt the trade, Bishop Laval persuaded the King to make it a capital offense punishable by death, to which the Bishop added excommunication. Two offenders were actually shot and one was publicly whipped. Public protest against such extreme penalties forced Governor D'Avangeur to suspend the law but after a couple of years of near anarchy in the colony Bishop Laval persuaded King Louis to reinstate the edict. That failed to stamp out the trade, however, and in 1705 Louis' intendant, Jean Baptiste Talon, decided on a new tack. He built a brewery in Montreal in the hope of weaning the populace from its addiction to brandy. That didn't work either.

In Upper Canada licenses to sell liquor were first imposed in 1792. By 1818 the magistrates were passing laws to regulate behavior in taverns and it was earlier reported that there were more distilleries than grist mills in one county and more taverns than schools. Just as the farmers took their wheat to grist mills and brought back flour they were hauling rye to distilleries and bringing home whiskey. During the severe winters, all members of the family were encouraged to knock back generous slugs of whiskey after breakfast before venturing out into the cold and their daily chores.

In the pre-Confederation Canadas the temperance movement drew inspiration and gained impetus both from the United Kingdom and the United States. When the State of Maine enacted the first outright Prohibition law in 1851 it became the example for the dry forces of both Canadas and the Atlantic colonies as well as for all the other American states.

Agitation for total Prohibition bedeviled the politics of United Canada until, in 1864, the Dunkin Act was passed which permitted local option votes on Prohibition and a number of counties went dry in both Canada East and Canada West. The ink was barely dry on the British North America Act before Parliament was being bombarded with petitions calling for the enactment of a national prohibition law. In 1878 the Canada Temperance Act, the Scott Act, was enacted. It enabled counties and municipalities to adopt Prohibition and scores of them did just that over the next twenty years.

In the United States thirteen other states followed Maine's example, but the dryness did not last and by the onset of the Civil War only Maine was still keeping the faith. In a real sense, Maine became the touchstone for the whole North American Temperance movement. It supplied glowing testimonials from a broad cross section of citizenry to the moral, social, and economic progress that followed on the heels of the adoption of Prohibition. Temperance missionaries embroidered their speeches with first-hand accounts of the Maine miracle. After the Civil War, Frances Willard got her Women's Christian Temperance Union into high gear on both sides of the border. Thereafter various American states were engaged in voting Prohibition in or out until, by the turn of the century, there was growing feeling that for Prohibition to work it had to be done on a national scale.

The way in which the tides of public opinion ebbed and flowed from wet to dry to wet on both sides of the forty-ninth parallel is well illustrated by the birth pangs of western Canada. The area literally was born of Prohibition. The primary motivation for the organization of the North West Mounted Police was to evict the American whiskey traders from the Northwest Territories and end the debauching of the Indians. That done, in 1874, the Mounties stayed on to enforce the Territorial ordinance against all importation of alcoholic beverages except when specially authorized by the lieutenant-governor.

Though open consumption of alcohol was allowed in Manitoba, Prohibition was the law of the land in the Territories until 1891. Then, in the amendments to the Northwest Territories Act which gave the area a measure of self-government, control of the liquor traffic was vested in the Territorial Council. It quickly opened the door to the sale of liquor in hotel saloons. While this was happening, six American states were opting for Prohibition, Carrie Nation was turning from physically hatcheting saloons in Kansas to verbally hatcheting audiences from lecture platforms on both sides of the border. The Women's Christian Temperance Union was sending down roots all across Canada adding new impetus to already vigorous temperance movements in the Maritimes and Ontario. And with the movement of the first masses of migrants from Ontario into Manitoba came a substantial advance guard of the temperance crusaders.

Midway through the 1890s the clamor for Prohibition reached such a volume that it could no longer be safely ignored but Sir

Wilfrid Laurier sought to dampen down the uproar by resorting to a national referendum. When the vote came in 1898, the Prairies voted three to one for Prohibition — 18,567 to 5,802.

In that plebiscite, all the provinces except Quebec voted in favor of the adoption of National Prohibition. The vote in the dry provinces was 249,944 in favor to 141,933 against, a majority of 108,011. Quebec, however, voted wet with even greater enthusiasm, 122,760 to 28,436. That cut the overall dry majority to 13,687, which, in the eyes of the Laurier Government, did not justify a national Prohibition law.

Laurier's decision rocked the western Prohibitionists back on their heels, but not for long. Until the plebiscite of '98 there had been debate over whether control of the sale of alcoholic beverages was a provincial or federal responsibility under the BNA Act. As a result the drys had to carry on their campaigns on two fronts. With the Laurier decision the Prairie drys concentrated on getting the sale and consumption of beverage alcohol outlawed by provincial legislatures. And this change of focus came at a time when worsening social conditions spawned by a massive resurgence of immigration into western Canada was adding arrows to the reformers' quivers almost by the hour.

Daily arriving boat trains from the east jostled with immigrant trains from the United States for platform space on which to disgorge their passengers. While the homesteaders and land agents fanned out across the Prairies the cities bulged with invading armies of building tradesmen, ironmongers, machinists, bookkeepers, and strong-backed laborers eager to fill the insatiable demand for human muscle. Between the dawn of the twentieth century and the outbreak of the First World War, Manitoba's population doubled and there was a fourfold increase in Saskatchewan and Alberta. Instant towns sprang up all across the Prairies and the cities doubled and redoubled in population, almost by the hour it often seemed. In a single decade Winnipeg skyrocketed from 40,000 to 200,000; Regina from 2,200 to 30,000; Edmonton from 4,000 to 30,000; and Calgary from 4,000 to 45,000.

It was a country totally unprepared for any such influx. The shortage of sleeping space in the cities reached a point where single men in Edmonton were bedded down six to a room and frequently slept in shifts. Calgary and Edmonton broke out in year-round tent villages to accommodate those who could not find suitable permanent shelter.

A natural consequence of the population implosion was a boom in the hotel business. In the small town, jumping off place for the farmers and homesteaders, a local hotel was on the way up before the last shingles were in place on the railway station. Some kind of shelter from the elements was, of course, the sine qua non of survival on the western plains. In many cases the hotel was a crudely built frame structure of half a dozen sparsely furnished rooms over a ground floor dining room, pool room, and bar. In the cities the enterprising Bonifaces were surrounding the railway stations with their hotels, or, as in Regina, and Calgary, stringing them out cheek-by-jowl across from the station in both directions. In Winnipeg more than fifty hotels were spotted along Main street, both ways from the CPR station, and down the crossing side streets.

Not only did the hotels serve the needs of the armies of transient immigrants, but they evolved in to the social centers for the resident single settlers who seemed to outnumber the married men by two or three to one. The show place of even the meanest hostelry, city or country, was its bar with its shined oaken counter, glass mirror, brass rail, and occasionally emptied spittoons.

In this era of the ten-hour day and the six-day week, leisure time was at a premium, something usually indulgeable only in the short interval between late supper and early bedtime, or before holidays and during bad weather lay-offs. It was an age of "brute force and ignorance" when the worth of a man, or a horse, to an employer was measured by his ability to lift and carry. So for the muscle weary employees of the packing plants, warehouses, railway shops, steel fabricators, lumber yards and construction projects social custom centered, perforce, around after work thirst quenching. Dropping into a bar for after work drinks was as casually done as pausing for a quick cup of coffee became much later. And it led just as casually to the outbreak of street drunkenness in the urban centers after nightfall. The severity of the street problem rose and fell like the waxing and waning of the phases of the moon, depending on the distance from payday. The full moon phase always occurred when payday came on a Saturday.

Wage paying practices in the west in particular were in a state of flux. Some employers paid only once a month, some paid weekly, some every two weeks. Some paid in cash but most paid by cheque. By this time weekly payment of wages had become a trades union talking point, but progress on that front was slow. Regardless of the pay period, however, or the manner of payment, the nub of the family problem was how to get the pay packet to the kitchen table intact on payday.

For the workers who were paid by cheque, the banks were long closed before they got off work. So were most of the stores because one of the first civic by-laws passed by the new-born towns regulated hours of trade: only on Saturdays were retail establishments allowed to remain open after 6:00 P.M. But the bars were open from 7:00 A.M. until 11:00 P.M., legally, and the legal limits were notoriously elastic. The city hotel owners knew the paydays of all the large employers and negotiated whopping one-day bank loans to enable them to cash all the pay cheques tendered across their bars.

On paydays the bar owners could count on the standing room in front of their bars being jammed three and four deep by seven o'clock, with the atmosphere awash in the mingling odors of machine oil, wood shavings, street tar, draft beer, tobacco juice, and the pungent musk of honest sweat. By eight the good natured jostling around the bar would have given way to petulant pushing and the first of the evening's brawls would have brought the first bodily ejections into the street. Bar-room brawling was inevitable, but most bartenders moved quickly to eject the brawlers before a general melee ensued. Participants in anything that presaged a knock-down and drag-out affair were invited to finish their fight outside, where a couple of judiciously placed whacks from a patrolling policeman's billy club was usually enough to restore the King's peace and order. Wayfaring drunks were as common as street-walkers and were as benignly ignored by the minions of the law until they became obstreperously belligerent. A patrolman who allowed a street brawl to get out of hand on his beat courted verbal chastisement from his patrol sergeant.

The turn-of-the century bars, it should be emphasized, had but a single purpose — to accommodate the stand-up drinkers of beverage alcohol. Entertainment facilities or amusements of any kind were unknown. They were definitely not traditional English pubs where groups of friends could enjoy a social evening while nursing a couple of drinks. They were for down-the-hatch let's-have-one-more, knocking-them-back type drinking. And that, on paydays in particular, was what passed for socializing with workmates. Just as a man's ability to hold his liquor was a drinking man's measure of a man's humanity, drinking alone marked a man as a bit queer, a fellow not quite to be trusted. So the mores of payday drinking dictated the storming of the bars be done by workmates in groups of threes and fours who would take turns buying for each other or "treating" as the practice was known.

For too many husbands and fathers, the intended payday cheque-cashing drink became an inadvertent payday drunk, and to many temperance advocates "treating" was as great a menace as the bars themselves. The bars might conceivably have been tolerated if it were not for the "accursed practice of treating." Periodically efforts erupted to have treating outlawed. In Alberta the Temperance and Moral Reform Society opted for moral suasion. Realizing that refusal to buy his mates a drink might make a man look like a churl and a cheapskate the reformers focused their attention on the recipients of treats. They printed up batches of pledge cards and distributed them at church meetings and on street corners. On the card was a printed message:

I .... hereby swear that I will neither accept a gift of drink or offer to buy drink for others.
                                        Signed ....

The theory was that the person who had signed the pledge would show the pledge card to his friends and thus feel free to buy only his own drink and not stay for three or four rounds.

For the married settlers of the west there was a place to put every dollar they could earn without leaving *any* at the bars. There was furniture to buy, rent to pay, loans to repay to relatives who had financed passage, food and fuel and clothes to buy. Above all there was the absolute necessity to save money to live on when the snow came and a great deal of commercial activity ceased for the winter. In an age in which even the concept of public welfare was unknown, the alternative to saving for the winter was doing without and going hungry — or living off the credit of grocers, butchers, milkmen, and landlords.

At the time of the Prohibition crusade the cash-and-carry retail food establishment was a rarity, and chain stores were two decades down the road. The neighborhood grocers, butchers, and bakers carried their customers on credit between paydays, just as country general stores carried the farmers between crops. The merchants naturally expected their customers to settle their accounts promptly on paydays. Some did, but no grocer was in business long before the delinquent credit on his books exceeded his money in the bank. The merchants knew, as they watched the workers staggering home long after dark, which wives would be in the next day tearfully to explain they would only be able to pay something on account instead of their full bill. It was always the wives who had to face the merchants, never the tarriers at the bars. The distraught women seldom confessed the real reason for their plight. That would have been akin to publicly confessing the man they had married was an irresponsible wastrel. So they made excuses! In a sudden emergency they needed medicine for sick babies, a relative had become hospitalized, or had died; sometimes hospitalized one payday and dead the next.

The merchants could bluster; but what were their alternatives? If they shut off credit, the customers were likely to move away. They could hope they could recoup their losses, perhaps by raising prices to the delinquents above what their sober customers paid, and they did. And they could and did become enthusiastic supporters of the Ban-the-Bars crusade.

And not only the retail merchants. Factory managers looked on impotently as the Saturday night drunk extended into the weekend drunk and Monday became a day of lost production at the work benches. The private charity groups became flooded with appeals for assistance from families made destitute by the liquor traffic. Destitute wives of payday drinkers swelled the ranks of charwomen, washerwomen, nursemaids, and cleaners to feed their families on the pittances they could earn at such employment. Wives of business and civic leaders complained about the rowdiness in the streets. The magnitude of the problem may well have been exaggerated by the Banish-the-Bars evangelists for the majority of the population was probably composed of sober, responsible citizens with little thirst for beer or whiskey. But when all allowances are made, drunkenness remained a big enough social problem to raise public pressure to blow-out porportions.

The Banish-the-Bar crusade developed into the greatest mass movement the Prairies had even seen. It centered in the main around the Presbyterian, Methodist, Baptist, and Congregationalist churches and the Women's Christian Temperance Unions. The United Farmers of Alberta, the United Farmers of Saskatchewan, and the United Farmers of Manitoba gave it overwhelming support in resolution after resolution at conventions of upwards of 700 delegates. Most of the Boards of Trade across the Prairies were on the bandwagon with the merchants and bankers. With but a handful of exceptions, the country newspapers of the west supported the Prohibitionist campaign. So did most of the daily papers except the *Calgary Herald* and *Edmonton Journal*.

The Roman Catholic Bishop of Regina was an outspoken opponent of the bars although the French and German Catholics and the ethnic enclaves were opposed to Prohibition. On the other hand, there was hardly a Protestant clergyman with functioning vocal cords who was not talking it up for the cause at huge public mass meetings as well as from their home pulpits. The first dam against the flowing booze went up in Saskatchewan in 1915 when Premier Walter Scott, as a war measure, shut down all the bars in the province and created a government monopoly for dispensing wet goods through a dozen government stores. At the first opportunity the electors of Saskatchewan abolished the stores. When the votes were all in after the 1915-16 provincial plebiscites, the three provinces had voted:

	For Prohibition	Against Prohibition
Manitoba	52,000	28,000
Saskatchewan	95,000	23,000
Alberta	58,000	37,000
	205,000	88,000

It is true, as the myth makers have contended, that the women did make their votes count, but only in Saskatchewan. In Manitoba and Alberta the vote was taken before the women got the franchise. If they had voted there is scarcely a doubt that the dry majority would have doubled in those provinces.

With the verdict in from the electors, the provincial legislatures moved at less than lightning-like speed to dry up the Prairies. By the spring of 1917 the legislation was all in place, but it contained a loophole that the liquor trade proceeded to drive express cars full of booze through. The provinces closed down the bars and retail liquor dealers. But it was still legal for dealers in one province to ship liquor to customers in other provinces, except in Manitoba where such licences were withheld. Freedom of trade between provinces was, after all, constitutionally provided for in the BNA Act.

As a result mail order boozoriums sprung into business in British Columbia, Alberta, Saskatchewan, and Ontario. Through 1916 and 1917 liquor flowed into Manitoba from Saskatchewan and Ontario; into

Saskatchewan from Ontario and Alberta; into Alberta from Saskatchewan and British Columbia. It not only flowed to the thirsty who bought it by the bottle, it flowed to the upper crust who bought it by the case for hoarding in cellars, and to bootleggers who saw a chance of selling it surreptitiously by the drink. All this ended in 1918 when as a war measure the National Government abolished the use of food-stuffs in the production of alcohol and outlawed the inter-provincial shipment of beverage alcohol. Bone dry Prohibition therefore existed on the Prairies only during 1918 and 1919.

What the closing of the bars did, however, was to break drinking patterns that had survived for generations. It put an instant end to payday debauchery. The potent interplay of peer pressure disappeared with the closure of the bars. When there was a bar on every street corner, it was easy to be persuaded to drop in for a drink, and to stay for six. But when there were no convenient sources of supply the reverse was true.

The weakness of the human spirit in the face of temptation has been a concern of moral philosophers and religious leaders from time immemorial. Petitions for the strengthening of will in the face of temptation is an integral part of many prayers, and not the least important entreaty in the Lord's Prayer. But this awareness of the weakness of the human will was not confined to religious leaders. No one was more aware of the potency of temptation than those who yielded to it, and the remorse of the drinker who yielded to it was awesome to behold. And thus it was that the disappearance of the bars was welcomed, almost with enthusiasm, by many of their most persistent customers. And so it was too that, even with the mail order business in full operation, the intake of alcohol on the Prairies dropped drastically in 1917. So did convictions for drunkenness, from 7,493 in 1913 to 1,085 in 1917 in Manitoba, from 2,142 in Saskatchewan in 1914 to 770 in 1917 and from 5,710 in 1914 to 391 in Alberta in 1917.

When the bootleggers of by-the-bottle or by-the-drink liquor became established in business and expanded their operations there were slight increases for such convictions, but it would be well after the end of the Second World War before the statistics would be any way comparable with what they had been before the First World War.

It was generally assumed, indeed it was absolutely believed by the temperance movement in 1917, that a permanent solution had been found for the liquor problem. Inherent in that assumption was the taking for granted that the Dominion-Provincial legal status quo would be retained with the coming of peace. Such convictions were reinforced by the fact that the United States had completed the constitutional formalities necessary to bring in nation-wide Prohibition under the Volstead Act.

Behind the scenes in Ottawa, however, some effective lobbying had been going on by the booze interests. Out of the blue in November 1919 came the thunderclap announcement of a two-pronged change. The interdiction of interprovincial shipments would expire with the end of the war, officially on 11 November 1919. It would only be reinstated if the provinces reconfirmed their adherence to Prohibition by holding another plebiscite. Most shattering of all was the announcement that such plebiscites would not be held until October 1920, thus creating a year-long restoration of mail order booze shipments.

Among those who were instantly into the mail order business in 1917 were the Bronfman brothers, Harry, Abe and Sam, in Kenora, Ontario, and Yorkton, Saskatchewan. The Diamond Brothers opened warehouses in Calgary and Vancouver and Nat Bell was in business in Edmonton and Swift Current. Involvement in the 1917 mail order liquor business gave all the store owners invaluable on-the-job training for re-engagement in the business during the 1920 hiatus.

Of all those mail order pioneers of 1917 none gained more from that experience than Harry Bronfman who, from his Yorkton hotel, later became the multi-millionaire king of the whiskey trade. Bronfman saw possibilities everywhere — in having a drug wholesale company, a bonded warehouse, and in the establishment of a string of cash-and-carry border town stores for American rum runners. But most of all it sparked his determination to transform Yorkton into the rum, gin, rye, and Scotch whiskey blending center of Western Canada. All of which would happen instantly with the repeal of the ban on interprovincial shipments in November 1919. That Bronfman had advance warning of the coming change can be taken for granted. Within a month Scotch whiskey was arriving on the CPR Yorkton siding by the carload and shortly afterward by the dozen carloads.

All the western provinces save Manitoba broke out in new rashes of mail order boozoriums which proceeded to make odiferous mincemeat of provincial liquor statutes. In a trice a vast new industry developed in Saskatchewan, Alberta, and British Columbia supplying booze to rum runners from the only recently drying up United

States. For the next three years Scotch whiskey, Jamaican rum, and Holland gin, all coming out of the same straight grain alcohol vats in Harry Bronfman's blending plant in Yorkton, made "Canadian" and "from Canada" guarantees of excellence in the bootleg trade of the Great Plains states.

The lapsing of the Federal prohibition law in 1919 naturally set the Women's Christian Temperance Union on its collective ear, but not for long. Within a matter of months the dry forces in the small towns and rural areas were fully re-enlisted. In the cities, however, the dry campaigns seldom got underway until late September. Even then they were limited to a few moderate rallies and sermons in the Protestant churches on the eve of the plebiscite. As far as public interest was concerned, the dry campaign was the palest imitation of the early crusade. Gone were the parades, the boisterous debates, public confrontations, and demonstrations. Even the letter writers to the newspapers lapsed into silence. On the wet side there was no campaign whatever; until, that is, the day before the plebiscite.

The plebiscite was to be held on the Prairies on 25 October but in British Columbia the electors went to the polls on 20 October with a different choice of questions. On the Prairies the question was "Shall the importation and bringing of alcohol beverages into the province be forbidden?" In British Columbia there were two questions:

Which do you prefer:
1. The present prohibition Act? or
2. An Act to provide for the Government control and sale in sealed packages of spirituous and malted liquors but with no open bars?

In British Columbia the second choice was vigorously advocated by a group known as the Moderation League which was spearheaded by prominent politicians and war veterans. It laid special emphasis on the claim that huge profits being made by the bootleggers and mail order houses would then accrue to the government. It laid great stress on its promise that it was not in any way advocating a return to the open bars. To the shock of just about everybody on the Prairies the Moderation League carried the day in British Columbia. Two days after the B.C. results were in, Moderation Leagues erupted into life in Manitoba and Alberta with full page advertisements appealing for a "No" vote on the plebiscites. They were doomed to disappointment as the vote in favor of banning mail order shipments carried by comfortable majorities in the three provinces.

Despite the fact that women now had the franchise, which they did not have in Manitoba and Alberta in 1915-16, results were a disappointment to the temperance forces. The overall dry vote only increased slightly, from 205,000 to 209,000 while the dry majority for the three provinces dropped from 166,000 to 64,000. The increase in the wet vote from 89,000 to 145,000 might have been attributed in part to the returned soldiers vote but disappointment with the enforcement difficulties government seemed to encounter at every turn undoubtedly changed some dry minds to wet. In any event, there was a noticeable softening of attitudes on both sides prior to the vote. The Manitoba Free Press, which supported Prohibition in 1916 opted for a "yes" vote but thought some modification of the law might be considered at a future date. The shrinkage in the dry majorities encouraged the Prairie breweries to keep the Moderation Leagues in business and when British Columbia turned a $1,000,000 profit on its first year in the liquor business the campaign for replacement of Prohibition with government monopolies got under way in earnest.

CHAPTER THREE
BACK TO THE BOTTLE, RELUCTANTLY

The Prohibition era on the Prairies encompassed a scant decade, from the closing of the Saskatchewan bars in 1915 to the establishment of the Saskatchewan Liquor Commission in 1925. Yet the social mores of the repeal years were worlds removed and the furthest of cries from the atmosphere that had prevailed in 1915. True the fabulous fifteen-year construction boom was already in ruins by the outbreak of the First World War. But the collapse had done little serious damage to the spirit of optimism that permeated the Prairies. The overwhelming consensus was that once the war was over the west would return to its ever onward and upward course. It was a consensus fed by a manpower shortage for war industry that had quickly absorbed the unemployed from the stagnated construction industry. Indeed the shortage of manpower was becoming so critical by 1916 that there was talk of prosecuting men without gainful means of support, and women were replacing men in factories and shops at jobs no women had ever done before. Out in the countryside, the greatest wheat crop in history was in the bins and vast new acreages were being broken to the plow. The irrepressible confidence that permeated the west permeated the Ban-the-Bars crusade. There was no doubt in the minds of the reformers that they were riding the crest of the wave of the future.

The gaping crevasses that would divide the people into warring interest groups were as yet only minor cracks to which no one paid much concern. The Ban-the-Bars crusade which won the west for Prohibition was in reality only one aspect of a massive social and moral reform movement that swept across the Prairies in the decade preceding Prohibition. The women spearheaded the Prohibition crusade, of course, but they were just as deeply committed to a massive program of social reform. They were just as dedicated to women's suffrage as they were to the temperance movement, perhaps even more so. They were out agitating for factory acts to protect women at the work places, for laws against child labor, for compulsory school attendance laws, limitations of the hours of labor, one day's rest in seven laws, Dower acts.

The era was indeed a happy hunting ground for social reformers because in plain truth the social environment lacked even the rudimentary factory acts of Karl Marx's England. There were no provincial public health departments worthy of the name. Victims of smallpox were forcibly incarcerated in pest houses. The victims of the annual epidemics of scarlet fever and diptheria were quarantined in their homes. That was not all. Only a few years before it had been against the law to become mentally deranged; insane people were prosecuted in court like common criminals. No workmen's compensation acts protected injured workmen and there were no government agencies to succor the casualties of the economic system. What succoring there was was done by the private charities of the churches and religious orders.

For much of this the women were inclined to blame the male monopoly in elective office. It was a basic tenet of the suffragettes that the social indecencies of the time could only be ameliorated by the election to office of persons of feminine sensitivity. Indeed it might be argued that Prohibition was of secondary importance to the great votes-for-women crusade. Certainly women like Nellie McClung, Frances Beynon, and Lillian Thomas in Manitoba, Violet McNaughton and Jennie White in Saskatchewan, and Irene Parlby, Louise McKinney, and Emily Murphy in Alberta were as enthusiastic drum-beaters for women's suffrage as they were for Prohibition.

The personifications of everything that was wrong with male democracy were Sir Rodmond Roblin, the Conservative Premier of Manitoba and Walter Scott, the Liberal Premier of Saskatchewan. Once, in an effort to persuade Roblin to enact a factory act to abolish child labor and protect women in the workplaces, Nellie McClung took the Premier on a tour of the sweat-shops in Winnipeg. His reaction: "What is a nice girl like you doing associating with such people in such filthy places?" Ultimately the male electors disposed of Mr. Roblin and the succeeding Liberals quickly enacted most of the social reform measures the women had been demanding.

Permeating the social and moral reform movement of the

twentieth century's first two decades was a deeply held belief in the perfectibility of man. The Methodists led by Salem Bland, A. E. Smith, William Ivens, and J. S. Woodsworth; the Presbyterians, by C. W. Gordon, R. C. Henders, William Irvine were among the scores of social gospellers who were imbued with confidence that the brotherhood of man was within the grasp of man. All that was needed was for mankind to get on with the business of creating heaven on earth. In a way the prevailing spiritual euphoria was the obverse of the economic euphoria that gripped the west. As Ramsay Cook and R. C. Brown observed in a slightly different context:

> This sense of "righteousness" which was often associated with "Canadianism" was not smothered by the militant patriotism of the war years, but rather was stimulated and siphoned into the (Union Government) movement. The war became the great patriot challenge which would purge Canada of petty politics, materialism and corruption.[1]

This blood and guts devotion to the war effort was an integral part of the Prohibition movement. Premier Scott's rationale for closing the bars in Saskatchewan in 1915 was service to the war effort. The Federal government used the War Measures Act to dry up the country in 1918. But as the confident expectations of an allied victory became mired in the killing ground of Flanders the gloss began to fade from the unity of purpose. Idealistic wartime unity was undermined by outbreaks of fault finding, finger pointing, and name calling. "Profiteers" were blamed for the "high cost of living." Strikes broke out across the land and the farmers, already plagued with labor shortages, were in near open revolt against the conscription of their sons for military service. Then, the soldiers came home from the war to depression and unemployment. The Hon. T. A. Crerar, Borden's minister of agriculture and Prairie agrarian leader, bolted the Liberal party and the Union Government to return to the west with ten other Members of Parliament to found the Progressive Party in protest against high tariffs and the exorbitant prices of farm machinery.

Instead of a continuation of the triumphant march toward the promised land, peace brought social distress, industrial upheaval, labor turmoil, mass disillusionment and a terrible, killing influenza epidemic that left hardly a family untouched. Though the Liberal Government of Manitoba had enacted into law most of the social reforms in Nellie McClung's platform, it was replaced by the electors with a greenhorn group of farmers who had never sat in a legislature before. In Alberta, in 1921, the angry farmers turned out another Liberal administration in favor of a coterie of "group government" ideologues who followed Henry Wise Wood and the United Farmers of Alberta.

The pre-war unity of the social gospellers had been shattered in a dozen places. Antagonisms between the rural and urban populations sharpened, particularly after the election of farmer governments in Manitoba and Alberta in 1921-22. Class antagonisms sharpened after the 1919 general strike whose aftermath shunted many of the reverend clergy, men like Woodsworth, Ivens, Smith and Bland, into left-wing political activities of varying colors. The drive for unification of the Protestant churches into the United Church of Canada was splitting the Presbyterians into implaccable warring camps. The civil war between the One Big Union and the craft unions was doing the same thing to the trades union movement. In the countryside the energies of the farmers were turning from social issues to basic economics in their frantic search for an alternative marketing agency to the Winnipeg Grain Exchange.

By the time the plebiscites were held in 1923 and 1924, the price of wheat had fallen by two thirds, unemployed workers, many of them returned soldiers, tramped the streets, and everybody's focus was turned from the brightness of tomorrow to the urgent problem of surviving today. And that was as true of the deficit-plagued governments as it was of their citizens. So when the Moderation Leaguers pointed to the millions of dollars that would flow into government coffers, enough millions to finance the public schools and other services, with the repeal of Prohibition and the establishment of government monopolies, the social climate was receptive to the idea.

As the campaign to repeal the Prohibition laws began to heat up it was apparent that the opposing forces had switched ends. Throughout the long campaign for Prohibition the drys had been on the offensive and the wets had mounted hardly any defense at all. The drys had dozens of targets on which to focus — the disorder in the streets, the brutalizing of women, the pauperizing of the drunkards' families, the crime that accompanied the flowing liquor, the impact upon the children, the ruination of the health of the overindulgers, the unfavorable impact on industry and commerce etc., etc.

In the 1923-24 campaigns it was the drys who were forced to fight a rear-guard action in defense of Prohibition and the wets, spearheaded by the Moderation leagues, who took the offensive. From the public stance and printed words of the Moderation League one might well have assumed that it was an arm of the Loyal Temperance Legion, or even the men's auxiliary of the Women's Christian Temperance Legion. In their public rallies the Moderationists yielded nothing to either group in their denunciation of the pre-Prohibition bars. Their claim was that the eradication of the bars had given way to an even greater menace to society — the bootlegger. It was because of their devotion to temperance that the Moderationists wanted to erase the abuse of alcohol that the bootleggers were causing. The Moderationist catalogue of aims and objects were couched in the grandiosity of patriotic hymns. Here is the Saskatchewan league's description of itself:

1. Support constituted authority and promote obedience to the laws of the province;
2. Safeguard the right of self-determination for the individual within the limits imposed by the best British traditions;
3. Promote by education temperance in all matters of life and conduct and encourage high ideals of public service and citizenship;
4. Insist on such legislation respecting the sale and use of alcoholic beverages as will command the respect and obedience of the people.
5. Maintain at all times the liberties and rights of the people.

Out in the trenches where the battles for the public mind were being fought with circulating petitions it was the war veterans who carried the load. On their return from the war many of the soldiers had hankered for the retention of their wartime comradeship in the peacetime milieu. They tried to do so through membership in the war veterans' associations that sprung up across the country. But as enthusiasms diminished with time so did membership in those associations. Nevertheless the soldiers still retained fond memories of their introduction to the social amenities of the English pubs, of the relaxed atmosphere over pints of "arf'n'arf", Guinness, or Bass ale, with darts, drafts, and general jollification. The veterans' leaders saw transplantation of the pub-like atmosphere into their club rooms as the magnet that would rekindle the interest of the lagging membership. When the Moderation Leagues offered the veterans a dime a signature for circulating petitions asking for government control and beer by the glass the veterans groups enthusiastically joined the campaign for repeal. Ultimately after two years of agitation they got enough signatures to persuade the governments to hold still another plebiscite on the liquor issue. Manitoba went to the polls in June 1923. Alberta voted in October and Saskatchewan delayed its plebiscite until 1924. Ironically, for the veterans who did all the leg work, while Manitoba and Saskatchewan voted for repeal both provinces rejected beer by the glass, for war veterans and everybody else.

The cause of the repeal of prohibition on the Prairies was, at bottom, the failure of the 1920 plebiscite to do what it was supposed to do, completely to shut down interprovincial trade in booze. The failure was two-pronged. In the first place it took Ottawa weeks stretching into months to proclaim the prohibitory law. The vote was taken on 25 October and the law was not proclaimed until the following February. In those three months anyone with the wherewithal could stock a basement full of booze, and many did so, even if the number who could afford to do so was hardly that great in the economic climate of 1921. It cost Winnipeg, Calgary, and Edmonton customers of the Bronfman Yorkton dispensary eleven dollars a gallon for the Scotch they ordered in one gallon cans, or forty-five dollars a two-gallon case if they bought bottles. In the interval between the vote and the proclamation it was not uncommon for a mail order house to fill orders for thirty to forty cases of assorted drink from single customers. It was obviously possible for anyone intending to merchandise liquor by the drink to lay in a good stock before the supplies were cut off. On the last day of legal mail order shipment the Dominion Express Company worked through the night in Regina to get 5,000 cases of liquor aboard three special express cars for Winnipeg.

In the second place exemptions were granted liquor wholesalers who were engaged in the export trade. Thus those with the string of branches in the small near-border towns of Saskatchewan, Alberta, and British Columbia were still free to import all the booze they needed to service their American rum-runner customers.

The owners of the export houses ran the risk of having their entire warehouse full of liquor seized if they allowed any of it to leak into the domestic market. For example, in October 1920 Edmonton police seized 30,000 bottles and 2,500 cases of Scotch whiskey after employees of the Nat Bell warehouse sold a case of Scotch to a local resident. Despite the risk, however, leakage became such a problem for Saskatchewan in 1921 and 1922 that the government ordered all export houses confined to cities of 10,000 population where closer surveillance was possible. But still the leakage went on, to the rising clamor from the citizenry for more adequate enforcement of the Prohibition laws. And it was at this point that the drys themselves came to play an important role in undermining public confidence in Prohibition.

There seemed to have been an assumption among the general body of temperance adherents that, once manufacture and sale of alcoholic beverages were prohibited by law, the liquor problem would be solved; that once the supply was cut off the demand would disappear. It was a fatally flawed assumption which might have had a better chance of realization if the breweries had been shut down along with the bars. But the breweries were allowed to remain in operation to produce and sell "temperance" or two-percent beer. In fact the breweries continued to produce strong beer — for the simple reason that it was only after the strong beer had been made that weak beer could be produced by dilution. So with the weak beer that went out to the hotels went shipments of strong beer. The breweries, therefore, helped the hotels maintain secreted supplies of strong beer for drinkers who would settle for beer when booze was not available. Vigorous enforcement of the law inside the breweries and in the hotels might have sopped up that supply. But none of the governments had the slightest conception of how vigorously the law would have to be enforced to achieve total sobriety. Profits from surreptitious sales of beer alone were far from sufficient to provide a bonanza for breweries or hotels. But they kept the breweries and some hotels in business.

For the unreconstructible hard liquor addicts with money there was whiskey, rum, and brandy available on doctors' prescriptions in all the urban centers. When it became apparent that prescription issuing was getting out of hand, the governments limited the doctors to 100 a month and the size of the prescription to 12 ounces. But at $2 for the doctor and $2 for the druggist, that made 12 ounces of booze too expensive for all save the upper crust to afford.

In the countryside, particularly in the German, Ukrainian, and French enclaves in the more remote areas, the farmers went on doing what they had been doing for generations — making their own wine, potato and corn whiskey for ceremonial and familial occasions. It was a process almost as simple as doing the family wash, and utilized many of the same utensils. It was just a short step from making a few gallons of brew for home consumption to making a few gallons for sale to urban bootleggers. Unhappily for the moonshiners, they seldom managed to stay in business for long. Their operations came within the jurisdiction of the Royal Canadian Mounted Police rather than the provincial liquor enforcers. The Mounties operated a moities system under which the courts were permitted to award half the fines imposed to the informers who tipped off the Mounties to the location of the still. Such fines far exceeded those usually imposed for other liquor offenses, by a ratio of about $1,000 to $200. Snitching on one's neighbor thus became a profitable venture. However after repeal the Federal Government, in a rush of economy to the head, cut the moities in half and convictions for operating illicit stills dropped by the same rate and moonshine became more plentiful in the urban areas.

The Prairies, hence, in 1921-22-23, were not nearly as bone dry as they had been in 1918 and 1919. But they were by no means as wet as the Moderation Leagues' agitators led the electors to believe, either. Now and then raiding enforcers would gain great public attention by knocking over a big still, or a druggist doing a land-office business in prescription filling. There were indeed whole municipalities in southern Manitoba and Alberta where there was all but total suppression of beverage alcohol. One perspective on the extent of the liquor traffic can be gained from the Alberta Government report on the medicinal alcohol trade in 1921. At that time there were 474 licensed physicians in the province who were permitted to issue 100 twelve-ounce prescriptions a month. If each had done so they would have written 47,400 prescriptions for 568,000 ounces of whiskey. In fact they issued a total of only 14,000 prescriptions for 168,000 ounces, or roughly one ounce per month per adult male in Alberta.

To this must be added the amount of booze that became available from illicit sources following the lifting of the ban against interprovincial trade in 1919. The flow of bottled stock across the borders went not only to thirsty imbibers but to everyone else who wanted to retail the stuff by the glass. It went to the urban hotels, to the brothels, to apartment house janitors cum bootleggers, to salesmen for delivery to selected clientel by the bottle on demand, to restaurant owners prepared to take the risk of serving liquor by the bottle under the table. When the Federal Government had ended the interprovincial shipments at the end of 1917, there was little apprehended reason to bother with special liquor enforcement agencies. The provinces left that chore to the municipalities. The 1919 repeal of the mail order ban caught the provinces completely by surprise without any effective enforcement machinery. So they had to organize provincial police forces and later government liquor inspectors. They were swamped with complaints from the citizenry and enforcement was rudimentary at best. In the country a new ingredient was added to the law enforcement load when the American rum-runners from the United States turned bank robbers and began robbing the unprotected banks in the near-border towns of Manitoba, Saskatchewan, and Alberta as they came and went.

In summary, there was a multiplicity of minor liquor law infractions after 1921 and the drys kept a steady stream of protests going to government over laxity in enforcement of the law. Sometimes the protests took the form of sermons, sometimes letters to the editors, sometimes motions at municipal council meetings. Prohibition, clearly, was not turning out to be exactly what its advocates had so confidently expected.

The spreading public awareness over liquor law enforcement was all grist to the mills of the Moderation Leaguers. The dirtiest of dirty words in their propaganda was "bootlegger." They expanded its original meaning into a generic term for everyone in the trade. The ethnic farmers with their kitchen stills were bootleggers, so were hotels selling strong beer, brothels selling booze by the glass, export warehouses, druggists filling prescriptions from blank pads. It was allegedly a vast money-making business that was draining millions of dollars annually from the pockets of the people, money that in the hands of the government could have financed the educational system and cut the taxes of the citizenry. Moreover, the traffic was bringing law enforcement into disrepute, encouraging all other forms of crime.

In Alberta, J. R. Boyle, the Liberal attorney-general, complained about the lack of public support his enforcement officers received, particularly from local policemen. Where there was public support, as in the Mormon area of southern Alberta, law enforcement was no problem. The Mormon religion forbade the use of beverage alcohol and for the most part Mormons obeyed the tenets of their faith. In the mining towns of the nearby Crowsnest Pass, on the other hand, the local religion seemed to be getting drunk. On one raid in the

Alberta section of the Pass twelve arrests were made, including one town mayor and two chiefs of police, none of whom lost his job as a consequence of bootlegging convictions. From his public statements after the 1920 plebiscite it is clear that Mr. Boyle would have preferred sale by government commission to bone-dry Prohibition. But he never got a chance to have such a system. The Liberals were driven from office by the United Farmers of Alberta in 1921. The farmers spurned the demands of the Moderation League for another plebiscite and for the next two years gave enforcement the old college try.

In Manitoba the Moderationists were out circulating petitions immediately after the 1920 plebiscite. When the Manitoba legislature met in January 1922 they tendered a pile of forms containing 55,000 signatures asking for a plebiscite on package sale by government commission and the sale of beer by the glass. After weeks of debate, the petition failed by two votes. In the provincial election of 1922, the Moderationists elected their secretary to the legislature, circulated a second petition, and persuaded the new farmers' government to let the question go to plebiscite in 1923. The Alberta farmers' government did the same later that year but a difference in the wording of the two plebiscites produced radically different results.

Alberta submitted a confusing four way choice to its electors. They could vote for (a) Prohibition; (b) Prohibition and beer in hotels; (c) Prohibition and beer in vendors; or (d) government sale of all liquor coupled with the sale of beer in licensed premises. Thus those who wanted to vote for government sale of all liquor had to vote for the sale of beer by the glass as well. The official count was 93,490 for proposition (d), 61,780 for proposition (a), and a total of 7,000 for the other two. That there was a substantial proportion of the population who wanted government sale of all intoxicants without beer by the glass was demonstrated in Manitoba where there were two ballotings. In the first vote government monopoly was approved by 84,000 to 54,000 but on the second vote on beer by the glass the result was just the opposite — 64,000 to 27,000 against it. When Saskatchewan went to the polls in 1924 it too voted wet by a substantial majority but like Manitoba rejected beer by the glass.

Despite the substantial affirmative vote for repeal racked-up in the 1923-24 plebiscites the reaction of all Prairie governments to the replacement of Prohibition with sale of liquor by government commission was no better than grudging bowing to the will of the people. And understandably so. The bulk of the wet majority was in the cities and major towns while the legislatures were dominated overwhelmingly by members for the dry rural constituencies. Many, perhaps most, of the country members still favored Prohibition as befitted representatives of constituencies which continued to vote dry in local option polls long after repeal. Along the front benches too were many members who had campaigned actively for the dry side, as Premier Bracken of Manitoba had done in the 1923 plebiscite. When draft bills to set up the government agencies came before caucus, it became for many farmer members a question of reluctantly voting to conform to the democratic expression of the public will rather than for their own convictions. For those charged with responsibility for drafting the bills, the sadly depleted state of provincial treasuries made the task somewhat less distasteful than it otherwise might have been.

The lack of enthusiasm of the governments for the business into which the electors had pitch-forked them was made manifest in many ways. There was no headlong rush to accommodate the wet majority, and there is no evidence that the wet voters were jumping up and down with impatience to be launched into the first legal binge. As governments began considering ways and means, emphasis was clearly on providing minimal rather than maximum freedom of access to alcohol. Alberta, where the Prohibitionist sentiment had been thinner than in the other provinces, relaxed regulations most. It set up retail liquor outlets in all the cities and in 28 towns, granted beer-by-the-glass licenses to 362 hotels and 52 clubs and permitted brewery sales warehouses to be opened at 36 country points.

The Saskatchewan system was more restrictive. It opened cash-and-carry liquor stores in each of the cities and in sixteen of the larger towns. Government outlets in 100 small towns and villages were restricted to selling only beer. Farmers who wanted hard liquor had to resort to the mails if they lived too far from the larger centers.

Manitoba, the most restrictive of all, seemingly operated on the conviction that drinkers were not to be trusted in public with bottles of booze. To gain possession of a bottle of legal liquor Manitobans had first to visit a permit office and buy a numbered permit. This enabled them to pay for an order of liquor which the Government would deliver to the purchasers' homes, the following day, if possible, otherwise as quickly as conditions allowed. Beer was ordered the same way but could also be ordered directly from a brewery which did the delivering. Manitoba also made provision for mail-order deliveries of hard liquor.

All provinces continued provisions for supplying alcohol to druggists for the filling of doctors' prescriptions. Consumption of spirits anywhere but in the homes of the citizenry was forbidden, though registered hotel rooms were later made legally acceptable. All required their drinkers to buy annual permits for $2 in Alberta and $1 in Saskatchewan and Manitoba. Casual purchasers, and tourists, could get short-term permits for fifty cents.

In the beginning none of the provinces placed any restriction on the amount of liquor a citizen could purchase, but it was not long before Manitoba placed a limit of twelve bottles of spirits and two cases of beer a week. The change grew out of a whopping order from an American rum-runner and the change underlined the lack of enthusiasm which the governments brought to their merchandising of the product.

In Winnipeg an enthusiastic American had $2,000 worth of liquor, at $65 a case of 12 bottles, delivered to his hotel room. Upon its arrival he immediately transferred it to his car preparatory to running it back to Minnesota. As he was stowing the last case away the police arrived and seized the tourist and his liquor. In police court he was fined $200 for having liquor in a public place and the liquor was confiscated. He appealed the verdict, won his case, and got his fine and liquor back and, presumably, took it home to the States. The Manitoba government then amended its regulations to limit purchases to twelve bottles of spirits and two cases of beer per week. Selling whiskey to Canadians was clearly bad enough, but for provincial governments to function as whiskey wholesalers for American bootleggers clearly violated Prairie sensitivities about the fitness of things.

From almost the moment of birth of the government liquor monopolies there was a curious reluctance on the part of all governments to permit American access to Canadian liquor supplies. It was as if the governments saw something obscene in citizens of the United States trying to buy Canadian booze when it was against the law for them to possess it in the United States. It was an attitude which made no logical sense, given the fact that the government monopolies were in business to earn a profit, and substantial profits were there for the earning from American customers. In all this, Alberta reacted just as vigorously as Manitoba had done. When the government opened its first store in Lethbridge in June, 1924, one of the first customers through the door was an American tourist.

"Gimme ten cases of Scotch", he said unrolling a fist full of bills. The astounded clerk, who was still stocking his shelves, said that he did not yet have ten cases of Scotch on hand.

"Okay", said the American, "gimme ten cases of whatever you've got". He loaded up with an assortment of booze and headed back for Montana. Some days later, when a liquor store was opened in the town of Foremost, close to the American border 100 miles to the south east, it was besieged by a stream of Americans trying to buy out its entire stock to run back to the United States. Alberta wanted none of the rum-runners' business. It closed the Foremost store and amended its regulation to prevent establishment of any other stores within sixty miles of the American border. Thereafter the rum-runners had to rely on liquor warehouses in B.C. for their supplies. And when a large trade developed between the Americans and the Crowsnest Pass bootleggers, Alberta set special enforcement squads to work to prevent the stuff being run through Alberta on its way to Montana.

From the tardiness with which the governments moved to get into the liquor business it is clear that the wet versus dry issue was no longer one which was tearing the country apart. In Manitoba the electors ended Prohibition on 23 June 1923 but it was two months later before the government got around to appointing its first Government Liquor Control Commission. It took the Board another month to get around to putting its first permits on sale, and two weeks still later before it was open for business for the sale of whiskey, gin, brandy, and other spirits. If there was a massive stampede into the order offices it escaped the attention of the newspapers of the day. Interest in Winnipeg, where a half dozen offices were opened, was no better than moderate.

Alberta was even slower than Manitoba in putting its system in place. It was four months after the vote for repeal before the system cleared the legislature in February 1924. Only then did the government start making provisions to get into business and withheld proclamation of the law until 10 May. On 12 May it opened its first retail liquor stores, one in Calgary and two in Edmonton. After seven years of off-again-on-again Prohibition one might have expected a rush of patronage to the stores. In Calgary half a dozen citizens were in line when the store opened at 10:00 A.M. Half of them were brewery salesmen passing out promotion material for their special "brew with a real kick." The *Albertan* reported the next day that 1,200 permits were sold the first day. In Edmonton the *Journal* reported that six men, one woman, and a dog ushered in the new era and the first to emerge was the woman who had six bottles of Guinness under her arm. No rush developed during the day and during the busiest hour sixty-five permits were sold.

The commonality of the liquor stores in all provinces was that they were not set up speedily to serve the cash customers. First an annual permit had to be purchased at a special wicket. Then the customer proceeded to one of several tables where he filled an order slip along with the appropriate prices. At the top of the form in Manitoba was a space for his name, address, and permit number. From the order desk he proceeded to the permit desk where a clerk entered his purchase in his permit book. The next step was a cashier's cage and ultimately his receipted order was handed to a clerk who in Saskatchewan and Alberta filled the order from shelves in the back storage area. Once this system was in place there was little inclination on the part of the bureaucracy to modify or tamper with it. Yet cumbersome as it was, the system was seldom placed under any strain by any rush of customers to the stores. An insight into the interest of the public in whiskey on demand was provided a week after the stores opened by R. J. Dinning, the Alberta Commissioner. Province-wide, he said, the stores were doing only a modest business. It remained so modest that several weeks later the Commission reported that it was considering reducing staff.

Getting around to opening the beer parlors in Alberta took the government much longer than it did to open the liquor stores. Having advertised their intentions of applying for a tavern license, the hotels then had to wait for several weeks before getting a license. All premises had to be inspected to ensure that they had proper sanitary facilities and were properly furnished. Moreover in the rural areas provisions were made for holding local option votes before licenses were granted. That process could and did take weeks.

In the interval between opening the liquor stores and the opening of the first urban beer parlors almost a month later, public interest became modestly aroused over what the price of a glass of beer would be. The breweries decided they would charge about the same to the legal hotel pubs as they had been charging the hotel bootleggers prior to repeal — $25 a barrel. That would translate into 15 cents for a twelve-ounce schooner of suds. News of that price triggered howls of protest from the beer drinkers of the province, from the mayor of Calgary to motion-passing conclaves of the war veterans clubs. Whatever the traffic would bear during Prohibition — usually fifty cents a bottle — was one thing, but fifteen cents for a schooner of beer in licensed premises was ridiculous! So hotel keepers publicly worried about being faced with a buyers' strike before they were even in business. All the hotels, that was, except the Macdonald Hotel in Edmonton. Its management was so convinced that the public's reputed appetite for beer was exaggerated that it decided against even applying for a license. It had done the arithmetic and was convinced it would make more money in its coffee shop selling five-cent coffee than it would from converting it to a pub to sell fifteen-cent beer. The way the price was ultimately established was a standoff. The price of beer was set at ten cents per glass of eight ounces instead of fifteen cents for twelve ounces, and that seemed to satisfy all the malcontents.

During the first couple of days the beer parlors were in business it looked as if the Macdonald Hotel had miscalculated. As the deadline for the opening of the taverns wound down from days to hours the newspapers managed to whip up a moderate frenzy of public interest. The hotels had had their services in place some days before they got their permits from the commission, whose approach to permit issuing was as super-deliberate as a constitutional conference. So from May Day onward growing numbers of the thirsty would-be downers of "the first legal drink of beer in Alberta since the war" checked the hotel parlors periodically for the zero hour. Eventually, on the afternoon of 5 June 1924 door opening telegrams went out from the commission to a handful of hotels in Calgary and Edmonton. Word spread quickly and by supper time the taverns were filled to capacity, lines were formed outside, and other crowds were circulating from hotel to hotel in search of vacated chairs. The same thing happened the next day, and the next, before the novelty wore off with a thud.

The taverns of 1924 in no way resembled the bars of 1915. The new taverns were forbidden to have food of any kind on the premises. There was no bar for anybody to stand around. Service was by waiters to customers seated at tables from which it was unlawful to stand up with a drink in hand. The decor was Domesday austere and the chairs and tables were made to last, not for comfortable sitting.

The most striking difference between 1915 and 1924 was that women were permitted to patronize Alberta beer parlors. But not universally, nor for long. They patronized them with great timidity and less enthusiasm, except for the "wrong type" of women, enough of whom were to be seen in them that "respectable" women were discouraged from joining the men in meeting for a beer after work. In the end the patronage of the "wrong" type of women caused so much trouble in Calgary and Edmonton taverns that regulations were amended, in 1926, to confine the beer parlors in those cities to men only. A couple of years later the government relented to the extent of permitting hotels which so desired to open parlors for women from which men were barred. Almost none did. Those that did found, in the later words of one waiter, that "women are a confounded nuisance. Three women can want five different kinds of cigarettes, they all buy their own beer, and argue about the change. They want messages carried to men in the other room, and are forever going to the rest rooms." In later years the segregation of the city pubs added considerably to the drunken driving on highways as the gay blades from the cities took to squiring their lady friends to the country hotels where sexually mixed drinking was still permitted.

Once the novelty of the open taverns wore off, the rush subsided. High license fees, wages for waiters and tapmen, maintenance of the whole hotel to commission standards, drained off most of the profit. Nobody in the hotel business on the Prairies ever got rich selling ten cent beer and most went so deeply into hock to the breweries that they wound up as employees of the breweries instead of hotel owners.

CHAPTER FOUR
MANITOBA BOOTLEGGERS CAME WITH REPEAL

The sales pitch of the Moderation Leagues was that once Prohibition was repealed and government liquor stores were in place social tranquillity would return to the Prairies. The controversial liquor question would cease to acerbate human relationships and the people could get back to their everyday concerns. And that turned out, generally, to be what did happen following the 1923-24 plebiscites, except in Greater Winnipeg.

As a matter of plain truth, as far as the countryside was concerned, there was no longer much disruptive social controversy over liquor. The agitation to repeal Prohibition was an exclusively urban phenomenon. In many farming communities boys could grow to manhood without ever seeing a bottle of whiskey, let alone sampling the stuff. These were the areas where the people went to the polls in plebiscites to reject proposals to locate beer parlors or liquor stores in their midst. It was not to them that the Moderationists' everlasting decrying of the bootleg evil was directed. Curiously enough, it was the repeal of Prohibition and the opening of the government liquor stores that launched the real bootleg era in Greater Winnipeg.

Bootlegging there had been in Greater Winnipeg during the 1918-19 bone-dry period. But it was a miniscule, rudimentary thing compared with what developed after the repeal of Prohibition. In the first instance, bootlegging was confined almost entirely to the hotels that had closed their bars and transferred operations to converted bedrooms on the second floor. Here, because of the scarcity of spirituous liquors, the trade was mainly in selling beer to a recognized clientel. It was a trade carried on with little interference from law enforcement agencies. And for very good reason. There were no liquor enforcement agencies as such at that time. It was not until 1919-20 that the Prairie governments got around to putting their own liquor law enforcement agencies in place.

When the provinces enacted their Prohibition laws in 1916 there was a naive, almost universal conviction abroad that once the law was on the statute books the people would obey it, as law-abiding British people obeyed all other laws. For those who did not, ordinary police forces were there to take care of them. Unhappily the war decimated the city police forces and those who remained had enough to do without snooping around after illegal liquor sellers. Without enforcement, it was only to be expected that the illicit traffic would develop. This it did, but minimally and mainly through the changes the war produced in the sex trade. Many of the whores moved from the segregated houses into downtown apartments and rooming houses and dispensed alcoholic libations along with sexual favors. But taken in total, the Prohibition era bootleg business was hardly a patch on what the liquor traffic had been or what it would become after repeal.

What Prohibition did not do was eliminate deeply imbedded thirsts for alcohol that had been reinforced by prolonged indulgence. It was a thirst, an addiction, which drove those possessed to seek gratification by any means that came to hand. As the German military strategist, Karl von Clausewitz, once described the difference between war and peace — war was the pursuit of policy by other means — the alcoholics of the day pursued their objectives — an alcoholic glow — by every other means at their disposal, up to and including the ingestion of vanilla extract, hair tonic, and canned heat. It was they, the practicing alcoholics and not the casual drinkers, who kept the bootleggers in business. Without them and relying on the casual drinkers, the bootleggers would have starved to death on fifty cents a bottle beer.

The opening of the Government liquor stores in the cities was an immediate boon for the speak-easies, brothels, and taxi operators. No longer did they have to rely on inter-provincial bootleggers for overpriced liquor of dubious quality, or substitute home brew for whiskey, when their supplies ran short. Henceforth they would have access to all the liquor they needed at half the price they had to pay during Prohibition. Most of all it would be quality booze about which no customer would complain. The booze business in the brothels of the west, particularly in the red light districts — Annabella Street in Winnipeg, East Brandon, River Street in Moose

Jaw, eastside Calgary, Edmonton's Kinistino Street, and The Point in Lethbridge — all blossomed anew with an alcoholic glow from 1924 onward.

Ironically, it was their descent into the booze trade that created a vulnerability for the brothels where none had existed before. Periodic law enforcement drives to stamp out prostitution usually floundered on the difficulty in obtaining convictions in court. Police magistrates tended to view informers and spotters with bilious eye, and found-ins were notoriously unreliable witnesses; indeed there was no more unreliable witness than an erring husband caught *in flagrante delicto*. But when booze became a staple item in the houses of ill fame, rounded-up customers were more amenable to police persuasion to testify to the purchase of liquor rather than sex. When the police and the madam fell out, it became a relatively simple matter to get a conviction for keeping liquor for sale and run her out of town.

The Manitoba system which went into operation in 1924 could not have been better designed to encourage bootlegging. In turning its back completely on any form of cash-and-carry merchandising, Manitoba ignored a fundamental of alcohol consumption — the spur-of-the-moment, I-feel-like-a-drink aspect. Under the Manitoba home delivery system, a minimum of 24 hours and up to 48 hours could elapse between the determination to acquire a bottle of whiskey or a case of beer and a drink from a bottle. It could take that long for the Liquor Commission to process an order through its warehouse and home delivery system. It was hardly surprising that facilities sprang quickly into place to reduce the time between the urge and the satisfaction.

Small transfer operators, taxicab owners, and messenger services set up bottle delivery subsidiaries to service the thirsts of special customers. All that was needed was to keep a few bottles of Liquor Commission Scotch on hand and spread the word through the business community that it was available on telephone demand for a nominal — $1 to $2 — delivery charge. Many business and professional men were already sequestering a supply of liquor in office cabinets for use on special occasions. In the Winnipeg Grain Exchange an after-the-market drink was a long established custom with many brokers long before Prohibition. Some of them then simply filled their office vaults with booze and got through the arid stretches of Prohibition without missing a drink. For those for whom it was inconvenient to drink in their places of business, there were multiplying speak-easies in downtown apartment buildings where Liquor Commission booze was available by the drink in congenial surroundings.

This was the bootleg trade against which the reformers inveighed. It bore no resemblance whatever to the shoot-em-up, high-jacking, gang-murdering bootlegging of the sensational newspapers. The bootleggers of the Prairies, indeed, were really no more than sub-agents of the Liquor Commissions, whose activities enhanced the profits of the Commission. They filled a gap in the services of the commissions by supplying goods after the stores were closed, before they opened, and over holidays and Sundays. It took the government of Alberta fifty years to recognize that fact and give its blessing to a dial-a-bottle service for its customers when its stores were closed. But in the early days of government control, all governments took the existence of all such auxiliaries as an affront to law and order.

Manitoba's liquor order offices were barely in business before the province was wrestling with a law enforcement crisis of substantial proportions. By this time the province had its own provincial police force in operation throughout the rural areas of the province. The government expected the cities to maintain their own police forces and to be responsible for the enforcement of the liquor laws. The cities, however, expected the government to provide enough revenue to finance the hiring of all the additions to the police force that liquor law enforcement would require. Neither side would yield sufficiently to provide adequate enforcement machinery. As a result bootlegging in Greater Winnipeg became increasingly a wide open affair.

The Winnipeg breweries, which had worked overtime from day one to destroy the credibility of Prohibition, embarked on a campaign of civil disobedience against the new liquor laws. They encouraged the hotels to close down their undercover tap rooms and reopen their bars. They loaded their trucks to capacity with great oaken beer kegs and sent them out on delivery. Any half blind liquor inspector could have quickly identified the hotels that were selling beer by counting the kegs that came rolling off the brewers' trucks. Some inspectors did that. But in order to make an arrest on the spot they had to get a warrant. By the time that was achieved the truck would have moved off to another hotel. There it would require a new warrant.

When the enforcers raided the hotels and arrested the bartenders, the brewer's lawyer would have the accused out on bail in a trice and the bar would be quickly reopened. When the police raided a second time they would nab a different bartender. When they tried to have the hotel's license cancelled for repeated offenses, new licenses would appear as if by magic. Perhaps worst of all, the magistrates courts developed a positive aversion for recognizing second offenders when they saw them. The police felt that stiff jail sentences to second offenders would prove a major deterrent to the trade. But while the magistrates showed no compunction about sending shoplifters to jail for a first offense, second and third time liquor offenders got off with fines which, of course, the breweries paid. If the law enforcers had come to their task with any enthusiasm in the first place, which was doubtful, it was quickly blown away by the lack of support they got from the courts, and the lukewarm response of the public in general.

In 1925, the province moved to tighten up its enforcement machine by amending the liquor act to give the inspectors the right to arrest suspected violators without warrants. That move set up a hue and cry from all the civil libertarians within earshot and prolonged the legislature's debate for many hours. Eventually the amendment passed but had little effect on the Winnipeg situation. A year later the senior country court judge resigned from the Winnipeg Police Commission in disgust at the conditions still rampant in Winnipeg.

Across the river in French Catholic St. Boniface, where from the beginning Prohibition was regarded as an alien aberration, open bootlegging raised no eyebrows, civic or provincial. Under the benign administration of Chief Joe Gagnon, anybody who wanted to get into the booze business was free to do so, although no one could take the word "free" quite literally. Gagnon managed to keep static to a minimum by the raids he staged occasionally on major supply sources, like the seizure of dozens of cases of contraband hidden in warehouses or in box cars of coal or wood.

In Manitoba seized contraband was first placed in police storage in case it was needed as evidence in a prosecution and then either destroyed by the police or disposed of to old folks homes, orphanages, or hospitals for medicinal use. In either case a court order was issued authorizing disposal and that ended official interest in the stuff. But not the police department's. In St. Boniface the seized liquor quickly found its way into the bootleg trade, either from incomplete spillage of the liquor ordered destroyed, or by short circuiting deliveries to the charitable institutions. Some of it even found its way into the export trade to the United States.

On one particular occasion Gagnon called in one of his men and instructed him with a wink to load the police car with confiscated booze for delivery to an institution. The policeman had been changing the oil in the car and when he finished he did as instructed. The trouble was he was more skillful at loading booze than at changing oil. He neglected to tighten the oil drainage plug sufficiently so by the time the car got five miles down the south road to Minnesota the radiator steamed up, the engine seized up, and the operation came to a dead stop. There was then nothing for the driver to do but return to St. Boniface for a tow truck to haul the car back to the police station. While he was gone a Provincial Police constable happened upon the abandoned car, investigated, discovered the booze, phoned headquarters to trace the licence of the car, and discovered it was owned by the St. Boniface police. That discovery set off a chain reaction that not only blew Joe Gagnon and his crew clear out of the police station but ran most of the city's aldermen out of office at the 1928 election.

Saskatchewan's counterpart of Joe Gagnon was Chief Walter Johnson of Moose Jaw, whose likewise benign rule made River Street the second most famous sin street in western Canada in the 1920s. (Winnipeg's Annabella Street, of course, was the first.) Johnson's system, however, was different from Gagnon's. In Moose Jaw the bootleggers and the prostitutes were confined strictly to River Street and anybody trying to set up elsewhere had Chief Johnson to reckon with. Winnipeg combined both systems. Annabella Street operated wide open, as it had since it had been set up by the police commission in 1910. But by the mid 1920s there was hardly an apartment house or terrace in the Winnipeg core that did not have its resident bootlegger as well.

The uproar over law enforcement in Winnipeg, which was seldom absent for long from the newspapers, naturally brought the Moderation League back into action to circulate another beer-by-the-glass petition. Its first effort in 1926 was rejected because it contained too many fraudulent signatures but when it got its act cleaned up the Province agreed to another plebiscite. This one combined conversion from home delivery to cash-and-carry liquor sales along with beer by the glass in hotels and clubs. In June 1927 the electors approved the change, by 76,687 to 67,092 and the law was changed to provide for men-only beer parlors in 1928.

In Alberta, where beer by the glass took the breweries off the hook as far as markets were concerned, the bootleg problem was less acute than in Manitoba. Nevertheless the government was bugged by complaints from residents of the small towns in the dry constituencies about bootlegging in their midst. Some of the correspondents went so far as to name names in letters to the government. The province could not, of course, order its police on direct raids on the basis of third party complaints. It could and did send its liquor inspectors to investigate. But a stranger in town nosing around for a drink quickly aroused such suspicion that his cover as an inspector would be blown to the winds. While the inspector went off to the justice of the peace for a search warrant the miscreant would have been warned in time to secrete his supply somewhere beyond the boundaries of reasonable search. Often, the authorities suspected, the warning might have come from the justice of the peace himself, or from the local policeman. The authorities suspected, moreover, that the country bootleggers had some kind of a network that flashed the word from town to town when the inspectors were sighted on the highways. Like Manitoba, Alberta also moved to tighten up its enforcement procedures.

For advice, John W. F. Brownlee, the attorney general went to R. B. Bennett, the highest priced lawyer in Alberta and future Prime Minister of Canada. He had Bennett draft a clause that would give the inspectors carte blanche to conduct their searches as they pleased. The amendment approved by the legislature in 1925 reads:

Any inspector or constable who believes that liquor is unlawfully kept on hand, or kept or had for unlawful purposes in any building or premises may, if authorized by the Attorney General in writing, enter and search without warrant such building or premises and any part thereof for such liquor, and for that purpose break open any door, lock or fastening of such building or premise, or any closet, cupboard, box or other receptacle therein, in which liquor may be kept, contained or stored. The authority of the Attorney General to any inspector or constable may be general and continuing, and shall be effective until revoked.

What effect the change had upon the Alberta situation was never assessed. However, it can be assumed that bootlegging continued long after it was passed because, in 1929, Mr. Brownlee in an angry criticism of the way the hotels were managing their beer parlors said the situation was worse than it had been during Prohibition and if something wasn't done to improve matters drastic action would be taken.

The Manitoba beer by the glass campaign in 1927 differed from the first Prohibition crusade in the way in which extreme positions softened. Many of the lukewarm supporters of Prohibition, the wavering-not-quite-committed temperance supporters, became vulnerable to the claims of the totally dedicated wets that opening beer parlors would be an act of moderation. If Prohibition had not wiped out the drink evil, if Government monopoly was not working to perfection, perhaps allowing beer drinkers legal access by the glass might work. At the very least it would make enforcement easier and get rid of the disputatious political noise makers on both sides.

By the time the 1927 plebiscite rolled around in Manitoba a new generation of voters had matured since the Prohibitionist triumph, a generation the social gospellers might have described as the post-war looseners of the moral restraints of the Victorian age. Young women who had escaped the fetters of Victorian mores during the war and had taken jobs in commerce and industry, refused to be shuffled back into home and motherhood with the coming of peace.

They bobbed their hair, shucked their corsets, abandoned knee length bloomers for silk steps-ins, shortened their skirts first to the ankle and then to the knee, experimented with rouge, lipstick, and bare arm dresses, and went out on the town, to work during the day, in offices, banks, trust companies, and railways which had never hired women before. At night they cavorted with their "cake-eater" escorts in bell-bottomed trousers and Valentino haircuts on the floors of the ubiquitous dance halls to the seductive new music of the new dance bands. They enthused equally to the Charleston and Black Bottom and cheek to cheek swaying to the waltzes and two steps. Between dances they puffed inexpertly on their cigarettes and spluttered after occasional swigs of gin from the flask their boyfriends now carried on their hips.

For the Judy O'Gradys there were the moonlight dancing excursions to the beaches or resorts. For the colonel's ladies there were the Saturday night supper dances at the railway hotels, where the music was more pianissimo, and large bottles of liquor came with the guests for hiding under the tables, or for stashing away in hotel rooms, to which the ladies and gentlemen repaired for libations throughout the evening. If the evenings were for such galas as Burns Nicht, St. Patrick's, St. Andrew's, St. David's, or St. George's anniversaries, the back and forth treks to the rooms began early and went on far into the night.

Youth never flamed as brightly in the Prairie cities as it did in the United States and the extremes in women's or men's fashions never really caught on north of the border either. But there was enough token compliance to alarm the reverend clergy and other viewers. In 1925, for example, Monseigneur Jubinville of St. Boniface devoted a Christmas week sermon to a blast against his youthful parishioners. He deplored "the spectacle of half dressed girls writhing like snakes to the brutal dancing of jazz bands" and called their escorts "five cent sports" who came to confession smelling of booze, took holy communion and then rushed away, for another bottle.

There were dance halls and then there were dance halls. There was the Belgian Club in St. Boniface. There the Saturday night dances broke off at dawn to make way for morning mass, resumed in late afternoon, and continued until well past midnight. It was the Belgian Club that, in a gesture toward gentility, plastered a large sign up on the wall behind the band: No Rough Dancing Allowed. Then there were also the Norman Hall, the Roseland and Columbus Hall in Winnipeg, the Temple Gardens in Moose Jaw, Penleys in Calgary, where decorum was insistently maintained. In none of them was the number of couples that combined drinking and dancing ever a noticeable problem for the management.

The distaff mores of the 1920s had certainly moved well away from what had prevailed before Prohibition. But the movement, generally, was the epitome of circumspection. Dress styles had radically changed, but generally women took to drink as they took to cigarettes — sparingly, timidly, and amateurishly and most of all without public display. They smoked privately in the washrooms, never at their desks or work places or in public view in streets or in stores.

As for drinking, even the girls who nibbled at their escort's flasks at a dance were seldom prepared to knock back neat slugs of Scotch, rye or gin. If they were going to drink, they wanted something diluted, that tasted nice, or at least familiar — like Tanlac, Lydia Pinkham's, or the other alcohol based "women's tonics" to which many of the older women were unawaredly addicted. As booze spiked with a dilutant was much milder in its effect on the imbibers than straight alcohol it could be argued that the appearance of the women on the drinking scene in the 1920s had a tempering influence on the drinking habits of both men and women.

Another factor which influenced the drinking patterns of men as well as women was the emphasis all the governments placed on drinking in the home instead of in the stand-up bars. Manitoba's home delivery of all liquor purchases made it as inconvenient as possible to drink anywhere else. In the well-to-do homes the wives had equal access to the booze, and probably had invitations from the husband to share in his drinking experience. That such invitations were declined oftener than accepted can be taken for granted. Society, and particularly the women themselves, still attached a stigma to women who drank. As school girls, they had been special targets of the temperance missionaries who recruited them to membership in the Loyal Temperance Legion, to pledge in song that "lips which touch liquor shall never touch me." Such childhood influences were still, generally, strong enough to inhibit any burning urge to swig from the home liquor supply when a husband's back was turned.

An even greater suppressant of housewifely tippling was the economic reality of the 1920s, that dictated that only the upper middle class could afford to keep liquor in the house. The depression that had gripped the west for four years was receding but slowly when the liquor stores opened. The price of wheat, which had topped three dollars a bushel in 1919, was nudging one dollar again, and wages were declining instead of improving. The construction and transportation industries were severely depressed throughout the 1920s and the loss of the 1919 general strike had all but destroyed the trade unions.

The era of unemployment insurance, or even unemployment relief, was far beyond the horizon of time. Climate-enforced seasonal unemployment, moreover, was still the impoverishing burden in the working class of the Prairies. The elite of the class, the skilled building tradesmen, earned from $.85 to $1.00 an hour which, for a 44-hour week, seemed a good enough wage in relation to the times. Certainly it was double what the unskilled tradesmen, factory workers, and store clerks took home. But averaged across a whole year and carpenters or bricklayers seldom had much more than $1,000 to show for their year's work.

When the liquor stores opened in Winnipeg the price posted for

26 ounces of imported Scotch was from $4.50 to $5 a bottle while Canadian rye was priced from $3.65 to $3.85 a bottle of 26 ounces. Beer was $3.65 to $4.00 for a case of 24 pints. This, generally, was also the price level adopted in Alberta and Saskatchewan. Obviously, an ordinary wage earner had to give up very close to a day's pay in exchange for a bottle of liquor or a case of beer. It was small wonder that laying in a supply of booze to have on hand in case friends dropped in was the sort of extravagance that only a tiny minority could afford.

There were, however, some contradictory cross currents that were tending to undercut the strict adherence to economic logic. Motivations for taking to drink were changing. In the barroom era drinking to get drunk, particularly on Saturday nights, had become the ingrained intention of many of the imbibers, just as drinking to demonstrate how well one could hold his liquor was an acceptable measurement of manhood. Almost imperceptibly, when legal access to alcohol was restored, attitudes changed. The dancing daughters of the 1920s did not go to dances to get drunk; they went to dances to dance and the intake of liquor was incidental to the dancing. Drinking was something done to enhance the pleasure of the moment. If both drinking partners emerged from an evening of dancing in states of relative sobriety that came to be accepted as perhaps the way it should be.

There were other avenues of socializing where liquor was beginning to be used to lubricate personal relationships. Liquor was an occasional facet of the burgeoning bridge craze, first auction and then contract bridge. Hosts who invited friends in for a couple of tables of bridge might occasionally deal out a round of mild libations with the cards. What made the libations mild was the recent invention of ice cubes and the growing popularity of such soft drinks as gingerale, Coca-Cola, Orange Crush, etc. A jigger of gin in a tall glass mixed with a soft drink and lots of ice and spiked with a soupcon of sugar could be nursed through two or three rubbers of bridge by the women as well as the men. Mixing in this manner made the liquor go a lot farther and last longer, a not unimportant consideration. To the conscience-pricked women, drinking alcohol in this pleasantly diluted form did not really seem like "drinking". "Drinking" was ingesting that awful tasting stuff that burned your throat and made you sneeze and even throw up!

Keeping a supply of liquor in the home may have been economically unthinkable for the overwhelming majority of the population of the 1920s; but thinking about getting a bottle to enhance the enjoyment of an anniversary, the birth of a baby, a family reunion, Christmas, New Year's Eve, or a summer picnic frequently led to modest stretching of family budgets. And the fact was that having liquor to drink did add to the pleasure of the occasion for many people who, prior to Prohibition, had never touched the stuff. That was particularly true when the liquor came in the tasty new cocktail mixtures spawned by the American Prohibition era — drinks like the whiskey sour, planters punch, mint julep, daiquiri, manhattan, martini, cuba libre, etc. The enhancement of the occasion was reflected in shyness being overcome, conversation made easier, inhibitions being released, confidence being elevated. That there could be fatal consequences hidden in these pleasurable enhancements of the occasion went completely undiscovered at the time and would not begin to emerge until a full decade after the beer parlors were a fact of life.

The extent to which such changing mores influenced the affirmative vote for beer parlors in the Manitoba plebiscite of 1927 and the Saskatchewan vote of 1934 would be difficult to assess. Certainly the evidence is that the women voters had little interest in beer or beer parlors. When Alberta changed its regulations to bar women from Calgary and Edmonton taverns, few complained. Women were banned by law from entry into the Manitoba beer parlors for almost 30 years without engendering any overt sign of resentment or protest. The uproar over bootlegging and law enforcement deficiencies kept the politicians talking and the newspapers editorializing. But there is reason to assume that the attention of the public generally was usually elsewhere, on the stagnant economy, the low price of wheat, sporting events, and most of all on that newest of public fascinators, the radio.

As for booze itself — beer, wine, whiskey, gin, rum, whatever — there is convincing evidence that the citizenry generally was taking it or leaving it with only a modicum of interest. In Manitoba, where 84,000 had voted in favor of repeal and the opening of government stores, only 25,707 permits of all kinds were issued during the first six months of operation. By the end of the first fiscal year the number reached only to 35,759. During the first full year of government stores in Alberta only a skimpy third of the affirmative repeal voters took out $2 good-for-one-year permits. That was the equivalent of one adult male Albertan in five, one Alberta adult in 10. Over the same period another 74,557 Albertans paid 50 cents for a single purchase permit because they did not contemplate buying enough liquor over the year to make a $2 investment worthwhile. Quantitatively over the same year the Alberta consumption of beer was 9 gallons per capita, spirits of all kinds one quart per capita, and wine less than a pint each.

CHAPTER FIVE
THE THIRSTY THIRTIES BROUGHT CHEAP BOOZE

With its beer parlor plebiscite out of the way, Manitoba drifted into a period of social calm no longer disturbed by noisy controversy over beverage alcohol. But not so Alberta. Its beer parlors seemed to keep public tempers on edge, particularly in the rural areas. There were public brawls over local option votes, and over the decade the wets won a majority of the plebiscites that were held to establish beer parlors. But the drys were often able to head off the establishment of liquor stores or beer parlors by petitioning against them before the wets got organized. By 1928 the rowdiness and drunkenness of the beer parlor environs reached a point where Premier Brownlee himself began issuing warnings that the law would be changed unless the hotelmen cleaned up their act. That nudged the Prohibitionists back into action and in 1931 they gathered petitions containing over 55,000 names calling for the end of the beer parlors. Apart from provoking the legislature into days of angry debate over the validity of the names on the documents the episode passed without any action being taken.

In Saskatchewan the hot summers of the 1920s and early 1930s were rippled by desultory efforts of the Moderation League to get a beer by the glass plebiscite. But the intransigence of the Liberal Government and its refusal to pay the wets the slightest heed dampened down the clamor. It was not until 1934 that one of the last acts of the expiring coalition-Conservative administration granted the plebiscite and beer parlors were voted in by a grudgingly narrow majority.

Rum running to the United States there still was across the undefended Prairie border in the late 1920s but it was hardly a trickle compared with the volume of booze that had flowed from the

Saskatchewan and Alberta export houses of the early 1920s. By the tag end of the decade, U.S. supplies flooding onto the illicit domestic market from illegal distilleries and breweries, combined with leakage from industrial distilleries and medicinal alcohol production, to more than fill the demand. The demand for the more expensive, imported liquors shrunk to a point where it was confined mainly to the upper middle class who were leery of the quality of domestic booze. For them, breaking the government seals on bottles of Johnny Walker, Chivas Regal, Dewar's Extra Special, or Grant's Best Procurable was an exercise in status symboling oneupmanship. Such liquor, tediously accumulated by Prairie bootleggers from their government liquor stores and smuggled into Minnesota, North Dakota, and Montana commanded a premium of $3 and $4 a bottle. But it was a business for the ribbon clerks of the rum running trade, small-time runners of occasional automobile loads, and sleeping car porters running it across the border by the suitcase full.

In the American cities, domestic supplies had long since reached a point where the gangster overlords of the trade were resorting to violence to force their own produced booze into the outlets of their rivals. Violent crime was of course not new to America, but a climax of sorts was reached in Chicago on St. Valentine's Day, 1929 when a half dozen Capone hoodlums lined up seven O'Banion gangsters against a garage wall and machine gunned them into eternity. By that time, Capone was estimated to be earning $60,000,000 a year from his booze monopoly, protection rackets, and drug traffic in the Chicago area. It was a figure that far outstripped the combined liquor profits of all the governments of Canada.

There is no question that the gang wars, wholesale murders, and open defiance of the law by the entrenched gangsters brought the whole American Prohibition experiment into disrepute. As details of this unfolding of a national problem without a solution flowed across our borders in lurid news stories, magazine exposés and increasing volumes of radio news reportage, Prairie people too became restive about the threat of the gangsters spreading into Canada. And this perhaps may have explained why, once Prohibition had been repealed, no Prairie-wide counterattack was ever mounted by the drys. It was almost as if, contemplating the American scene with increased attention, Prairie people saw the gangster era as the inevitable result of Prohibition, and were thankful they had changed their minds before it was too late. So as the Prairie governments dipped their toes gingerly into operating liquor monopolies, there was a general disposition, even among the temperance people, to give the newest experimental venture a fair trial.

To head its liquor monopoly Manitoba reached clear over to the Saar Valley on the Franco-German border for Armistice Commissioner Hon. W. D. Waugh, a former mayor of Winnipeg. Alberta chose R. J. Dinning, a successful businessman with impressive UFA credentials. On the principle, seemingly, that high paid commissioners would be shielded from temptation to dip into the till, the governments amply rewarded their liquor bosses. Mr. Waugh received $7,500 a year and his two part-time assistant commissioners were paid $5,000 each. Mr. Dinning functioned as a one-man commission and was paid $750 a month. In relation to the times, these were princely stipends all, well beyond the earnings of ordinary bank managers and even of cabinet ministers on the Prairies. The stipends did indeed buy integrity; no breath of scandal ever touched the skirts of Prairie liquor commissioners over a stretch of fifty years.

Alberta's UFA Government, so eternally thankful that it was not a "political party government" like the others, went whole hog in revealing the totality of the commission's operation. Its first annual report ran to fifty exhaustively detailed pages. Every liquor supplier, no matter how insignificant, was listed with details of sales value. All the expenses were detailed even down to the salaries of warehouse men and office clerks. The less stuffy Liberal Government of C. A. Dunning of Saskatchewan invited its electors to take it on trust. Its annual report ran to barely twelve pages, two thirds of them reproductions of legal forms and lists of store locations. Manitoba, which also had a farmers' government, tended to follow Alberta's model, but at a considerable distance.

Perhaps the most interesting aspect of the settling into the liquor trade by the provincial governments was the humdrum way in which it was done. The head offices and storage facilities selected were used-up old warehouses in the backwaters of the capital cities. The stores themselves, when they got them opened, were unadorned by fancy eye-catching signs one might have expected of new business premises. The store fronts were devised completely to cut off the view of the interior from pedestrians on the street. The only adornment of the interior walls was a single wall calendar. The stock in trade was all safely stowed away behind partitioning and out of sight of the customers. It was delivered to the purchasers in plain brown wrapping, whether by hand in Alberta or by home delivery in Manitoba. Clearly the liquor business was not one the governments were proud to be in.

All this may simply have been keeping step with the times because the 1920s was a humdrum time in which the glorious promise of the Sifton immigration era had turned ashes on this northern fringe of the great American desert. Even though a steady stream of European immigrants continued to flow in to join their pioneer families, the great immigration binge was over. Only Alberta was able to retain its natural population increase, by a measly 25,000. More native westerners were migrating to the United States than the immigrants were able to replace. Over that whole decade less than a handful of noteworthy buildings went up in the three provinces. Boosterism was replaced with persistent worry over farm debt and insufficient taxation bases to support provincial services.

As things turned out, the government liquor business was the best thing that ever happened to the provincial treasurers. In 1926 for example, the Prairie provinces had budgets totalling $35,000,000 to provide all the health, education, and other services for their 2,100,000 people. Of that sum roughly $6,000,000 or 17% came from liquor profits. Liquor was not only reliable as a revenue source, it was also slowly but steadily increasing. Nevertheless all the governments seemed to regard their enterprise with a sort of jaundiced toleration, almost like straight-laced spinsters who inherited a string of lucrative brothels. Each government went to great pains to establish the sort of commissions which would shield the reigning politicians from contamination with the liquor traffic.

Missing from the records of the governments is any statement of principle or philosophy which would govern the operation of the government boozoriums. What was to be the primary objective of the liquor control commission? To serve as a sort of stalking horse for the temperance movement by providing minimal accessibility to alcoholic beverages consistent with the suppression of illicit trade in the stuff? Or was it to engage in commercial enterprise like other publicly owned utilities? Should it provide service at cost, like the street cars, or earn profits like the electric companies? And if the latter, how much profit was it expected to earn to meet political expectations? On this last point there had been a measure of direction from the voters. In the referenda controversy a strong point was made of the fact that British Columbia was earning $1,000,000 a year from its liquor business, that by earning that profit the burdens on the taxpayers could be reduced. Perhaps, with an eye on the referendum vote, the commissioners decided that a profit of $1,000,000 a year would be a nice round sum at which to aim.

A search of the archives of the three provinces failed to turn up anything in the way of formal correspondence between premiers and chief commissioners on the governments' expectation of the commissions. What probably happened was that the premiers talked privately with their commissioners, and law officers of the Crown drafted regulations based on models borrowed from Ontario and British Columbia.

Premiers John Bracken, Charles Dunning, and Herbert Greenfield were all staunch temperance supporters, if not downright Prohibitionists. John Bracken had been a featured speaker at Prohibition rallies in Manitoba in 1923 and Premier Greenfield was a veteran United Farmers of Alberta wheel-horse. The bone dry UFA was a Prohibition supporter with resolution and muscle from the beginning and was continuing to pass resolutions attacking the liquor outlets long after the repeal of Prohibition. Premier Dunning may have been somewhat less committed, but while he had bowed to the demands of his electors for a plebiscite in 1924, he steadfastly refused to grant a beer-by-the-glass vote as long as he was premier of Saskatchewan. Simple logic would have dictated that none of the premiers would have chosen a commissioner who was not on his own wave length. A typical exchange could have sounded like this:

About all that we are really required to do by the plebiscite is to provide reasonable legal access to alcoholic beverages for those who want them. Well suppose we kept the stores open from 9 or 10 A.M. to 6 P.M. The one thing we must keep in mind at all costs is this: there must never be a return to pre-Prohibition conditions. Public drunkenness simply cannot be tolerated. We must adopt measures which will make it difficult, if not impossible for degenerate drunks to obtain access to our supplies. We should establish a reasonable mark-up on our stock so that the trade will return a reasonable profit on our investment. In view of the type of goods we're going to handle, we will have to take extraordinary measures to make absolutely certain there is no leakage between our suppliers and ourselves or between our stock and the public. And we must do all our trading in the absolute open so that there can be no scandals about petty graft, secret commissions, kick-backs, or favoritism for friends of the government. And what else should we think of . . .?

Nothing in the history of the government monopolies is inconsistent with such a catalogue of considerations. But the liquor commissions, like most other government enterprises, gradually assumed lives of their own. And as time passed the interest of the governments dwindled to concern, almost exclusively, with the bottom line on the profit and loss statement. The commissions, for their part, came to regard that same bottom line as a measure of the success of their enterprise. After all, what other yardstick was there?

They had no mandate to increase the consumption of alcoholic beverages by the promotion of their sale. If they could do all the business there was to be done from one store, they were content with one store. If an inconvenienced public complained loudly enough to the government a second store might be opened, but only after long sieges of prayer and meditation. There was no advertisement of wares, no bargain sales of slow moving lines and brands, not even a placarded counter or wall announcement of the stocking of new lines. There were open front doors, order desks, and cash registers, and that was all. As time passed governments came to rely on liquor profits to balance budgets, the commissions became accustomed to providing the profits, and when there was a sudden turn-down in profits there was considerable soul searching in the back rooms.

In these times before business administration majors, the liquor commissions seemed to have worked on a combination of "by-guess-and-by-God" and "follow-the-leader" business principles. Each commission seems to have taken a quick look at prices being charged elsewhere and priced their own stock accordingly, give or take differences in freight rates. Alberta had the advantage of British Columbia, Manitoba, and Quebec already being in business, so Mr. Dinning took a short tour around before opening his doors for business. As a result of neighbor watching, liquor prices from 1924 tended to remain relatively uniform across the Prairies. In 1925, for example, the following prices prevailed for representative brands:

	Alberta	Manitoba
Scotch (26 ounces)		
Dewars	$5.25	$5.45
Dawsons	4.75	4.90
Grants	5.00	5.10
Rye (26 ounces)		
Corbys	3.50	3.45
Gooderham & Worts	3.50	3.50
Canadian Club	3.75	3.65
Gin (26 ounces)		
Gordons	3.75	3.80
Gilbeys	3.70	3.70

Once established the prices stayed put. Price lists were issued spring and fall but changes were minor for established brands. What did happen was that all the distillers began price probing to find markets at the bottom of the scale. Thus by 1929 all Canadian distillers were marketing a 26 ounce bottle of rye whiskey for $2.85 and a 13 ounce flask for $1.50. For the younger crowd the 13 ounce "mickey" became exceedingly popular for stowing away on hips for consumption at dances, and with it the silver flask's popularity began to slip badly.

Tracing the growth of the liquor business and comparing consumption, sales, and profits for the early years is fraught with difficulties that arise out of differing systems, time frames, and accounting procedures. In Alberta until 1936 beer sales were separate from liquor sales. Liquor was sold only through government stores while the breweries were allowed to retail their beer through their own stores and keep the profits. In return they were charged $220,000 a year in brewery licence fees, which did not go through the liquor board. Manitoba had a somewhat similar system until 1928-29 but Saskatchewan sold both beer and spirits and its sales and profit figures reflect the difference. Alberta began operating on the calendar year, then went to a March 31 fiscal year. Manitoba operated on an April 30 fiscal year end for many years. Nevertheless, for discerners of trends the statistics are fascinating. Here are some categories for the 1920s. (Saskatchewan kept no statistics on permits):

	Manitoba $000's			Saskatchewan $000's		
Year	Permits	Sales	Profits	Permits	Sales	Profits
1924-5	58,865	$3,639	$1,346			
1925-6	45,090	3,745	1,315		$ 7,812	$1,898
1926-7	49,811	3,794	1,367		10,305	2,115
1927-8	68,499	3,985	1,345		11,709	2,444
1928-9	92,595	7,372	1,999		14,067	3,083
1929-30	93,091	7,620	2,045		12,380	2,398

	Alberta $000's		
Year	Permits	Sales	Profits
1924-5		$3,734	$1,552
1925-6	31,000	4,268	1,803
1926-7	33,800	4,858	2,038
1927-8	43,343	5,997	2,561
1928-9	43,136	6,551	2,661
1929-30	35,488	6,283	2,410

The trends which are indicated by the sales and profits figures for the 1920s are probably indicative of the way in which the public reacted to whiskey and beer on demand. As the population grew slowly and matured slowly, so did the consumption of liquor. Sales were undoubtedly spurred by the sharp rise in economic conditions from 1926 onward, particularly in Alberta, a development also seen in the boom in sale of electric stoves, electric refrigerators, electric radios, and automobiles.

The Manitoba permit figures may perhaps reflect accurately the number of moderately steady drinkers in the province but can hardly include many casual, once-in-a-while drinkers. The Manitoba home delivery system, it should again be emphasized, was downright discouraging to impulse drinkers. When the cash and carry system was adopted in 1928 there was a sharp jump in the number of customers and the number increased again in 1929 when beer sales were brought completely within the scope of the government monopoly.

The Alberta permit figures also substantially understate the facts because of the two permit system. The figures in the tabulation are only for the $2 annual permits. Two or three times as many fifty-cent individual purchase permits were sold, many of them unquestionably to purchasers previously of the $2 numbers which were printed on rather flimsy 2 x 3 inch slips of paper, crumpled easily, and were easily mislaid. In short they were a nuisance to carry around so many Albertans simply bought the fifty centers when the annual permit self-destructed.

Minor aberrations aside, the conclusion which flows from the 1920s statistics is that when times are good, and liquor is available, its purchase and consumption will increase. It can even be argued that liquor and beer sales figures constitute a fairly accurate barometer of the economic climate. Certainly liquor sales on the Prairies signalled the peak of the 1920s economic improvement; the sales decline in 1930 arguably signalled the onset of the Great Depression. That was the year of a fairly good crop in Manitoba and Alberta but a below average crop in Saskatchewan. It was also the year in which the price of wheat fell to below fifty cents a bushel at the country elevators, less than it had ever been before on the Prairies.

Fiscal Year

Manitoba	1929-30	1930-31	1931-32	1932-33	1933-34
Permits	93,091	83,195	68,915	53,049	47,092
Sales	$7,620,000	$6,507,000	$5,399,000	$4,116,000	$3,767,000
Profits	$2,044,000	$1,867,000	$1,630,000	$1,094,000	$ 992,068
Saskatchewan					
Sales	$12,380,000	$9,158,000	$5,774,000	$4,787,000	$4,823,000
Profits	$ 2,398,000	$1,516,000	$ 843,000	$ 864,000	$ 919,000
Alberta					
Permits	35,488	24,426	19,447	15,828	N.A.
Sales	$4,678,000	$3,571,000	$2,929,000	$2,697,000	$3,224,000
Profits	$1,738,000	$1,305,000	$1,319,000	$1,178,000	$1,484,000

It took a while for that shattering disappearance of farm purchasing power in 1930 to work its way through the economy, but the result of that process can be seen in the 1931-34 figures. There was a near crop failure in Manitoba and Saskatchewan in 1931 which, with even more ruinous prices, brought on the unemployment relief crisis that was to become a permanent feature of Prairie politics and economics. At a time when all government revenues were shrinking, and the demands on government revenues were greater than ever for unemployment and agricultural relief, the anchor to windward — liquor profits — came unstuck. In that regard, Saskatchewan, which had profited the most from the liquor trade suffered the most, and continued to do so.

And then came 1934 and the onset of the dust bowl years. That

June blowing top soil from the plains of Nebraska clouded Washington in a perpetual haze, and could be seen to the height of 10,000 feet off New England. Blowing dust from Saskatchewan obscured the sun in Winnipeg before being blown eastward to western Ontario.

That was really only the beginning. With the dust came grasshoppers in clouds that also obscured the sun, stripped the soil of everything green, laid their eggs, and were swept forward into the north east. That was the year when it was, frequently impossible to see across the street in Regina, when the Moose Jaw Creek dried up and Wascana Creek was a hard-caked mud hole. As the destitute farmers went out to try to windproof their fields amid the swirling dust, an ice cold beer would have been ambrosia from heaven, but nobody had any ice. There wasn't one farmer in fifty who had a quarter for a bottle of beer, or would have spent the quarter on beer if he had. But there were people around somewhere with money for beer. Albertans that year consumed almost 3,000,0000 gallons of it plus 108,000 gallons of whiskey, gin, and rum and 127,000 gallons of wine. And as Saskatchewan ran almost $2,000,000 worth of beer (at cost) through its monopoly it is a reasonable estimate that the people of that province almost equaled Alberta's consumption.

The shattering drop in liquor board profits confronted the governments and their commissioners with several dilemmas: should they take positive measures to counteract the trend? Should they jack up their profit margins and risk buyer resistance to higher prices? Or should they reduce prices to increase patronage and achieve a restoration of profits from greater volume, even though this would run counter to every precept of the Temperance cause? Between 1932 and 1935 the governments all quietly crossed the Rubicon by choosing the latter course. It had been the impression of the temperance people, when they voted for repeal, that government control would mean the taking of stringent measures to reduce consumption. That notion was filed and forgotten forever during the depression. The word "control" was left permanently imbedded in the titles of the Manitoba and Alberta boards, but after 1935 the boards became purely and simply sales agencies concerned only with merchandising the product.

As patronage shrank with the incomes of the people, the liquor boards did what they could to keep their books in the black. To increase patronage Alberta dropped the permit price from $2 to 50 cents and all boards allowed their prices to sink 30 to 40% below the

1925 levels. Here, for example, is a comparison of the prices in Manitoba and Alberta for 1925 and 1935:

	Alberta		Manitoba	
	1925	1935	1924-25	1935
Scotch				
Dewars	$5.25	$3.25	$5.45	$3.25
Dawsons	4.75	3.00	4.90	—
Grants	5.00	3.00	5.10	3.80
Teachers	—	3.10		3.00
Rye				
Corbys	$3.50	$2.15	$3.45	$2.15
G & W	3.50	2.15	3.50	2.15
Canadian				
Club	3.75	3.00	3.65	3.00
Gin				
Gordons	$3.75	$2.00	$3.80	$2.40
Gilbeys	3.70	2.00	3.70	2.00

The price of liquor did not proportionately follow the price of wheat and steers, but the price cuts nevertheless were substantial. The Commissions were quietly edging into more profitable areas as well. Thus Alberta was marketing its own Control Board Rye at $1.75 a 26 ounce bottle and $1.00 for a 13 ounce mickey. Manitoba also had a house brand mickey of rye for $1.00 and Scotch for $1.15. Its imported house brand brandy in the 26 ounce bottles was listed at $3.40 while Hennessys XXX brandy sold for $4.10.

Anyone with $2 to spend in Alberta had available a wide selection of imported table wines: a bottle of Chateau Margaux was $2, Pontet-Canet was $1.75, Chauvenet Red Flag $1.25, and Heidsieck Champagne was $2.10 a half bottle. For the punch makers and ordinary winos, Bright's Catawba was available at 60 cents a bottle or six for $3.25 in Alberta, or for 50 cents a bottle in Manitoba.

If the commissioners had retained even a trace of interest in reducing public consumption of beverage alcohol, they would hardly have expanded the number of brands and varieties carried the way they did during the depression. Indeed substantial savings might have been made in inventory costs by confining their stocks to no more than two or three brands of each liquor. Before Prohibition, tipplers seldom had a choice of more than two or three brands of rye or Scotch at their favorite bars. When the Bronfman's blending plant at Yorkton was going full blast in the hiatus period, it gave buyers a choice of several labels, but the contents of all the bottles on which the varied labels were pasted came from the same vat. And nobody seemed to know the difference.

In the 1930s Manitoba especially, provided its customers with an unbelievable breadth of choice: in 1935, for example, it offered a selection of red and white wines and champagnes from Australia, South Africa, France, Germany, Italy, and Spain, plus eighteen Ontario and three British Columbia wines. It offered fifteen Canadian ryes from seven distillers and Scotch in almost infinite variety: there was Canadian blended Scotch, imported-in-wood and bottled-in-Canada Scotch, thirty-nine brands of imported-in-the-bottle Scotch and three brands of imported-in-barrels-and sold-by-the-gallon Scotch. Nine brands of brandy were on sale along with two imported gins and fifteen brands of domestic gin, a dozen varieties of rum, and no less than twenty liqueurs.

Neither Alberta nor Saskatchewan provided the customers with quite such a broad selection, perhaps because the demand was not there. Nevertheless, Saskatchewan stocked the products of fifteen Scottish distillers and a dozen French, Spanish, and Italian vintners. But by far the greatest portion of its business was done with Canadian wineries for the people of Saskatchewan clearly preferred Canadian wine beyond any other libation except beer. Alberta offered about as many brands of wine as Manitoba but only ninety brands of hard liquor compared with Manitoba's one hundred-and-twenty.

The most expensive bottle of liquor stocked on the Prairies was the Bols' four compartment liqueurs decanter, priced at $13.50 in Manitoba. A 26 ounce bottle of Hudson's Bay 50 year-old brandy came next at $9.60, a 40 ounce bottle of Chivas Regal Scotch was $6.20, and 40 ounces of Seagram's V.O. and Walkers Canadian Club sold for $4.40. Neither of the other provinces stocked any of these high priced items. Alberta with but very few exceptions confined its stock to 26 and 13 ounce sizes. It offered the lowest-priced hard liquor — 85 cents for a mickey of gin while Manitoba offered the lowest-priced French wine in the country — 65 cents for a bottle of Danglade's St. Emilion claret and the same price for the vintner's Fronsac semi-dry Bordeaux.

It is clear from the foregoing prices that a liquor dollar in 1935 was worth at least half as much again in terms of the beverage alcohol it would buy as it had been ten years before. In the crop year 1925-26, a better than average wheat crop was harvested all across the plains and it went to market at better than average prices. Unemployment was minimal, in the low range of seasonal joblessness. Compared with it, 1935 was a crop failure year at ruinous prices, and mass unemployment gripped the land. Single unemployed men were hived off in bush camps puttering away their lives on make-work projects at twenty cents per day and their board. In 1925-26, the first year for which figures are available for all provinces, the people spent a grand total of $15,825,000 on beverage alcohol of all kinds. In 1934-35, the total had dropped to $13,148,000. But in terms of the volume of liquor the $13,148,000 would buy it is obvious that the people of the Prairies were putting away more booze at the nadir (to then) of the depression than they had been doing in the most normal year of the normal 1920s.

And then everything went down hill.

Coincidentally with the change in the Federal government in 1935, urban unemployment eased and business generally picked up in the cities over the next couple of years. But out in the Palliser Triangle of Saskatchewan and Alberta in 1937 the dryest summer within the memory of man gripped the land. Not only was the Saskatchewan wheat crop reduced to cinders, but by the first of July the pasture lands were so badly burned that the government was faced with moving 400,000 head of starving cattle off the land into the packing plants. At the University of Saskatchewan at Saskatoon, an emergency task force was dispatched into the countryside to harvest random growing Russian thistle — tumbleweed — in the hope of being able to use it to bring its prize cattle herd through the winter.

Here again, however, it took time for the full impact of the Palliser disaster to work its way through the economic system. The steady increases in liquor sales that were being recorded annually from the 1933 low point continued into 1937 and only began to reflect the economic retreat in 1938. In doing so the statistics serve to focus attention on a seldom recognized aspect of the Great Depression — there was never a time when it victimized everybody on the Prairies.

It is true that there were municipalities in Saskatchewan where eighty percent of the people were on relief. It is true that upwards of 150,000 people fled Saskatchewan as a result of the depression. It is true that thousands of farm families in southern Saskatchewan loaded their possessions onto farm wagons and headed north out of the dust bowl. It is true that between a quarter and a third of all the families in Winnipeg went through the relief rolls during the depression. But it is also true that outside the dust bowl many thousands of farmers had good crops and stayed off relief. And in the cities and towns there were thousands of people who never missed a day's work and who constituted the hard core of the population who had never had it so good. They were the doctors, lawyers, merchants, chiefs, policemen, firemen, civil servants, bus drivers, railway employees, bank employees, etc. etc. True their incomes were reduced and everybody in a job was forced to take salary and wage cuts, but the cost of living dropped to an all-time low and stayed there. Food, clothing, and shelter all glutted the market and the prices reflected that fact.

The endless days of rainless weather may have destroyed the crops but it was great for golf and tennis. Labor was plentiful everywhere for twenty-five or thirty cents an hour and for the convivially inclined working class with jobs a gallon of Catawba wine, spiked with an Imperial pint of straight grain 100 proof alcohol, could put a party of ten to singing and dancing well into the night for less than five dollars.

As will be seen from the final tables of statistics of the 1930s, the people of the Prairies spent more money in their liquor stores than they had in 1931. On a per capita basis, the expenditures were not large, about nine dollars per capita in Manitoba and Saskatchewan and twelve dollars in Alberta. The expenditure on liquor per adult male was around thirty-five dollars per annum in 1937 in Manitoba and Saskatchewan and fifty dollars per year in Alberta. Translated into a little over a bottle of whiskey a month for Manitoba and

Fiscal Year

Manitoba	1934-35	1935-36	1936-37	1937-38	1938-39	1939-40
Permits	51,248	58,465	66,496	74,544	76,378	108,380
Sales	4,209,000	4,540,000	5,190,000	5,890,000	5,947,000	7,887,000
Profits	1,086,000	1,293,000	1,912,000	1,753,000	1,742,000	2,135,000
Saskatchewan						
Sales	5,203,000	5,735,000	6,715,000	6,042,000	6,012,000	7,273,000
Profits	1,027,000	1,279,000	1,451,000	1,245,000	1,289,000	1,704,000
Alberta						
Sales	3,224,000	3,725,000	*7,661,000	8,194,000	8,645,000	9,365,000
Profits	1,484,000	1,802,000	2,332,000	2,532,000	2,676,000	2,873,000

*Beer sales included for first time.

Saskatchewan and two bottles in Alberta that does not seem to be all that extravagant an involvement with booze. But when the numbers are compared with some vital provincial expenditures they appear in a different light: the people of Manitoba and Alberta in 1937 spent three times as much on liquor as they did on education, over twice as much in Saskatchewan. Similarly Manitobans spent twice as much for liquor as they did for law enforcement and agriculture combined, Saskatchewan spent four times as much and Albertans five times as much.

The figures are also a commentary on the Moderation League contention that Prohibition was the root cause of crime on the Prairies. Convictions for crimes of all kinds, which touched bottom in 1917-18, jumped sharply in 1920 during the export hiatus, declined in 1922, and then rose steadily until 1929. The figures for Manitoba were 16,334 convictions in 1914, 8,155 in 1917, 12,516 in 1920, 10,718 in 1922 and steadily upward to 28,524 in 1929. For the same years Saskatchewan dropped from 13,782 in 1914 to 7,072 in 1917 and ultimately rose to 13,331 in 1929. Alberta showed the same trend — 19,426 in 1914, 6,627 in 1917, and 16,140 in 1929. And when the consumption of liquor dropped during the 1930s so did crime of all kinds. Manitoba criminal convictions dropped by a third from 1929 to 1936, Saskatchewan by almost a half and, Alberta by better than a third. Then as the Prairie economy began to inch its way out of the depression, and liquor sales began to rise again so did criminal activity of all kinds. By the end of the decade liquor sales and profits were nudging the 1929 levels across the plains and so were crime statistics.

With the correlation between booze and crime now so clearly established one would have expected that the temperance forces would have been launched on a counter-offensive to bring back Prohibition sometime during the 1930s. After all, the Moderationists and the beer-by-the-glass campaign in 1927 in Manitoba had made much of the law and order argument. The explanation for the silence of the Prohibitionists was simple: they had disappeared without a trace from the face of Western Canada. The raising of the 50,000 signature petition in Alberta to abolish the beer parlors in 1931 had been the dying paroxysm of the Temperance cause. Though antipathy toward boozing would survive in scattered rural enclaves in Manitoba and Alberta, it was a completely spent political force.

The United States in 1931 was, of course, long gone on the road to repeal of the Nineteenth Amendment. Alfred E. Smith, the

Democratic Party candidate for President, had started the process in 1928 in repudiating his party's dry platform and coming out for repeal of Prohibition. Urban newspapers were increasingly taking the same stance. The election of Franklin D. Roosevelt in 1932 and the nationwide sweep of the Democrats led to the passage by the U.S. Senate in 1933 of a resolution calling for repeal by passage of the 21st Amendment to the constitution. A succession of States voted for repeal and in December 1933, Utah became the 36th State to do so and that made it official.

There is little question that Prohibition had been so thoroughly discredited in the United States by the utter inability of its governments to enforce the law against the massive opposition of the liquor interest, criminal elements, and the urban population. Only Kansas and a handful of other States kept the faith. On the other hand on the Prairies of Western Canada the operations of the liquor boards were shaking down so well that public interest in the subject diminished to vanishing point. As far as the politicians were concerned the Liquor Commission became just another government agency, but a rather distinguished one able to operate profitably year after year without ever doing anything to make political waves for political parties.

As for the public generally, there seemed to be a wide consensus that the kind of government control that had been devised for Western Canada was giving the public the best of both worlds. There was liquor available for those who wanted it, and on any given day of any given week that was a minority of the population. For the rest no intolerable problems were being created by drinkers. Under government control consumption of liquor had been shunted from the ubiquitous bars of the pre-war Prairies to the homes of the drinkers. As a result there was little evidence of excessive consumption except in the vicinity of the beer parlors of Alberta. Even there, arrests for drunkenness dropped from around 2,000 a year before Prohibition to between 300 and 400 during the 1920s and to under 200 during the depression. Saskatchewan, without the beer parlors, arrested an average of less than 150 a year in the 1920s, and touched an all-time low of 47 in 1933. Manitoba which had averaged 1,800 a year before the war was down to less than 200 during the depression.

This lack of pervasive physical evidence of excess consumption distracted attention from the way consumption of alcohol was steadily increasing over the years. During the first five years of government control, sales increased at the rate of twenty percent a year. If that rate had continued for the next ten years there might have been some public worrying done by 1939. But the depression intervened to dampen down demand so that by 1939 overall sales had only risen to $21,000,000 from the $15,000,000 recorded during the first full year of government control. In any event there were few problems associated with drink that were not being managed with reasonable satisfaction by constituted authority. Even with the onset of the Second World War, and the development of horrendous problems for the drinkers, there was no disposition on the part of either the drinkers or the abstainers to blame the liquor boards. Not from the press, the pulpits, nor the street corner weisenheimers.

CHAPTER SIX
FIGHTING THE WAR ON THE LIQUOR PERMIT FRONT

To tell the story of Prairie participation in the Second World War as a chapter in a book about booze may seem an affront to that event. It is far from intentionally so but the war experience in many ways impinged as forcefully upon the social fabric of the Prairie Provinces as the Ban-the-Bars crusade and Prohibition had done. It took 50,000 young Prairie Canadians off the streets, welded them into cohesive groups, gave them a reason for living, and for dying, and endowed them with a sense of self-worth and dignity they had never had before. As single unemployed they were nudged from soup kitchen to soup kitchen, from town to town, into and out of relief camps. As soldiers in uniform they were welcomed everywhere. Few motorists ever refused a soldier, sailor, or airman a lift. A soldier walking into a beer parlor in search of his buddies would be invited to a vacant place at the tables as he passed. Civilian families, who might have served him a meal in the kitchen when unemployed, competed to serve him in their dining rooms when he was on leave from the service.

A couple of decades later, a thousand Alcoholics Anonymous confessionals could have begun with "Well, looking back on it I guess I really learned to drink in the army" or, "I can remember like it was yesterday the first time I ever got stinking drunk. It was our first payday at Fort Osborne and we all went down to the Exchange Cafe to look for girls and all the guys had mickeys of rye. That was in the summer of 1940." And that — in the summer of 1940 — was when the war really started.

Until the early summer of 1940 it had been a strange almost

business-as-usual, 40-hour-week kind of war. The Polish conquest was over in a matter of days as the Russians invaded from the east to divide that unhappy land with the Germans. On the western front the British and French in their Maginot Line exchanged token artillery barrages with the Germans in their Siegfried Line. Token air raids were flown, sometimes with planes dropping propaganda leaflets, occasionally by planes dropping bombs. Then in a matter of days the German army blew the French out of the Maginot line and clear out of the war, overran Belgium, Holland, and Denmark, conquered Norway, and drove the British army in headlong flight from Dunkirk.

A sense of urgency descended on Canada for the first time and in the west the summer was spent in the frantic construction of air strips, hangars, and barracks for what would become the British Commonwealth Air Training Scheme. Recruiting for the three services was taken off "hold" and placed on the full-on front burners. Eastern Canadian textile plants worked overtime turning out uniforms for the army, navy, and airforce. Industrial plants went out of consumer production and into war production. In the west the change to a war footing was noticeable mainly in the increasing number of uniforms on the streets, in the gradual closing of the soup kitchens, and in the slowly dwindling relief rolls in the cities and towns. But behind the scenes things went forward at a frantic pace.

By the late fall of 1940, more than thirty new air training establishments were in operation, mainly on the Prairies. There were initial, elementary, and advanced training schools, navigational schools, wireless schools, and bombing and gunnery schools. There were hangars full of training planes scrounged from England and the United States. In June of 1940 there had been 500 airmen in training, mainly in Ontario. By December there were 8,000, mainly in western Canada, on stations dotting the Prairies from Penhold, Claresholm, Lethbridge, Medicine Hat, Swift Current, and Moose Jaw to Rivers, Portage la Prairie, and Gimli. Soon the stations would be turning out aircrew at the rate of 16,000 a year, ultimately to be raised after Pearl Harbor to 26,000 a year. The heavy impact the British Commonwealth Air Training Scheme would have on the liquor trade on the Prairies was made doubly so by the vast expansion in the army and navy establishments.

To bring the air training scheme to fruition at the same time as the army and navy installations were being expanded and multiplied set off a many-sided construction boom. For the first time in ten years, there was work for everybody who wanted work, steady work at good wages and frequently with overtime. And it was spread evenly across the west although Alberta did get the major share of the air training plan facilities.

As quickly as the service bases were in operation canteens were opened to provide for the leisure time comforts of the service personnel. At each establishment there was an officers' mess, a sergeants' mess, and a mess to serve all other ranks. All the canteens operated under license from the Liquor Control Boards, the offices' mess to serve liquor as well as beer, and the others to serve only beer. All drew their supplies from the liquor stores on the same basis as the civilians, by individual purchases. Before liquor rationing the regulations presented no problem in keeping the messes supplied. A lorry full of service men could pick up enough liquor and beer to keep all the canteens in stock for a week. In Manitoba it might have taken two lorries because, unlike the others, that province limited permit holders to the purchase of one forty-ounce bottle of liquor and a case of beer a day.

Problems for Alberta drinkers came after the Japanese bombing of Pearl Harbor. A week after that happened the Americans discovered Canada — and the fact that, unless the door was slammed quickly, Alaska could provide a landing place for a Japanese assault on the American heartland through north western Canada. Slamming that door, however, first required overland access to the Alaskan territory. More, it required instant access to that territory over an all-weather road. So the Americans rushed in and built the Alaska highway through Alberta and the Yukon. Alaska also had to be supplied with fuel for ships and planes and trucks and tanks. So the Americans ordered up the construction of the Canol oil pipeline from Norman Wells to Fairbanks.

No accurate estimate can be made of the number of Americans who descended on Alberta after Pearl Harbor because they came and went in such numbers. Some stayed in Edmonton, thousands worked on the Alaska Highway both on the site and bringing in equipment and supplies. There were units of the American army and airforce coming and going on mysterious missions; squadrons of planes would descend on nearby airports, linger awhile, and take off. There were 10,000 American troops and upwards of 16,000 civilians employed on the Alaska Highway alone and the Canol pipeline project required thousands more. Most of the civilians were

Canadian, but there were thousands of Americans involved as well, particularly as heavy equipment operators, engineers, surveyors, and, above all, truck drivers on the trains of heavy transport that were constantly on the move northward from the United States.

No liquor was allowed on the big construction jobs so there was a steady flow of construction workers south to Edmonton on three and four day leaves. There they competed for sleeping space with the coveys of American service wives who were regular visitors to Edmonton on conjugal reunions.

The impact of the American invasion on Edmonton and northern Alberta was a many splendored thing. It zoomed Edmonton's population well over 100,000 and above that of Calgary for the first time since 1883. The high wages of the Alaska Highway work camps denuded the Edmonton restaurants and the hotels of the surrounding countryside of their cooks, waitresses, and chambermaids. The rural hotels were all required to operate dining rooms in order to qualify for liquor licences. For the rest of the war what passed for meals were cooked and served by whoever happened to be handy, whether they could cook or not. Ordinary Edmontonians who did not carry their lunches from home started queueing up at the restaurants at 11 o'clock in order to be fed by noon. Hotel rooms in Edmonton were so overfilled that drummers from eastern Canada frequently slept in the lobbies, in competition for chairs with construction workers and service men on leave.

The influxing Americans quickly learned they would have to bring their cigarettes, bourbon, and beer with them if they were to continue their American way of life. American military convoys were soon so loaded with contraband cigarettes that cheap Camels and Lucky Strikes threatened to displace Players and Millbanks in the Edmonton market, though bourbon never reached the status of a potable alcohol by Alberta standards. One thing more valuable than cigarettes, liquor, or even money for the tom-catting Americans was nylon stockings because there was a nylon famine in Canada throughout the war. For an Edmonton secretary to turn up for work in a pair of new nylons was prima facie evidence that she had been out on a date with an American soldier the night before.

When Edmonton's Blatchford Airport runways were adjudged inadequate the Americans whistled up battalions of Seabees and rebuilt them. When even greater accommodation was needed they took over 2,000 acres of Namao farmland and turned it into an instant airport which for a while was reputed to be the largest on the continent. Such was the traffic in and out of these fields that in 1943 the Blatchford Airport claimed it had established a continental record when it handled 860 plane landings or takeoffs in a single 24-hour period.

The American influx was concentrated mainly in Edmonton and the north. The uncounted thousands of Commonwealth Air Training Scheme trainees as well as the Canadian servicemen in the airforce, army, and navy were scattered all over the province. Midway through the war a Liquor Board spokesman said the stores were trying to service a population that had risen by 60,000 almost overnight with reduced supplies of beer and hard liquor. It was noted further that whatever the number of newcomers or where they came from they all applied for liquor permits and used them when they got them.

The combined effect of full employment, the American influx, the expansion of the armed services establishments, and the Common-wealth Air Training Scheme was to place a strain on the Prairie booze supply. Surprisingly, that supply held out better than for any other consumer product.

As the country moved through 1941 and 1942 the consuming public was beginning to learn the meaning of total war on the home front. Wages and prices and profits were frozen more or less solidly at the 1941 levels. Taxes were doubled and redoubled and compulsory saving became an added taxpayer's burden. Butter, sugar, tea, coffee, and meat were all rationed, gasoline rationing had started, and severe restrictions were imposed on car purchases, instalment buying, and credit accounts. But nothing happened to liquor, except that demand for it was increasing daily as more and more people acquired permits. Then, in December 1942, the Federal Government moved in with a whole series of restrictions. It shut down the distilling of beverage alcohol, severely cut back the supply of malt for the breweries, limited liquor boards access to supplies to a percentage of what they had purchased in 1942. Beer sales were cut back by 10%, wine sales by 20%, and spirits by 30%, and the alcohol content of spirits was diluted by 30%.

The result of the government restrictions was to catch the Prairies up in the "if there ain't any I want some!" syndrome. The number of permits in public hands, which had increased rapidly with full employment, skyrocketed with the implementing of rationing, particularly in Saskatchewan and Alberta.

Liquor Permits Issued

Year	Manitoba	Saskatchewan	Alberta
1940-41	95,000	0	110,000
1941-42	134,000	0	149,000
1942-43	173,000	46,000	195,000
1943-44	258,000	171,000	400,000
1944-45	272,000	154,000	410,000
1945-46	285,000	185,000	393,000

The public was off on a frantic paper chase. Citizens who had never before owned a liquor permit not only rushed out and got them, they took their wives along as well. As the demand increased and the ration was cut it became almost a condition of employment for secretaries, clerks, cashiers, and receptionists to acquire liquor permits and hold them inviolate for the zero hour when their bosses wanted a purchase to be made. It is interesting to note that in 1943 the 400,000 permits issued to Albertans constituted one for every adult in the Alberta population, not excluding the reverend clergy, ladies of the Women's Christian Temperance Union, and card carriers in the various do-good organizations centered on the churches of the province.

All the provinces eventually rationed permit holders to forty ounces of spirits and a case or two of beer a day. As the number of permitees increased it was cut to one forty ounce bottle a week and then to one bottle a month. Saskatchewan and Manitoba cut it to one twenty-six ounce bottle and two cases of beer a month. Alberta did likewise and ultimately was forced to reduce its liquor ration to thirteen ounces a month.

The liquor store hours were cut in half, from noon until 6:00 P.M. Then they were reduced further to closing for the day when they ran out of supplies. In Calgary the queueing up habitually began an hour before the store opened and by noon the line stretched clear down the block. The odds were that those getting to the back end of the line as the store opened would find supplies exhausted before they got to the order counter.

The difficulty which all drinkers experienced in finding stuff to buy with their permits resulted in a modification of tastes in beverages. What people drank depended on what they could get, not what they preferred. The tastes of the Scotch drinkers were first to suffer as supplies of Scotch were cut by the submarine war on the Atlantic. Reluctantly the Scotch drinkers turned to rye, if it was available, or even to obscure brands of liqueurs that were left over in the stores from pre-war purchases. Manitoba and Saskatchewan did not experience so severe a shortage of Canadian rye and beer as Alberta did. As a result many former Scotch drinkers in those provinces acquired a taste for the better grades of Canadian rye, a factor that ultimately contributed to making it the favorite libation of the liquor consumers of the Prairies.

Of all the drinkers on the Prairies it was the civilian beer drinkers of Alberta who fared worst. Because of the shortage of malt, the Alberta breweries ran at seventy-five percent capacity. They might conceivably have kept the taverns reasonably supplied if they had not been seized by a rush of patriotism to the head. They made the enlisted men's canteens their special concerns and risked the displeasure of the control boards by "backdooring" enough suds to those canteens to make sure they did not want for beer. That did not mean that the "other ranks' "messes were ever awash in beer. It did mean they seldom encountered the fierce kind of droughts that regularly engulfed the civilian taverns. On the beer parlor front anarchy reigned throughout the war. Some taverns put their entire daily ration on sale when they opened, closed the tavern when it ran out. Some divided their daily supplies into hourly alotments, shut up shop when the hour's supply ran out, reopened when the next hour arrived. Finally there were taverns that put the month's allowance on sale until it ran out midway through the month. Casually dropping into a tavern for a glass of beer on a hot day was no longer worth a second thought. Locating an open pub with beer on tap required as much foresight and planning as a military exercise.

The armed services took care of their own without too much difficulty. The officers at the basic training camps made the first assignment of their new recruits a visit to the nearest liquor store to get a permit and what liquor they could for the officers' mess, along with beer for their own. For many of the young servicemen that assignment had to wait until they were into their uniforms because they were under the legal permit-buying age of twenty-one years. (The anomaly of being old enough to fight and die for their country at eighteen, but not being old enough to buy a case of beer, would be given wide circulation, decades hence, in the campaign to cut the official drinking age to eighteen.)

The permit issuers tended to lean to strictness in dealing with callow looking civilians, but an eighteen-year-old recruit in battle dress was seldom refused. Nor were they refused access to beer in the mess. Peer pressure from the old-sweats-in-the-making veterans of at least six weeks in the service, was irresistible. Initiating the youngest and newest recruits into the Canadian army by getting them drunk for the first time in their lives was the equivalent of freshman hazing in the colleges. As a result many of the wet-behind-the-ears, straight-off-the-farms, under-aged recruits learned very quickly how to get drunk, without ever learning how to drink.

But it was also true that many more provisional privates acquired such a respect for alcohol power from their first couple of brushes with it that they avoided further deep involvement. The dilemma which confronted the young servicemen was indeed painful. On one hand, they had an imperative need to establish a comradeship with their fellows, to become one with them in respect and affection, and that often meant full participation in the drinking escapades. On the other hand, getting drunk often gave rise to an almost allergic revulsion for ever again becoming involved in such a biliously degrading experience. Those who developed a technique for zigging around Scylla and zagging past Charybdis easily survived the drinking-to-get-drunk armed services environment. Those who did not would have a lifetime to struggle with alcoholism.

The drinking to get drunk proclivities of the servicemen was little more than a mildly accentuated reflection of the Prairie Canadian drinking mores; a set of circumstances which militated against having a casual drink or two and then turning to other things. The circumstances were the regulations of the liquor boards which forbade the transportation of opened bottles of liquor, or possession of such bottles outside one's home. Unopened bottles had to be taken directly from liquor store to home or hotel room and entirely consumed there. Any wayfarer who carried a half consumed bottle from one hotel room to another, or one town to another was breaking the law, so the custom developed of polishing off a bottle wherever it was opened.

Drinking in the army, and to a lesser extent in the other services, quickly acquired connotation of pleasurable experience. Vision of the quiet quaffing of an ice-cold bottle of beer in the cool shade of the Camp Shilo canteen enabled many a sweating recruit to finish the last couple of miles of a full-pack route march through the blistering Manitoba sand hills. Where the beer was the young recruits went looking for their friends when they had a day pass or weekend leave. Drinking was what one did for relaxation when the hard stuff was behind them.

More and more, as time passed, liquor became identified with both pleasurable occasions and with relief from the frustrations of wartime. Frustrations there were by the barrel-full in civilian Canada as business was entangled in bureaucratic regulations and families were beset with shortages of everything.

The entire society was undergoing drastic changes that would profoundly influence its future development. The manpower short- age that submerged the unemployment problem brought the two-income family into existence, made it a permanent fixture of the economic system. The substantial improvement in the standard of living of two-income families made the spending of a few dollars on liquor once a month a budgetable item. Even for those with little appetite for the stuff, the fact that it was a rationed scarcity item made its purchase a monthly necessity. It was almost unpatriotic to let a month slip past without latching onto the bottles of liquor and cases of beer to which all permit holders were entitled by law. Under such circumstances it was not long before a trend of having liquor on hand in the home became established, a trend which by wars-end would be found by the Gallop poll to have been acquired by the majority of Canadians.

For the people who acquired permits to accommodate drinking bosses, husbands, or friends, the fact that people whom they respected or admired used the stuff was a cachet of sorts. What could the harm be in drinking if a respected employer did so without noticeable ill effects? By 1944 a sort of permit protocol developed which dictated that the person for whom the liquor was bought should at the very least offer the permit holder a drink as a matter of courtesy. It thus became rather common for a secretary to stop at her boss's desk at quitting time to share a drink from the bottle she had bought for him on her permit.

For the overwhelming majority of the new permit holders, who tentatively sampled the wine and liquor they bought, the sampling was pleasurable, non-addictive and totally without concern for side effects. The psychology jargoneers had not yet invented such phrases as "mood altering drugs," "awareness enhancement," "inhibition sublimation," "self-doubt neutralizing." If they had, and described what they were talking about to civilian or soldier, the response would have been that the Liquor Control Boards were actively supporting the war effort because the products they sold were an enhancement to civilian and service morale. Certainly they were financial morale builders for all the Prairie governments whose income from liquor profits doubled during the war. Despite the restrictions imposed on public access to supplies, the dollar value of sales and profits rose steadily.

	Manitoba		Saskatchewan		Alberta	
Year	Sales	Profits	Sales	Profits	Sales	Profits
1940-41	—	—	$ 8,509,000	$1,940,000	$10,753,000	$ 3,316,000
1941-42	$ 9,983,000	$2,842,000	—	—	13,197,000	3,812,000
1942-43	12,368,000	3,743,000	12,092,000	2,983,000	16,968,000	4,908,000
1943-44	12,571,000	3,831,000	12,155,000	3,335,000	17,250,000	5,112,000
1944-45	15,298,000	4,380,000	13,623,000	3,776,000	20,564,000	5,820,000
1945-46	20,267,000	6,101,000	20,592,000	6,605,000	27,351,000	8,051,000
1946-47	21,291,000	6,527,000	25,182,000	8,104,000	31,395,000	9,534,000
1947-48	23,743,000	6,989,000	25,421,000	7,921,000	33,361,000	9,820,000
1948-49	25,429,000	7,291,000	27,656,000	8,546,000	37,186,000	11,045,000
1949-50	—	—	29,298,000	9,112,000	39,850,000	11,814,000

Part of the explanation for the steady increase in the dollar value of sales was the gradual increase in prices during the war despite the price ceilings. By 1940-41 prices for most liquor except Scotch had fully recovered from the depression lows and were back to the 1929 level. Thus Canadian Club rye, which had sold for $3.65 for a 26 ounce bottle in 1929, dropped to $3.00 in 1935, was back up to $3.80 in 1941 and was selling for $4.70 in 1945-46. Dewars Scotch sold for $5.00 in 1929, for $3.25 in 1935, $4.10 in 1941 and $5.50 in 1945-46. However, these changes could have accounted at most for perhaps a third of the increased revenue and the balance would have been made up in increased sales as indicated by the number of permits issued.

The Federal order of December 1942 did seriously curtail the supplies to the Liquor Control Boards. But the objective of the government to curtail spending on liquor was frustrated by two serious flaws in Federal thinking. No account was taken of the inventories on hand in the Control Boards' warehouses. Nor was there anticipated the mad public rush for permits after the curtailments were announced. When that rush developed, the boards were able, for a while, to meet public demand by dipping into inventory. It soon became the apprehended birthright of every free-born, non-interdicted, non-Indian Canadian to own a liquor permit. Any attempt to abrogate that right might well have triggered some nasty whiskey riots. On the other hand, there was no way for Alberta to divide supplies adequate for 125,000 drinkers among 400,000 permitees. The only alternative to shutting down completely was rationing, and as previously noted rationing was more severe in Alberta than anywhere else..

There was a compelling rationale for the Canadian government's decision to try to reduce the public spending on liquor in 1942: there was an urgent need to direct manpower from an unessential industry into the armed services and to war industry; a need to conserve food products; a need to divert money into the war effort. But perhaps most important, and least emphasized, was the conviction that there was something unseemly for Canadians to be boozing it up at home at the most critical period of the war when our allies were being slaughtered on a dozen battle fronts. The crowning irony must be that the measures taken to reduce the consumption of alcohol beverages not only increased the number of drinkers, they introduced thousands of Prairie Canadians to alcohol for the first time, with the result that when the war ended the number of drinkers had doubled.

There is, of course, no way of arriving at precise figures for the drinking population, before or during the war. All that the skyrocketing permit figures proved was that many more people were buying liquor, sometimes for themselves and sometimes for others. Perhaps a quarter of the permits might have fallen into the second category. Perhaps another quarter might have been the here-today-gone-tomorrow people: the American army personnel, the Canadian soldiers going through the boot camps, the Canadian, Australian, New Zealand, and British enrolees in the air training scheme. Yet even with such discounts the only conclusion to be drawn from the following table of permits issued is that the drinkers had at least doubled in number during five years of war.

Year	Manitoba	Alberta
1940-41	95,000	110,000
1945-46	285,000	395,000
1946-47	223,898	335,000
1947-48	235,820	294,000
1948-49	217,711	298,000
1949-50	213,968	320,000
1950-51	222,529	331,000
1951-52	228,573	353,000
1952-53	240,380	401,000
1953-54	249,963	454,000

(Saskatchewan did not keep comparable statistics.)

It was over two years after the end of the war before liquor supplies reached a point where rationing could be completely abandoned. Thereafter there was no longer any need for non-drinkers to buy liquor permits. If a husband had a permit there was no compelling reason for a wife also to have one, unless the neighboring wives were substituting gin klatches for coffee klatches. So there was a sharp drop in liquor permits after the war, but the decline never reduced the numbers to the pre-war level.

The conclusion from all of this is the number of permits in circulation is a fairly accurate yardstick of the number of drinkers in the population. That the number rose much faster in Alberta after the war than in Manitoba is an indication of a more rapidly increasing population after the Leduc oil discovery in 1947. Alberta gained 300,000 in the decade after Leduc while Manitoba gained only 100,000 and Saskatchewan, which abandoned permits altogether in 1947, gained only 50,000.

One remarkable aspect of the wartime liquor consumption was the decorum that prevailed everywhere across the Prairies. Over the three provinces in 1940 there were 3,378 convictions for drunkenness. When recognition is given to the spectacular change thereafter in economic and social conditions, it is remarkable that the total number of convicitons for drunkenness rose barely one third to 4,971 in 1945-46.

Obviously from such statistics the public seemed to be handling its liquor about as well as could be expected, perhaps more so. And though there was undoubtedly a lot of griping from the heavy drinking fraternity with unslakeable thirsts, the liquor control system, even with rationing, seemed to be working to the public's satisfaction. A Gallop Poll taken in early 1947, for example, found that thirty-nine percent of the Canadian public, nationwide, believed that liquor rationing should be retained as a permanent method of controlling the liquor traffic.

That thirty-nine percent figure is more impressive than it might appear thirty years after the fact. The war ended for a population fed up to the gills with rationing and other governmental restrictions. When the regulation forcing all adult Canadians to carry National Registration cards on their persons was repealed many thousands made the disposal of the cards symbolic ceremonial occasions. They ripped the cards to shreds and tossed them to the winds; they collected them and burned them in office waste baskets; they flushed them down toilets with discardable ration tickets, tokens, and books. They did it with such enthusiastic abandon that years later Prairie archivists were hard put to find national registration certificates, ration books, and stamps for their museums.

Nevertheless as the first half of the century was winding down, mutterings against the system were beginning to be heard. Most of the criticism centered on the beer parlors. Throughout the depression, operating a beer parlor had been more a ticket to the poor house than a road to riches. That was to be seen in the way the hotels fell like nine-pins into the maws of the breweries, who lent them money to keep them selling beer, and ultimately foreclosed their loans. With wartime prosperity the beer parlors were humming with customers as long as their supplies lasted.

But there never was any such thing as a quiet Prairie beer drinker, or a fully patronized beer parlor that could keep rowdiness in check. Too many timid souls became raging bulls after three or four beers. It was the bedlam that reigned in the Prairie beer parlors that gave the women's libbers of the time their most persuasive argument for access to the beer halls.

The barring of the bars to women patronage, save in the small towns of Alberta, was a continuing Prairie phenomenon throughout the war. Women's Lib, as an important social force, was still over a generation away. The earliest rumbling of revolt against feminine subservience exploded into the open in Winnipeg on 7 May 1945, the false V.E. Day.

The German surrender had been scheduled for simultaneous announcement from Moscow, Washington, and London and in battle zones for 8 May 1945. However, Edward Kennedy of the Associated Press broke the story prematurely by cabling New York that the surrender had taken place early on 7 May. The conflict between the official version and the Associated Press story gave the Winnipeg news media an early morning conniption fit. The end of the war in Europe was a news story of unequalled importance, the story the public had awaited for almost six years. Once it was released there would be an explosive celebration! While the news editors dithered, Winnipeggers went to work.

When the Kennedy story began flashing over American radio it was no longer possible for the Winnipeg media to hold back. The story went on the air and Winnipeggers erupted into the streets, and stormed into the nearest beer parlor. Participating in the storming of the pubs were hundreds of young women bent on reliving the creation story by sampling forbidden elixir instead of forbidden fruit. By noon downtown Winnipeg beer parlors were half full of women demanding to be served, not only while seated at the tables as the law required, but bellying up to the service counters as no man had done in Manitoba for thirty years. Some hotels, fearful for the loss of their license, formed flying squads of waiters and hustled the women back onto the streets. Others, rolling with the punches and careless of the consequences, served the ladies along with the men. When the parlors were permitted to reopen two days later nothing was made of the episode. The occurrence opened no cracks in the male-only dike.

Elsewhere in the west peace came in a more orderly fashion. Because of the time zone difference, Regina and Edmonton got the news in time to shut everything down before normal opening hours. Alberta not only ordered its liquor stores and beer parlors not to open on 7 May, it kept them closed for the next forty-eight hours until all the formal ceremonies had been completed. Albertans who had not been foresighted enough to lay in a supply of toasting material for the war's end simply went without.

Prairie history came a full circle in 1945 when the troops came home from the war with their mental pack-sacks filled with the same pleasant memories their fathers and uncles had brought back from the First World War, memories of the English pubs and continental bistros in which they had whiled away so many happy hours over a glass or two of beer or ale with their girls and comrades. What was more, many of the returnees this time brought back their girls with them, war brides for whom an evening in their pubs was a way of life, and who joined them, in season and out, in singing the praises of that way of life.

By 1946, however, the Prairie drinking environment had changed considerably from what it had been in 1919. There was no longer any bone-dry Prohibition against which the organized war veterans could fight a war of words. Beer was now available in veterans' club rooms, in private golf clubs, in military messes, and in hotel taverns. But it was available to men only except in Alberta's country towns.

The conviction that women and the public consumption of alcohol did not mix was an article of the deepest faith on the Prairies before Prohibition, during Prohibition, and long after the repeal of Prohibition, even to the end of the Second World War. But it was a state of mind to which the women themselves were beginning to enter an occasional mild caveat. The thousands of women who had served with the armed services overseas were permitted access to draft libations in their Canadian Legion clubrooms, or in the reserve establishments. But they were barred from the civilian taverns frequented by their husbands, and from which increasing numbers of patrons who dropped in for a beer after work went reeling home at closing time. When public controversy appeared over unseemly tavern behavior, street brawling or drunken driving, distaff writers of letters to the editors were quick to blame it on discrimination against women drinkers.

Open the beer parlors to women, the argument ran, and the drinking habits of the men will be quickly improved. The mere presence of the women would force the men to clean up their act, moderate their behavior. There would be less bandying about of profanity and obscenities, less brawling, and a great deal more going home while they were still able to navigate.

Unfortunately for the women, letters columns of newspapers proved to be no Wittenberg church doors on which they could nail their theses for the reformation of the liquor trade. The only evidence that any government was listening was in the steps taken by the Alberta government to force the taverns to close during the supper hour. In addition Alberta amended its regulations to permit private clubs to serve liquor to their members and wives. Otherwise women were ignored.

There was of course no good reason why the governments should pay any more attention to the women than they paid to the murmurings of the men against the liquor laws. All Prairie governments were headed by teetotal premiers. The legislatures were still all controlled by the numerically dominant rural consti-tuencies in which the dry vote substantially exceeded the wets. So the Prairie governments were reasonably secure in paying no attention to agitations for radical changes coming from the cities. As long as the farmers were content there was no problem.

In the countryside antagonism toward liquor was softening as memories of the wide-open bars dimmed. The changing attitude, however, was more apparent in the larger towns than among the farmers. The businessmen in the towns saw the location in their midst of a beer parlor or liquor store as a plus for business. Not only would the odd farmer be lured to town for a case of beer or a bottle of liquor, he would probably bring his wife along to do her shopping. Additionally, the patrons of their competitors in the nearby towns and villages might become accustomed to combining shopping for liquor with shopping for groceries, dry goods, or even automobiles.

There was provision in all the Liquor Control acts for the holding of plebiscites if ten percent of the electors petitioned for such a vote. The businessmen became prime circulators of beer parlor and liquor store petitions, just as the local clergy sponsored petitions to close either or both of such establishments. With the presentation of a qualified petition to the government the holding of a plebiscite was automatic. But an affirmative vote for a liquor outlet did not automatically produce one because the majority in favor had to exceed sixty-six percent. If it were only sixty percent it was lost, and in Alberta another vote could not be held for at least three years. Plebiscites had rougher going when they encompassed an entire rural municipality than when confined to the larger towns. Nevertheless, over the first couple of decades of government control most of the plebiscites that were held gave majorities to the affirmative action petitions and the bone dry areas of the Prairies shrank and shrank.

Another factor which may have helped stiffen the official reluctance to change was the steadily rising post war sales and profits of the dispensaries, as the following table shows:

	Manitoba		Saskatchewan		Alberta	
Year	Sales	Profits	Sales	Profits	Sales	Profits
1939-40	$7,887,000	$2,135,000	$7,273,000	$1,704,000	$9,365,000	$2,813,000
1949-50	25,149,000	7,291,000	29,298,000	9,112,000	39,850,000	11,814,000
1954-55	33,546,000	8,621,000	39,118,000	11,332,000	52,712,000	15,028,000

Beverage alcohol was reaching the point in the postwar Prairie environment where it was achieving immunity from impact of changing economic conditions. It was becoming a government money machine that nothing could interrupt or even slow down. Thus 1950 was the year of the historic flood of the Red River Valley which brought normal life to a full stop in Manitoba during the months of May and June and caused more than $100,000,000 in property damage. In that year Manitoba's liquor sales increased over $3,000,000 and profits were up by $600,000. In 1954 the Prairies experienced the worst region-wide crop failure since 1937. It was a year in which all the viewers with alarm were looking over their shoulders for the return of another great depression. But in that year of acute economic depression liquor sales and liquor profits were up slightly in Manitoba and Saskatchewan and down only minutely in Alberta.

Verily this was indeed a golden goose which no one had envisioned when the egg had first appeared a quarter century earlier.

CHAPTER SEVEN

FORGET THE FACTS, LET'S GET BACK TO THE BARS

The extent to which newspaper editorializing influences public opinion — if at all — has never been susceptible to precise definition. It is probably as indefinable as whether opposition members of legislatures have an influence on the course of action governments pursue; or if an ordinary citizen can change, retard, or advance the course of history. Yet there is some evidence that one newspaper in Alberta, one maverick oppositionist in the Manitoba legislature, and a young Winnipeg entrepreneur collectively upended a liquor control system on the Prairies that had existed for twenty-five years. The newspaper was the *Calgary Herald*, the politician was Jack McDowell, the independent Conservative member of the Manitoba Legislature for Niverville, and the citizen was thirty-seven-year-old Stephen Juba, a Winnipeg building supply company owner and bird fancier.

When it came to the liquor traffic, the *Herald* stood four-square on the side of anarchy. It fought Prohibition in 1915, 1920 and 1924, waged a journalistic guerrilla war against liquor regulations throughout the depression, war, and the return of peace. It railed against all government intrusion into the liquor trade on principle and, in season and out, on specific detail. All the other Prairie newspapers were reconciled by mid-century to living in peace with government liquor monopolies. But not the *Herald*, despite the obvious fact that nobody in the Alberta Government paid the slightest attention to its criticism. But as the 1950s succeeded the 1930s-1940s it was becoming apparent that the liquor control systems were becoming entangled in the back-lash of social change and might be forced to make some accommodation with the revolution taking place in public attitudes. The *Herald* seemed to sense a change of winds and redoubled its efforts.

The Prairies of the 1950s were moving with Brobdingnagian strides away from conditions of the 1930s and 1940s. The root-hog-or-die economy that had ruled from the first days of settlement was being replaced by a cradle-to-the-grave welfare state. Unemployment insurance had become an established fact in 1940; children's allowances in 1944; old age pensions were being enlarged and liberalized; comprehensive medicare was just over the horizon. The 1950s saw increased fertility and profitable prices for everything the farmers were producing. The service men had returned to become beneficiaries of generous government grants to rehouse and rehabilitate them educationally and economically. A return to mass unemployment which all governments feared with the ending of the wars in Europe and Asia did not happen. There was, instead, plenty of work for just about everybody and at living wages.

The wartime revival of the trades unions gave the working force more muscle than it had had in thirty years. Where it had once been possible, in the pre-war west, to hire the most skilled artisans for 50 or 60 cents an hour, building trades wages were now well over $1 an hour. Owning a $6,000 home of their own became an achievable goal for Prairie Canadians. Though they had doubled in price to $2,500, Fords, Chevrolets, Dodges, Studebakers, and Henry J's were, through extended instalment plans, becoming purchasable to increasing thousands, either new or newly second-hand.

Most important of all was the way in which women at long last were achieving the status of persons. Welcomed into the work force during the war, they insisted on staying there when the war ended. Rosey the Rivetter and Winnie the Welder may not have avoided redundancy but the thousands of other jobs in retailing, government, and in the service industries that were once filled by men were taken over by women. As soon as they had done their bit for the post-war baby boom, the women were back into the work force. In the process they laid waste forever the proposition that woman's place was in the home, that a mother's place was with her children, that working married women were social outcasts.

Throughout the depression the proposition was universally accepted that married women who worked outside the home were stealing jobs from husbands and fathers who had families to support. It was the fixed policy of most governments clear down to the smallest school district that once a female employee married she was gone from the payroll. So firmly entrenched was that conviction that the practice of firing marrying employees survived long after the justification for it disappeared. When a serious shortage of teachers developed with the onset of the 1950s, many rural areas in Alberta and Saskatchewan were forced to hire underqualified personnel in order to keep their schools open. As the war babies flocked into the elementary grades the shortages extended quickly to the cities. Thus in 1953 the superintendent of schools in St. James, Manitoba, appealed to his board to repeal the restrictions against hiring married women to fill vacancies on his staff, at least until single women again became available. Despite reluctance, it eased enforcement, and, as elsewhere across the west, the discriminatory regulations were quietly allowed to wither away, in private employment as well as in the government service.

Within the working force, however, the pressure of protocol where women were concerned still existed. During the war the consumption of cigarettes more than doubled and much of that increase was attributed to the enthusiasm with which women were taking to cigarettes. But with women tobacco like alcohol was very much a private thing: it was well into the 1950s before smoking at the work place became generally acceptable for women. Even then some offices, and most of the chartered banks, frowned on the practice so the women employees confined their puffing to coffee breaks and their rest rooms.

During the war then, women had taken to drink, to cigarettes, and to life outside the home. When the mumbling started in favor of "liberalized" liquor laws, the women were part of that too. But it was not something for which they marched with picket signs gesturing. It was more quiet nodding of agreement when men argued that as women were allowed to drink with men in all the veterans' clubrooms and in private clubs they should also be allowed to drink in the taverns as well. As has happened so frequently in the Prairie West, the main pressure for change developed outside the borders of the area rather than from within, from eastern Canada and the United States.

When the government liquor monopolies were established in Canada after the repeal of Prohibition it was taken for granted that they were the only workable and acceptable alternatives to the wide open bar, on the one hand, or complete Prohibition on the other. The United States had adopted Prohibition just when the Canadian west was having second thoughts about it. As long as the United States had Prohibition comparisons were possible. On balance it seemed to most reasonable people that in Canada the government monopoly systems were working a lot better than the American Prohibition. Then, while nobody in Canada was paying much attention, the United States repealed its national Prohibition law and went back to a variety of state control systems. Some states stayed with Prohibition. Some established state monopolies similar to those of the Prairie provinces. Some had government monopoly at the wholesale end and public drinking in taverns, cabarets, cocktail bars, and restaurants. Two things brought these other alternatives to the attention of Prairie drinkers; and the closer they examined them the less enthusiasm they were able to work up for their own system.

The first root of dissatisfaction was the opening of the cocktail bars and the sale of liquor in restaurants in Toronto in April 1947. The traffic between the west and Toronto had never been all that great, but the occasional westerner who visited the Toronto watering holes was favorably impressed. The word that drifted back across the west was that the atmosphere in the new cocktail bars was delightful, that the meals certainly were improved and how nice it would be to have something similar in Winnipeg, Saskatoon, Edmonton, and Calgary! It was, however, more lukewarm interest than the beginning of a boisterous agitation. But it was an interest that spread steadily with the changing post-war social and economic conditions.

After foreign exchange controls were lifted in 1951, and Canadians were again able to travel freely in the United States, the American experience began strongly to influence western thinking. That was particularly true of the thousands of urban citizens who were acquiring cars, often for the first time. On any Canadian long weekend, and on many regular Canadian weekends, from early spring to late November, such centers as Spokane, Kalispell, Great Falls, Shelby, Minot, Devil's Lake, Fargo, Grand Forks, Detroit Lakes, and Moorhead were overrun by Prairie Canadians on shopping-cum-drinking sprees. After assaults on the marts of commerce they stayed up for hours savoring the freedom to sit around drinking in bars and listening to juke box music or, infrequently, live entertainment. It was in the American bars, for example, that Prairie Canadians made their first acquaintance with that fabulous instrument of revolutionary social change — the television set.

On the way home the comparisons they now made was that the

Americans had a much better system, one which Canadians might do well to copy. Inevitably they came home with vague intentions of doing something about reforming their own "archaic" liquor laws. Their disenchantment was reinforced now and then when visiting tourists who sounded off on the impediment to a profitable tourist trade that Prairie liquor regulations had become.

When the complainers happened to be foreign visitors who compared the Alberta milieu unfavorably with the way they managed things in their homeland, the *Calgary Herald* found front page space for the critical interviews. More, as in the case of the absentee English owner of a string of national parks hotels, it used the interview as a peg on which to hang editorials meat-axing the Alberta Government and its liquor laws, as for example, this editorial on 27 April 1951.

OUR HOPELESSLY ARCHAIC LIQUOR LAWS

Sir Norman Watson, Bart., who has had an interest in mountain resort lodges for some years, entertains harsh views about the Alberta liquor laws. He described them in Calgary this week as "archaic", "tragic", and "simply unbelievable".

Now let us admit that the British baronet has a commercial interest in the relaxation of the liquor laws. Let us admit that he, and many others, would benefit if, say, cocktail lounges were permitted in Alberta hotels. Admitting all that does not make what he said any the less true. Alberta liquor laws are beyond doubt archaic and simply unbelievable. But what is to be done about it?

Over the years, we have tried to point out in these columns the stupidities of the liquor laws: the doctrine, for example, that for a man and woman to drink beer together is sinful in Calgary but perfectly all right in Okotoks or Cochrane, or the doctrine that it is proper for men of substance to buy whiskey by the glass at their club but improper for working men, who do not belong to clubs, to do the same thing. So far, our efforts and the efforts of others like us have gotten nowhere; they always run into the stone wall of rural bigotry and the bland refusal of an all-powerful government to concede that public opinion even exists.

It is said that relaxation of the laws would lead to drunkenness, disorder and various kinds of unmentionable crime — which is patent nonsense. The English, who have far more liberal liquor laws than the province of Alberta, are, on balance, more law abiding. You can travel the length and breadth of France, where there are virtually no restrictions at all, without ever seeing a drunken Frenchman. (Can you travel the length and breadth of Ninth Avenue on a Saturday evening and say the same thing?)

We believe that the freer sale of liquor would tend to lessen, not increase, its consumption. We believe that wines and spirits should be sold freely to both sexes, by the glass, in any reputable hotel that wishes to do so; that beer should be available in grocery stores (as it has been for some years in Quebec without any disastrous consequences), and that if responsible private citizens want to operate wine and spirit stores and sell these products by the bottle, they should be allowed to do so. And if men like Sir Norman Watson happen to make a little money in the process, why, then, we cannot see much harm in it. The government makes about $11,000,000 a year out of alcohol, and we have yet to hear it argued that this is wrong.

Such editorials became grist for the critical mills of the opposition members of the legislature, and for the urban business men hankering for the profits they could make from expanding the tourist trade. With the return of adequate beer supplies there were appeals to curb the rowdiness of the beer drinkers. The Government had tried years before to water down the criticism by closing all the Alberta taverns during the supper hour. But there was nothing much it could do about the problem of under-age drinking then reaching serious proportions. The legal minimum age was twenty-one years, but how could tavern waiters in Lethbridge, Medicine Hat, or Red Deer be expected to know that the pregnant wife of the customer at table twelve was two years shy of the legal minimum? Or what was the waiter to do if the friends of a fellow who looked no more than seventeen insisted he was twenty-two?

In most cases, the tavern operators tended to do nothing unless forced into action by threat of license suspension. That only happened after parents of teenagers fired off angry complaints to the government when their daughters came home drunk from nights on the town. Except for the *Herald*, however, nobody was beating the drum loudly for abandonment of the government monopoly system, in Alberta, Manitoba, or Saskatchewan.

While the Liberal-C.C.F. opposition in the Alberta Legislature kept pressing the Government to set up a committee to study the liquor situation, Premier E. C. Manning tried to placate the liberalizing forces with minor adjustments. In 1950 private clubs were permitted to set up liquor dispensaries for members and their wives; golf clubs and military canteens were permitted to serve beer on Sundays and to both sexes. Such minor concessions satisfied nobody but a few club members, golfers, and soldiers and the legislative pressure on the government hardly abated at all. In 1952 the Government asked the chairman of its liquor board, the attorney general, and the superintendent of the RCMP to investigate the workings of its control system and recommend how it might be improved, if at all.

Months later the committee's report shattered Alberta's political calm. It suggested that mixed beer drinking be restored to Calgary and Edmonton, that wine be allowed with meals, and that cocktail bars be allowed in high class hotels. Far from achieving an immediate change, the report set up a clamor from the drys against change of any kind along with demands for more vigorous law enforcement. In one month alone Premier Manning received over 200 letters opposing change and that was enough to nudge the committee's report off the front burners, and into the warming oven.

In Manitoba, vigorous enforcement of the liquor laws had never been regarded by the Winnipeg Police Department as one of its categorical imperatives. High court judges and police magistrates tippled quietly from bottles in their office drawers; the annual policemen's ball was notorious for the boisterousness of its wassailing; policemen never entered beer parlors officially unless called specifically to put down small riots. The city's restaurants and hotels turned nary a hair when their customers brought their own liquor to dinner. On the city's outskirts a number of road houses — Don Carlos', The Highwayman, The Copacabana, The Edgewater — imported American entertainers to amuse their dine-and-dance, bottle-under-the-table, customers. Far from being a mailed fist in an armed glove, Winnipeg liquor enforcement was more a padded mitt in a feather pillow. As a result, scarcely a legislative session passed without two or three outbreaks of criticism of the liquor laws and the need for better enforcement. In all such debates, the most prominent participant was Jack McDowell, the independent Conservative and Manitoba's most strident advocate of the *Calgary Herald's* abolitionist point of view.

Jack McDowell had two bête noirs, the Canadian Wheat Board and the Government Liquor Control Commission. He worked up his greatest head of steam over the continuation of the wartime regulation that diluted the potency of all spirituous liquors. McDowell was the first elected politician in Manitoba to climb aboard the liberalization-modernization bandwagon, but the man who got the wagon rolling down hill was Stephen Juba.

At a time when most other Winnipeg Ukrainian-Canadians were still refighting the Russian revolution and choosing sides in civic politics between the Communists and the anti-Communists, Juba was bitten by the cocktail bar bug. He propagandized his customers so assiduously at his building supplies store that they began urging him to take his message to the hustings and run for the city council. The more he thought about it the better he liked the idea and so he became an aldermanic candidate for Ward Two in Winnipeg's 1951 civic election. Running on a one-plank platform — legalization of bi-sexual drinking in cocktail bars — he ran a surprising fourth in a three-to-be-elected ward, missing out by a scant 500 votes. Thus encouraged, Juba decided to run for mayor the following year against the establishment's Garnet Coulter, then rounding out a dozen years in office as one of the most popular mayors in Winnipeg history. This time Juba's cocktail bars platform garnered him 33,443 votes compared to Coulter's 45,000. It was like a hundred to one Kentucky Derby shot missing by half a length, for he ran without the endorsement of either the Communists, the CCF, or the Citizens Election Committee. When the provincial election rolled around in the summer of 1953 he was into that too and this time was rather easily elected.

Juba naturally made himself heard in the Legislature on his favorite theme and to the surprise of just about everybody the Liberal Government of Premier Douglas Campbell listened. It did more than that. It appointed a Royal Commission to investigate the operation of the liquor control system and come up with some practical advice. So grateful were Winnipeggers to Steve Juba for his dam-breaking exploits that they elected him mayor at the next civic election; and went on re-electing him for the next twenty years.

The commission which Premier Campbell named on 15 April 1954, was about as close to being all things to all men as ever achieved in the business of royal commission appointing. Its chairman was Hon. John Bracken, a one-time professional agronomist who served as premier of Manitoba for twenty years. Bracken was also the former leader of the Progressive-Conservative Party of Canada and a lifelong temperance advocate. Its members were:

— Dr. Paul L'Heureux, medical director of the St. Boniface Hospital and a noted public health expert;
— Clifford McCrae, reeve of the rural municipality of, Westbourne and president of the Union of Manitoba Municipalities;
— Mrs. Jean Whiteford, a school teacher and successful Manitoba poultry farmer;
— Major General Harold Riley, former director of mobilization for National Selective Service and president of the Manitoba Bar Association.

The commission was charged with studying: (a) the adequacy of the present liquor law; (b) the advisability or otherwise of changes; (c) current problems and those likely to exist under any amended act and; (d) matters considered by the commission to be incidental to the foregoing.

The establishment of the Bracken Commission gave the Alberta Government an excuse to do nothing. Instead of yielding to opposition pressure and appointing a legislative committee of its own, it announced it would wait and see if Manitoba's problems were applicable to Alberta. Curiously enough, Saskatchewan was profoundly indifferent to the excursions and alarums on its flanks: there were in its legislature no demands for changes in the liquor laws. The perennially burning issue in Saskatchewan was not booze but the way in which the standard time zones split the province down the middle and created endless confusion for the citizenry. The eastern half of the province was never on the same standard as the western half and Regina was never in step with either for more than half a year.

The Bracken Commission did about as thorough an investigation as an unlimited budget and exemption from time constraints could make possible. It visited Quebec, Ontario, Alberta, and British Columbia, New York, Pennsylvania, and fifteen other American states to investigate the workings of all manner of liquor control systems, from no control to Prohibition in action. It called upon the services of Dr. E. M. Jellinek, founder of the Yale University Center for the Study of Alcohol and a world renowned expert, for advice and direction. It listened to everybody in Winnipeg who had an opinion to express, then toured the province from border to border taking more testimony. It interviewed and consulted with thirty Canadian agencies and with fifteen American institutions. Its hearings ran from early in May 1954 until well into 1955. It took the better part of three months to complete its report which was presented to the Manitoba Government on 1 September 1955.

The hearings of the Bracken Commission might have been expected to become simply a prolonged replaying of all the old arguments between wets and drys of bygone plebiscites. That did not happen, although perhaps a quarter of the 165 witnesses favored the dry side and perhaps half of them were for Prohibition. Thirty years of government control and the attrition of time had decimated the Prohibitionist legions. The Women's Christian Temperance Union itself was down to only 200 active members. It now accepted the existence of beer parlors, provided they were allowed to serve food with drink. In northern Manitoba an Anglican missionary on an Indian Reserve claimed Indians could "handle their liquor" as well as white men could and wanted it made available to them on reserves, "as it was made available to them as soldiers during the war". At the town of Swan River, a group from the United Church laid its emphasis on permitting liquor advertising to appear in weekly newspapers. Even the Provincial Council of Women and the Women's Institute of Manitoba had become reconciled to the present system and wanted food served in beer parlors although they both rejected cocktail bars. Only in Brandon and Portage la Prairie, and among the Baptists and Mennonites did the commission encounter substantial support for Prohibition.

The most eloquent presentation to the commission against any liberalization of the liquor laws came not from any of the women's groups or Protestant clergymen but from the Jewish proprietor of the Marlborough Hotel, which was so strategically located in the heart of downtown Winnipeg that it might have expected to profit handsomely from the wide open drinking.

"Let me warn you," he told the commission, "if you bring the sale of whiskey by the glass into this province, Manitoba will be a province of alcoholics within 25 years! If I want to make a dollar, I want to do it with clean hands. I do not want blood and tears running out of the palms that are counting the money!"

Within the hotel business Nathan Rothstein was a minority of one. The Winnipeg Chamber of Commerce reported that seventy-five percent of those who replied to its survey favored cocktail bars, the sale of liquor in clubs, hotels, and on trains and the service of wine with meals. The Retail Merchants Association presented a petition signed by 50,000 asking for the sale of beer and wine in grocery stores and a petition against such a proposal containing only 5,000 names.

What set the Bracken Commission apart from anything that had happened before on the Prairies was the way in which it brought the burgeoning problem of alcoholism out of the closet and focused public attention upon it. This was done not only in the presentation of briefs but in the massive amount of material it accumulated in the working papers of the commission.

Judge Ralph Maybank, representing the Manitoba Committee on Alcoholism, and himself a former alcoholic, urged the commission to recommend that the government establish treatment and rehabilitation centers for the province's estimated 10,000 alcoholics. It should be coupled with an on-going educational program and a prisoner rehabilitation program. Dr. Morley Lougheed, director of public health services, was prepared to settle for a lot less — a special ward in all hospitals to treat alcoholics who were by now disrupting the services of the hospitals. His was an almost verbatim copy of an appeal that went out from Dr. Alex Pincock more than a dozen years before. A. J. Kitchen, the chief probation officer of the Juvenile Court System, called attention to the "alarming increase in the use of alcohol by juveniles" every year. Judge E. J. Heaney of the family court identified liquor as the major factor in the breakdown of marriages in Manitoba. Judge M. S. Watson said his study revealed that liquor was a factor in fifty percent of all the cases that came before him in family court. Spokesmen for the Salvation Army blamed liquor for seventy-five percent of the cases it had to deal with. The WCTU claimed that alcohol led to the downfall of eighty-five percent of the delinquent girls in shelters for unwed mothers.

There was indeed a dark underside of the pleasurable experience which people were getting, and hoped to increase, from the consumption of alcoholic beverages. It was a darker side that was emphasized in the mass of factual material which the staff of the commission turned up from the history of liquor control in Manitoba. In the fifteen years from the outbreak of the war to the sitting of the commission, Manitoba's population had increased by fifteen percent. During the same period the expenditure of Manitobans on alcohol increased by 300% — from $10,500,000 to $42,700,000; the number of identified alcoholics doubled, from 5,000 to 10,000; convictions for drunkenness increased from 160 to 420 per 100,000 of the population; convictions under the Liquor Control Act increased from 1,000 to 3,686.

What this all meant was Manitobans in fifteen years had increased their annual consumption of spirituous liquors by almost 200% — from 192,000 gallons to 554,000 gallons. Consumption of beer went from 218,000 gallons to 719,000 gallons and wine from 157,000 gallons to 265,000 gallons. Accompanying these local statistics were background papers gathered from the literature of the world and published as a kind of 234 page preface to its final report.

The 751-page Report of the Manitoba Liquor Inquiry Commission is one of the most fascinating unread books in the history of Canadian publishing. Certainly it could hardly have been read by four of its five authors, or by the governments of the Prairie Provinces which embraced its findings. The first 234 pages of the report were a compendium of extant information on the effects of alcohol consumption. The works of Dr. Haver Emerson and the joint works of Drs. J. A. Waddell and H. B. Haag are quoted extensively, the tone of this prefatory material set by the following quotation from page 49:

Dr. Emerson in the closing chapter of his book, *The Effects of Alcohol on Man* summarized the prevailing view on alcohol and its effect when used in beverages as follows:

Those of us who grew up in the nineteenth century under the misinformation, the extravagance of expression, the biased and the fanatical teaching of the effects of alcohol, will welcome for ourselves and our children the balanced and reliable statements which modern medical science offers in simple terms carrying conviction. In the press, among politicians, in social converse, among economists, the clergy, men of business, contradiction of fact and irreconcilable opinions appear to be the rule.

It is therefore with relief and added courage that we find a remarkable unanimity of opinion expressed impersonally on the subject of alcohol by physiologists, immunologists, clinicians, psychologists, psychiatrists and medical statisticians. There is agreement among the students and teachers of the medical and associated sciences on the following points:

1. Alcohol is a narcotic which, by depressing the higher centres, removes inhibitions.
2. Outside of the nervous system and the digestive tract, alcohol used as a beverage has little demonstrable effect.
3. It is a food used as a source of energy and sparer of protein, but it is such only to a very limited extent.
4. It is improbable that the quality of human stock has been at all injured or modified by the long use of alcohol, although the effects on the individual are often devastating.
5. The therapeutic usefulness and value of alcohol are probably slight.
6. It may be a comfort and a psychological aid to the aged.
7. It does not increase and sometimes decreases the body's resistance to infection.
8. By releasing inhibitions, it makes for social ease and pleasure and herein lies one of its great dangers.
9. Its effects are best studied by changes of conduct.
10. It impairs will, reason, self-control, judgment, physical skill and endurance.
11. It may produce situations in which crime and social lapses result.
12. It is a frequent destroyer of health, happiness and mental stability.
13. Its use commonly lowers longevity and increases mortality.
14. It is used primarily for its psychological effect and as an escape from unpleasant reality.
15. It constitutes an important community health problem.

There followed page after page of physiological data from British and American sources leading into chapters on the social impact of its use. There were chapters on what other countries did to control alcohol use, with side excursions into its impact on ancient history.

Eventually the commission located Dr. E. M. Jellinek, secretary-general of the International Institute for Research on the Problems of Alcohol, at his headquarters in Geneva and persuaded him to spend two weeks in Winnipeg giving the commission the benefit of his vast expertise in the problem of alcoholism. Dr. Jellinek took the commission on what amounted to a world booze tour, from France which had the world's worst alcoholism problem — 5% of the entire population compared with 1.9% in Denmark and 1% in Ireland — to India and the Moslem countries where it scarcely existed.

In all these more than 700 pages, a diligent reader will encounter nothing in the shape of a persuasive argument in favor of drinking beverage alcohol. In the words of that defrocked American vice-president, Spiro Agnew, the experts consulted by the commission were "nabobs of negativism" as far as booze was concerned. Yet in the end, despite the overwhelming weight of such evidence, the commission recommended a plebiscite which would let the people decide whether they wanted beer parlors, cocktail bars, cabarets or dining lounges; or all four of them; or none of them.

There was one dissenter, Dr. L'Heureux. He argued that the cause of temperance could best be served, and anti-social behavior avoided, by actively encouraging consumption of beverages with low alcohol content, like beer and light wine. Further, drinking should be confined as much to the home as possible and consumed with food rather than by itself. So he rejected cocktail bars and advocated sale of low alcohol wine and beer in grocery stores. He wanted to restrict the opening of all places serving stronger liquor to late in the day, and to limit the size of all liquor outlets in order to encourage family or small club atmosphere.

The commission was clearly convinced that the public wanted wide open boozing and confined itself mainly, in the bulk of its report, to drafting regulations for a new liquor act. In this opinion it was on solid ground. When the questions were put to plebiscite in October 1956 all Manitoba's main urban centers voted for the licensing of beer parlors, cocktail bars, cabarets and liquor in first class dining rooms.

The exception to the trend, as was only to be expected, was in southern Manitoba which had an unbroken record of keeping the temperance faith. Yet even in areas which had voted dry in 1898, 1915, 1920, and 1923, there was slipping from grace in a number of pockets. Thus while Killarney, Morden, Neepawa, and Manitou were still solidly dry, Minnedosa, Boissevain, and Deloraine all went whole hog for public drinking.

The impact in Alberta of the Bracken Commission Report and the vote in Manitoba was immediate. The Manning Government announced that with the completion of the Bracken study it was now appropriate to appoint a legislative committee to study the Alberta system in conjunction with the Bracken Report. After due deliberation the committee came down on the side of a system roughly similar to that which Manitoba had adopted. Like Manitoba it insisted that constituencies that wanted more liquor outlets declare their desires in plebiscites. Unlike Manitoba, which accepted the verdict on a simple majority, Alberta insisted on two thirds majority. In the City of Lethbridge, which had a large teetotal Mormon population, the city's cocktail bar majority was less than 60%. As a result there was no extension of services and the city had to wait for three years before it got another chance to vote and get the needed majority.

In Saskatchewan a legislative committee also took a look at the province's liquor control system and the Bracken Report. It recommended the province join with the other provinces in widening the provisions for drinking in public.

On the recommendation of the Bracken Commission, all provinces ended the discrimination against women drinkers and opened their facilities to the women on the same basis as to men. In one aspect at least they also took the advice of Dr. Jellinek. He was convinced that alcoholism was a disease, and ought to be treated as such by provincial health authorities. He was also convinced that effective control of the liquor traffic was impossible as long as large numbers of alcoholics existed. Moderate drinkers might be willing to forego access to alcoholic beverages under strict control measures, but the confirmed alcoholics would search out the illegal suppliers regardless of cost. So anything the governments could do to reduce the number of alcoholics in society would be a plus for law enforcement and social tranquillity.

In Alberta the efforts of Dr. Donovan Ross had already born fruit by the time the Bracken Commission was in session. The Alberta Government in 1953 provided the Alcoholism Foundation of Alberta with a $100,000 grant with which it set up the first treatment center on the Prairies. Following the Bracken Commission, both Saskatchewan and Manitoba followed suit.

Surprisingly, in view of the cocktail bar agitation, there was no headlong rush into opening such establishments once the legal impediments had been removed. One retarding factor was the capital expenditures which the hotels were forced to make before they could qualify for licenses. The enforcement agencies would not settle for a once-over-lightly paint job but required extensive, tasteful, and costly refurnishing of the establishments. At the time of the Bracken Commission many Prairie hotels had either been taken over by the breweries or were so indebted to the breweries they were no longer free agents in the operation of their property. And there seemed to be little profit for the breweries if they lent the hotels more money to build in cocktail bars which would switch drinking tastes from beer to hard liquor. The Bracken Commission devoted much attention to the concentration of hotel ownership in brewery hands and urged stringent measures to retard the process. Saskatchewan never permitted breweries to own hotels and Alberta already had regulations barring any further lending by breweries to hotels.

So the change in the system of liquor control proceeded, if not at a snail's pace, at no headlong rush either. For the first couple of years it even seemed that Premier Campbell's economic projection of the course drinking would take might be on target. In December 1955, he said that except for federal subsidies, liquor was the largest single contributor to government income. He noted that Manitoba obtained about $8,000,000 a year from that source and expected that it would peak there or decline because liquor was a luxury people could get along without.

As things turned out, liquor sales and government profits did increase but slowly the next couple of years as the cocktail bars got into business. But over the longer term Premier Campbell could hardly have been farther out of the ball park in his calculations. During 1958, the first year of the cocktail era, Manitoba's sales were up less than five percent. And that figure was barely exceeded in Alberta where the oil and gas boom had increased its population by fifty percent in a decade and its prosperity beyond anything experienced in Manitoba or Saskatchewan.

Two other discerners of trends would prove to be much more accurate forecasters than Premier Campbell. Premier John Brownlee of Alberta in 1929 enunciated the principle that "you cannot make it easier for people to get liquor without the logical result being that consumption of liquor will increase." Twenty-six years later Dr. T.

A. Pincock, the Manitoba superintendent of psychiatric services and a consultant to the Bracken Commission said: "The more alcohol becomes available the greater number of excessive and problem drinkers there will be."

Ten years into the cocktail era Manitoba's liquor sales were $73,557,000 and its profits were $23,404,000 — an increase of almost 80% in sales and over 100% in profits. Saskatchewan sales were up 50% and its profits up 100% between 1958 and 1967. Alberta's sales rose from $66,683,000 to $105,487,000 and its profits from $19,574,000 to $41,511,000. Over the same decade, Manitoba's population grew from 875,000 to 970,000, Saskatchewan's from 891,000 to 955,000 and Alberta's from 1,206,000 to 1,500,000.

In the next decade a compounding factor became apparent in Prairie liquor consumption. More people were drinking more each year, even though the rate of population growth had slowed. Between 1967 and 1977 Saskatchewan actually lost population but its liquor sales increased from $62,746,000 to $151,388,000 and its profits from $20,941,000 to $50,327,000. Manitoba had a population increase of barely 5% but its sales were up 130% to $171,819,000 and its profits were up from $23,000,000 to $62,000,000. Alberta's population increased 25% during the decade but its liquor sales were up by 250% to $359,000,000.

In the early days of the beer-by-the-glass campaigns the proponents had argued that their cause was the cause of true temperance, that if beer were available to the populace less hard liquor would be drunk. Dr. L'Heureux had argued that point in his minority report of the Bracken Commission. The twenty-year record of the cocktail bar era demolished that contention. Manitoba recorded an increase in beer sales from 11,000,000 gallons to 18,000,000, but during the same time hard liquor sales climbed six times as fast from 700,000 gallons to 2,123,000 gallons. Alberta's beer sales doubled but its hard liquor sales quadrupled from 1,022,000 gallons to 4,700,000 gallons. Wine sales were up 300% in Manitoba to 1,328,000 gallons and in Alberta by 600% to 2,890,000 gallons. The spectacular increase in wine consumption was probably a concomitant of the reduction of the drinking age to eighteen in 1970 and the introduction of carbonated and fortified native wines like Baby Duck and Gimli Goose at about the same time. These bubbly wines had a pleasanter impact on the taste buds of the teenagers who found the harsher tastes of beer and hard liquor took a lot of getting used to. But they got used to it, in spades, and it was not long before the hotel owners were knocking out walls and expanding their taverns into Grand Central Station size to accommodate the teenagers.

Obviously a multiplicity of factors contributed to the steady, even spectacular growth in liquor consumption in the second post-Bracken decade. The aging, disciplined generations of the thirties and forties were being infiltrated by a generation reared on the gospel according to Spock in homes where ever-increasing numbers of mothers were going out to work, educated in schools where attendance was everything and performance was nothing, in a milieu in which permissiveness was in and discipline was out.

Profound as were the changes taking place in society, the transitions were glacier-paced rather than precipitous. From crew cut to long hair took at least five years; the high-schooler's journey from defiant cigarette smoking in the school yards to marijuana puffing in the parking lots took the better part of a decade. And that might have taken a lot longer except for the massive marijuana advertising campaign by the media that broke out in the late 1960s. They regarded themselves as viewing a social problem with alarm, bringing a social malaise into the open so that constituted authority would be forced to take appropriate action. But as the young people were to testify, the effect of all the publicity on them was to arouse their curiosity and interest in trying what everybody else seemed interested in trying. By the fall of 1968 Ottawa was wondering about launching a probe into marijuana use. That winter the RCMP set up special drug squads and the following summer were knocking off illicit drug rings in Winnipeg, Calgary, and Edmonton in batches of two and three dozen marijuana traffickers and possessors.

All this was accompanied by choruses of contradictory advice from the sidelines. Doctors checked in with statements that so little was known about the effects of marijuana that it was wrong to put it in the same class as heroin and other hard drugs. Agitation increased to treat marijuana users more leniently. The LeDain Commission was appointed and embarked on its transcontinental tour of the drug scene. In the public debate, an occasional small voice was to be heard protesting that none of the newly popular drugs was as harmful as alcohol. To that voice, nobody listened, least of all any provincial governments. Their reaction in 1970-71, following the example of the United States, was to reduce the minimum legal drinking age from twenty-one years to eighteen years. It was as if somebody had the idea that the way to wean the young people from the so-called mood altering drugs was to make alcoholic beverages more readily available to them. All the change did was make it easier for the young drinkers to combine booze and "pot" and compound their reactive experiences.

The contribution of the young drinkers to the steadily increasing liquor consumption in the 1970s is unknown. But one fact did emerge from exhaustive studies of one aspect of drinking alcohol: a sharp increase, almost everywhere, in highway fatalities involving the eighteen to twenty-four year age group. As the result of such information, the government of Saskatchewan in 1974 raised its minimum drinking age to nineteen years.

Part of the explanation for the steady ten percent annual increase in liquor consumption, perhaps the most important contributing factor, was the synergistic impact of steadily improving economic conditions on the Brownlee-Pincock-L'Heureux principle that the greater the availability of alcohol the greater the consumption. For the adult working class, bulging pay packets added a new dimension to the meaning of availability. The increasing number of two-income families added another. Finally, the pricing policies of the government liquor boards expanded availability beyond anything ever before experienced on the Prairies.

The consumer price index remained steady almost to the point of stagnation during the 1950s while there was a steady rise in both employment and wages during the second half of the decade. Across the west wages rose by twenty-five percent between 1954 and 1961 and employment was up just over twenty-two percent, an indication of improving economic conditions and the entry of increasing numbers of women into the labor force. It was a trend that would continue unbroken for the next fifteen years.

By 1976-77 the Dominion Bureau of Statistics employment index was more than double what it had been when the Bracken Commission was in business. Its estimate for the average wage earned in the Prairie cities for 1954 was $54 for a 40-hour week. Carpenters at that time, representing the high side of the average, earned $76 a week. By 1976-77 the D.B.S. average was up to $220 a week and carpenters were earning $275 a week.

Compared with increases of that order, the price of liquor increased very slowly indeed, as will be seen from the following table:

	1955	1976
Canadian Club Rye	$4.95	$7.75
J. Walker Red Label	6.25	7.55
Capt. Morgan Rum	4.30	7.30
Corby's Gin	3.95	6.55
Domestic beer	2.35	3.25
(12 bottle case)		

The result of the sharp rise in the income of the workers and the slow rise in the price of alcoholic beverages was to reduce the cost of alcoholic drinks to within ballpark comparison with the price of soft drinks. At the time of the Bracken Commission it had taken the better part of a day's pay to buy a bottle of liquor. Twenty years later, the same size bottle of Scotch or rye could have been acquired for little more than an hour's work. A worker might have been understandably reluctant to work a day for a bottle of rye, but he might not have hesitated if the energy expenditure was reduced to an hour or so or to half an hour for a case of beer.

Entertainment was forbidden in taverns and then permitted. Establishment of beer services on University campuses was rejected and then permitted. Sale of liquor in Provincial Auditoriums in Calgary and Edmonton was banned and then permitted. The hours of sale were extended in government stores in Alberta and then provision was made to allow special agents to deliver booze by the bottle to phone-in customers. Advertising of liquor in newspapers and periodicals was first forbidden and then approved in Manitoba and Alberta. Saskatchewan, however, maintained its ban on liquor advertising of all kinds and was one of the few Canadian provinces to use television to broadcast educational programs designed to discourage drinking by young people.

By the time the cocktail bars opened in 1958 television was well established on the Prairies but like the rest of the media it was barred from accepting liquor advertising of any kind. The breweries, however, had discovered long before a way of driving trucks through holes in the regulations. They came out with soft drinks named after their beer brands, plastered the countryside with billboards extolling the virtues of "Calgary Gingerale" and "Drewry's Gingerale" confident that the beer drinkers would identify the trademark with their brands of beer. They did, but it was not until 1965 in Alberta and 1967 in Manitoba that the governments permitted print media advertising of beer or spirits. Manitoba, in 1967, also dropped the

bans against television and radio advertising, but only after 10:00
P.M. Alberta kept its ban on television advertising until 1973, then
lifted it only for wine and beer.

Here again, however, the advertising geniuses of the beer industry
were able to make mince-meat of government regulations and
indeed, by conforming to the regulations, devise a more effective
campaign than they might have done had there been no restrictions.
The restrictions were these:

> A distiller, vintner or brewer may advertise brands and
> products by referring to trade marks, brand names, body
> labels and established slogans and recipes. No advertisement
> may encourage the use of liquor, state prices, depict family
> scenes involving liquor, refer to persons who may be minors,
> portray drinking scenes, or claim theraputic effects. . . . The
> overall emphasis is on good taste, and the elimination of
> "obnoxious" advertising techniques directed at young peo-
> ple.

The breweries, with liquor commission endorsement for every
advertisement that appeared, spent their money promoting a
lifestyle in which beer is the icing on the cake, the cherry on the
topping of the sundae. With hard liquor barred from television, the
breweries across the country zeroed in to monopolize the programs
with the widest young audiences: the hockey broadcasts, the football
broadcasts, and the baseball broadcasts. Thanks to the incessant
huckstering, one-hour hockey and football games were blown into
three-hour television commercials for beer. For the youngster sports
fans, beer became inseparably identified with their favorite sport,
and salubriously associated with every kind of fun they might expect
to indulge in for the rest of their lives.

Nor have the provincial restrictions inhibited the effectivess of
the distillers advertising in the print media. The lifestyle all liquor
ads identify with is the tastefully elegant and emphasis is on
superiority of its taste, the message seductively whispered rather
than shouted from the house-tops.

In the 1970s the breweries and distilleries went their separate
ways. While the former dominated television sports broadcasting to
a point where it relied on the brewery advertising to finance the
sports themselves, distillery advertising became the life blood of the
Canadian magazine industry. Such national publications as

MacLean's, Saturday Night, and the *Financial Post Magazine* could not long survive without the steady infusion of revenue from liquor advertising.

In their campaigns to persuade the liquor boards to allow them to advertise, the agencies insisted that advertising beer and liquor would not increase the consumption of either product. All they wanted to do, they pleaded, was familiarize the public with their particular brand names. Then when the imbibers went shopping they would be encouraged to substitute the identified brand name for another brand. But if all brands were advertised would the clamor for public attention not increase the desire to drink? The answer to that question was frequently a Trudeauian shrug indicating that if there was such a result the increase would be insignificant.

Was it?

Between the onset of the cocktail bar drinking on the Prairies and 1976 the breweries, nationally, increased their advertising expenditures from $4,000,000 annually to $17,000,000, the distillers from $3,300,000 to $19,000,000 and the wineries from $576,000 to $4,695,000. In total, over approximately two decades, the liquor industry increased its advertising budgets by 400%. During the same period liquor sales on the Prairies increased by $546,000,000 or 360%. It by no means follows that there is an exclusive cause and effect relationship between these remarkably coincidental figures. Availability and price-effective demand are obviously more important. But to argue that advertising did not play an important role in increasing consumption of all kinds of alcoholic beverages would be to challenge the entire body of doctrine on which advertising is based.

The maturing of the cocktail bars era marked the completion of the evolution of government liquor commission from agency to control the liquor traffic to promoters of it. As demand increased the sales outlets proliferated until, in Alberta at least, no new shopping center could be considered complete without a liquor store. That change of terminology is important for as time passed by only hide-bound senior citizens any longer identified them as "liquor commissions" rather than "liquor stores."

That was what the Liquor Boards had become — operators of glorified chain stores. As the brewers and distillers poured out their millions of advertising dollars to attract the consumers, the governments provided the retail outlets. There was no discernible difference, surely, between that operation and the way in which General Foods and Proctor and Gamble poured out their millions of advertising dollars and the chain stores provided the consumer outlets. Indeed the liquor stores came more and more to imitate the chain stores. They also shelved their products in the open for cash-and-carry purchasing. They too provided shopping carts and baskets for the convenience of customers. Their goods were ticketed with identical machines to those used to stamp prices on corn flakes. Both set up occassional displays of bargain-priced discontinued lines to tempt the impulse buyers.

The public-be-damned attitude that was the characteristic stance of early liquor board operations was long gone. In its place were bevies of hovering sales assistants forever eager to help customers locate their favorite libation. The profits flooding into provincial government coffers became a vital source of revenue from which modest trickles were allowed to flow out to the welfare agencies that had been established to succor the human flotsam and jetsam of the liquor traffic.

CHAPTER EIGHT
WHERE THE SOLUTION
IS THE PROBLEM

Of this there is no doubt — the alcoholic hell which Indians by the thousands would experience was paved with the good intentions of Canadian politicians. The paving project began in 1946-49 when the Canadian Parliament had a joint committee look into the operation of the Indian Act. Eventually the committee considered the interdiction of Indians to access to alcohol, which had been around in one form or another since long before Canada was invented. Under the Indian Act it was forbidden: for non-Indians to give or sell alcoholic beverages to Indians; for Indians to have alcoholic beverages in their possession off the reserves; or to take the stuff onto their reserves. The purpose of such discriminatory legislation, of course, was to prevent the obliteration of the Indians at the hands of the white race, whose debauchery of the Indians with booze was the original holocaust.

Discrimination of whatever sort went out of fashion with the end of the Second World War, and the spread of the humanitarian euphoria with which the United Nations came upon the world stage. At the Parliamentary committee witness after witness boggled at the racial discrimination in the Indian liquor laws. Biologically, it was asserted, Indians were no different from whites when it came to being able to "handle their liquor". Several thousand Indians had served in the Canadian armed services during the war, had access to liquor in the canteens on the same terms as their white comrades, and had behaved no differently.

Indian and white spokesmen alike testified that the liquor laws gave the Indians a feeling of inferiority. Civil libertarians could isolate scores of inconsistencies. An Indian as a soldier could drink himself under a mess table, but as a civilian he could not enter a

116

Prairie pub for a bottle of beer. A white woman who married an Indian soldier could not, when they returned to civvy street, serve her husband a glass of beer legally on their own kitchen table. Certainly there was something patently ridiculous in a system which permitted an Indian to risk his life for his country but denied him access to a bottle of beer. In the aptly turned phrase of an Indian witness, "you allow us the right to get shot but deny us the right to get half-shot." Eventually the conscience-pricked Parliamentary committee recommended a number of changes in the Indian Act.

When the Government got around to trying to work the changes into the Act in 1951 it immediately stumbled over the fact that control of drinking in Canada was vested in provincial governments. Some of them had their own restrictions on the sale of liquor to the Indians. Eventually Ottawa found a formula for shunting responsibility for Indian drinking to the provinces. It left the prohibitory sections of the Indian Act intact but added a rider that they would be nullified when any provincial government formally requested such action within its jurisdiction.

If the provinces were content to have the Indians drink, they would be able to drink. If the provinces objected, or did nothing, the Indians would still be forbidden access to beverage alcohol. British Columbia immediately passed the required legislation to exempt its Indians from Section 94 of the Indian Act and opened its facilities to them. None of the Prairie Provinces, however, were moved to any such precipitous action. Meanwhile the government of the United States was also doing a lot of soul searching about discrimination against its Indians. In 1953 it removed all Federal restrictions on the sale of alcoholic beverages to Indians although, as in Canada, some state and local restrictions were still in force.

While the American Congress was acting, Ontario launched an investigation of its own by a select committee of the legislature. As a result of that committee's recommendation, Ontario in 1954 passed the necessary legislation to exempt its Indians from the Indian Act restrictions. The committee's recommendations contained the following sections which defined Prairie attitudes as well:

The Committee made a special effort to find medical evidence on the question of consumption of alcohol by Indians. At no time was any evidence submitted to show that Indians are any more prone to alcoholism than non-Indians, nor that they are constitutionally any less capable of using alcohol with discretion than non-Indians.

The Committee found a very strong feeling, not only among the Indians questioned, but among expert witnesses, that Indians should be fully equal with non-Indians in the matter of consumption of alcohol. Members of the clergy, Indians Affairs Branch officials, Royal Canadian Mounted Police Officers, Ontario Provincial Police Officers, welfare and recreation workers, and others favored allowing Indians to buy packaged goods and take it home to consume in their homes on the reserves. The Indian Act specifically forbids this.

Several bands took the attitude that allowing an Indian to drink in a public place would not be any help. These bands considered the problem will be solved when the right to purchase packaged goods is extended. At every reserve, the Committee ran into the same complaint. Indians are now obtaining liquor through illegal sources. Bootlegging is almost uncontrollable. Prices are as high as $18 for a bottle of the cheapest whiskey sold. In many cases, there were reports of home brews being sold to Indians, with subsequent deleterious effects.

In the course of its investigation the Ontario committee visited eighteen reserves, of which ten favored giving Indians free access to liquor, three were opposed, and three could not make up their minds. The Federal Government in its 1951 amendments to the Indian Act discovered that it had stepped on a great many Indian toes in permitting liquor onto the Indian reserves without regard to the wishes of the residents. In 1956 it re-amended the Act to insert a clause to stipulate that liquor could not be legally taken onto a reserve until the Band had petitioned for a referendum to be held on the question and approved it by a majority vote.

There was still the interdictions in provincial law in the way, however, and these had to be removed before the Indians could obtain legal access to the booze to take onto the reserves. Manitoba and Saskatchewan moved rather quickly, in 1960, to amend their regulations but Alberta did not get around to changing its liquor act until 1966. Thereafter, if the right to legally consume beverage alcohol be the criterion, the Indians joined the human race.

They did more than that. They began a trek to the cities of the

Prairies which would ultimately move a good third of the Indians off their reserves. It was a population movement that would cause horrendous social problems for the cities and for the Indians. The upending of the government's attitude toward Indians and alcohol was the first step in reconsideration of the whole business of a government acting as custodian-guardian of one particular race of people. That would ultimately end, in 1968, by the decision to launch a concerted campaign to Canadianize the Indians by making them responsible for managing their own affairs. What changed everything for the Indians before that, however, was the way in which money began to trickle out of the government coffers into the hands of the Indians in the 1950s. It was in truth a mere trickle, but compared with the pre-war volume it was a raging torrent.

From Confederation until the onset of the war the Canadian Indian population grew so slowly that there was an impression abroad that the Indians were dying out. The Department of Indian Affairs in the Canada Year Book for 1939 made reference to that impression when it noted the Indian population had grown from 102,000 in 1871 to 123,000 in 1931 and said this proved that "the popular notion that the race was disappearing was not in accord with the facts".

What was in accord with the facts was that the Indian reserves were more concentration camps and economic slums that habitations for people. In 1937, according to the same year book, the 45,000 Indians in the Prairie Provinces had a gross income of $1,924,000 or $43 per capita or $250 per family. Of that total $632,000 came from farming operations, $344,000 from fishing, trapping, and hunting, while wages accounted for $135,000. Much of the farm income total was from Indian lands leased to white farmers rather than from the Indians' own farming operations.

Indian income was supplemented by five dollars a head treaty money and welfare payments in the form, usually, of food allowances which were doled out when the bands were facing starvation. Hived away as they were on reserves the Indians were hardly a pimple on the conscience of any Canadians, least of all the people of the Prairies. For one reason, one could live and die in almost any city of the Prairies without ever seeing an Indian in the flesh, except during the annual fair weeks. Then in the afterglow of the summer fairs, an occasional Indian might still be seen dazedly walking the streets, seemingly in search of a way out of town and back to the reserve. In August, vacationers traveling across the country would encounter Indian women and children on railway station platforms selling baskets of fresh-picked blueberries, toy birchbark canoes, trinkets, and beadwork. For the rest of the time the overwhelming Indian majority vegetated on the reserves, huddled in shacks that would have merited instant condemnation in any city skid-row slum, utterly untrained for any viable role in the white society that harbored them.

The social watershed of the Second World War, which changed everything for the white population, even more profoundly changed the Indian way of life. Out of that war came the conviction that Canadians were never going back to the social conditions of the 1930s. A niggardly welfare system, with rock-bottom minimum benefits grudgingly granted, was replaced by a system which recognized the right of the casualties of the economic system to be sustained in relative dignity by the state. A system of unemployment insurance was in place; a pension system for the blind; old age pensions of $25 a month, with a means test, for the over 70s was replaced by benefits of $65 a month without a means test. A children's allowance scheme provided a monthly subsidy of $6 for each child payable to the mothers in their family.

All these, moreover, were as much a part of the anti-discrimination package for the Indians as was the freedom of access to booze. Each of these items, considered individually, could have but a minor impact on the daily lives of the Indians. But in aggregate, to people who had been existing on near nothing for almost a hundred years, it must have been tantamount to reaching the promised land.

Obviously, however, such payments could have had but little effect on Indian consumption of alcohol if Indian annual income had remained within the fifty dollar per capita range. It did not. In addition to the welfare package, all kinds of other financial goodies were pressed upon them so that they had both access to booze and the wherewithal to acquire it.

With the election of the Diefenbaker administration in 1956 Indian Affairs embarked on a program of encouraging young Indians to leave the reserves to seek their fortunes in the white world. Highly selective at first, the Department's program sought out the brightest young Indian high schoolers and set up agencies to place them in city jobs. They were provided with training for the jobs, provided with room and board and given day by day counseling to enable them to adapt to the culture shock the change in environment made inevitable.

This program was rapidly expanded in size and scope. Provision was made to supply the Indians with tools, clothing, and twenty-five dollars a month in pocket money. While the federal government was getting into high gear the Saskatchewan provincial government of Premier Ross Thatcher got into the act. As part of a program to get the Metis and non-reserve Indians off welfare, Thatcher announced that he would find a job in his government for any natives with high schools diplomas.

During the 1960s the Saskatchewan government did find jobs for a number of Indians, but unhappily in positions that kept them imbedded in the second class citizens category. Because of the opposition of the white civil servants, the Indians were placed in a special supernumerary category doing odd jobs in a make-work environment. They got none of the fringe benefits allowed the white employees, had no job security, no paid vacations or pension plans. In the end the program was quietly abandoned and the Indians had to compete for the government jobs on equal terms with everybody else. The exception was when work was being done in or near the reserves where it was possible to give preference to native people.

Neither Manitoba nor Alberta followed even the token program of Saskatchewan and when the Bill of Rights legislation came into being across the Prairies any hope of affirmative action programs to assist the urban Indians went down the drain. The Federal Government, of course, did find ways and means of placing hundreds of natives in its Indian Affairs Branch, but the deficiencies in the Indians' educational achievements barred all but a minority from these jobs.

At no time did the employment opportunities for the Indians ever keep pace with the flood of Indians into the Prairie cities. The following table shows the growth of the urban treaty Indian population. The figures for 1941 to 1971 inclusive are from the Dominion Bureau of Statistics. In 1974 Statistics Canada stopped taking racial origin statistics. The figures for 1976 are Indian Affairs

Indian Population

	1941	1951	1961	1971	1976
Winnipeg	24	210	1,081	4,945	6,000 - 16,000 .
Regina	7	160	539	2,860	5,300 - 10,000
Saskatoon	6	48	207	1,070	2,000 - 10,000
Calgary	14	62	335	2,265	5,000 - 10,000
Edmonton	5	616	995	5,205	10,000 - 15,000

estimates and include, on the high end, non-treaty as well as treaty Indians. It estimated that there were 42,000 female and 38,000 male treaty Indians living off reserves across Canada.

The availability of welfare in the cities, coupled with a chance for employment that did not exist on the reserves, proved an irresistible magnet for the Indians. So also, and perhaps to an even greater extent for some Indians, was the existence of the liquor stores and taverns in such conveniently located cities and towns as Kenora, Broadview, Regina, Lethbridge, Fort McLeod, Gleichen, and Calgary. In the cities the drinkers discovered the Salvation Army and other welfare agencies willing to supply them with temporary bed and board while they located relatives with whom to live. But most of all they discovered the skid-road slums, the slum taverns, and other Indians with whom to share bottles of cheap wine. And they found drunk tanks, police courts, and jail cells in numbers far outweighing their proportion of the population.

All this was accompanied by massive growth of services being offered to the Indians by the Federal Government. The Department of Indian Affairs, which in 1937 got by on a budget of $5,000,000, spent $829,000,000 in 1978-79. That total included $104,000,000 for social assistance, $24,000,000 for child care, $5,600,000 on alcoholism, and $94,000,000 for medical services.

The best intentions in the world, coupled with the lifting of a century old discriminatory law from the backs of the Canadian Indians and a cloudburst of money combined to bring about the ultimate Canadian tragedy — the alcoholic degradation of the Canadian Indian.

That degradation was documented to the hilt by the Department of Indian Affairs and Northern Development in 1980 in a publication entitled: *Indian Conditions: A Survey*. The survey found that between fifty and sixty percent of all Indians' illness was alcohol related; the Indian death rates range from twice to four times the national average; Indians died violently at three times the national rate; died in auto accidents at twice the national rate and committed suicide at two and a half times the national rate. Indians in the twenty-five to fifty-five years group were admitted to hospital for alcoholism at five times the national rate. The rate of alcoholism for reserve Indians, however, was twice the rate of Indians living off the reserves. Forty-five percent of Indian births were outside wedlock, compared with ten percent for the national average. The number of Indian children in government agencies increased by fifty percent. There were seven times as many Indians as whites in prisons in proportion to population. In Manitoba and Saskatchewan forty percent of the inmates in provincial jails were Indians. The Indian rate for juvenile delinquency was three times the national average.

The picture is not, of course, one of totally unmitigated disaster. In all the cities progress is being made. Some Indians are finding permanent employment and are doing well. More and more children are staying longer in school and emerging with the tickets that will enable them to find a place in white society. The Indian Studies departments in the universities are expanding. The Saskatchewan Indians Federated College at the University of Regina has seen its full-time enrollment grow from 23 students in 1977 to 150 in 1980 and its off-campus enrollment increase from 257 to 450. Similar growth rates are expected at Winnipeg, Brandon, Saskatoon, and Lethbridge. All across the west Indian teachers are increasing in numbers in the school systems and the hundreds of Indians and Metis self-help organizations being funded by Ottawa are being staffed and operated mainly by native employees. Indian women in particular are finding employment as secretaries and administrators in increasing numbers of government agencies.

On the reserves themselves progress is also being made. On the huge Blood reserve west of Lethbridge more and more Indians are making a success of cattle ranching and grain farming. The province of Manitoba has recruited several hundred Indians for its special agricultural courses for native people. Several reserves have been trying with some success to establish manufacturing businesses staffed by natives. On the Sarcee reserve adjacent to Calgary a housing development based on long term leases of land is being experimented with. The development includes a public golf course. The project is being financed with resources accumulated from oil and gas royalties.

The crux of the status problem being encountered by the Indians in white society is the super-visibility of the drunken Indians compared with the low visibility of the sober and successful Indians. Senior police officials in Winnipeg, Regina, Calgary, and Lethbridge all testify to the fact that what whites see as masses of drunken Indians on their streets are in reality the same relatively small numbers of Indians being seen over and over and over. The monthly tabulation of drunks taken into protective custody by an urban police department may contain 2,000 names, half of them Indian. But the bulk of the Indian detainees may be accounted for by no more than a few hundred names, repeated again and again.

In the flow of the Indians into the cities a good many found the way open to a better life and they grasped the opportunities to become lawyers, teachers, social workers, and community leaders. But for the great majority city life was as much a life of frustration and spiritual deprivation as life on the reserve had been. They were as lost, as alien to the urban white culture of Prairie Canada as immigrants from the moon.

The Prairie Indians were prisoners, products of their 15,000-year history on the western plains. Anthropologically a primitive people, they had lived with and off the buffalo for thousands of years. The buffalo provided them with their food, shelter, clothing, and fuel for their fires. So vast were the herds, and so teeming with game were the adjacent woodlands, that no Indian ever had to take thought of the morrow. What they had to take thought of was physical courage of the kind needed to engage in hand to hand combat in battle and in the struggle against the predators that also lived off the buffalo. Only after the arrival of the white man were their skills in horsemanship and in the use of the white man's weapons to be developed.

Within the Indian culture the men were the warriors and hunters, the women labored to supply all the creature comforts. Then one day in the 1870s the American slaughter of the buffalo was complete and nothing remained for the Indians but a Prairie landscape white with buffalo bones. The Indians' food and shelter were gone forever and they faced mass starvation.

The Canadian Indians were rescued from that fate by the Canadian government who decided to settle them on special reserves of their own where they could learn to become farmers like the homesteaders who would soon be pouring onto the lands vacated by the buffalo. A concerted effort was made by the government to teach the reserve Indians how to farm: farm equipment was bought and shipped to the reserves, instructors were hired to teach the Indians how to yoke oxen, plow, harrow, disc, and seed their land. Some of that land was ill-suited for farming, some of it was superb wheat land. But whether the land was good, bad, or indifferent was of no consequence. The notion that a nation of warrior-hunters could be instantly converted into sod-busting grain growers was tinged with lunacy, just as 100 years later the idea that reserve Indians could be pitch-forked into the cities was also sheer madness. The farm equipment rusted on the reserves and, if the Indians evolved at all from the status of hunter-warriors in the hundred years that followed, the change was hardly discernible from their thought processes or work habits.

The Indians moved into the cities without any of the skills needed by modern urban employers. They brought to such employment as they could get, the work habits and thought-processes developed in 15,000 years with the buffalo and 100 years of reserve dependency. What white people have seen as Indian improvidence, of living a day at a time and working only when they needed money, was rooted in the hunter-warrior practice of hunting only when food was needed. It was a process of thought that certainly disrupted Indian-employer relationships.

In Alberta white farmers who leased Indian lands for grain production employed Indians in their operations. They always began spring seeding or harvesting with a full compliment of Indian help. But when the Indians drew their pay the work crews melted by half and were seldom restored to full size until the absent workers ran out of money. Then they returned fully confident that their jobs would be waiting for them. The farmers understood the Indians and made provision for replacing them, but urban employers who saw their work disrupted by such absences were neither understanding nor forgiving. To the drunken-Indian stereotype was added the absentee-Indian stereotype which caused employers to look elsewhere for their work crews the next time.

The cultural shock which the reserve Indians experienced in the cities was horrendous. The housing accommodation they found was little better than they had left on the reserves. They found skid row drifters eager to introduce them to city vices, sharp-cornering merchants swindling them with shoddy merchandise, thieving taxi-drivers willing to let them sleep off a drunk in the back of a cab with the meter running. In the process of discovering the cities, they demonstrated that the expert witnesses who had urged the repeal of the liquor restrictions had been wrong. Indians were in fact different from white people when it came to managing alcohol. A hundred years on the reserves had conditioned their drinking reflexes in a way that made them peculiarly vulnerable to the chemistry of ethanol.

By the middle of the 1960s the drinking habits of the Indians, from the Gulf Coast to the Arctic, were undergoing the scrutiny of small armies of earnest sociologists who were reporting their finding in the publications of the learned societies. The researchers discovered that there was a pattern to Indian drinking that held consistently from the Gulf Coast to the Arctic, a pattern whose roots could be easily traced to a century of lives of dependency on Indian reserves. There were, of course, variations between the behavior of members of different tribes, but as a general rule the following factors seem to be almost universal: American Indians were group drinkers just as Canadian Indians seemed to do everything in groups. In addition all Indians seemed programmed psychologically to share whatever they possessed with other Indians. Two Indians, for example, might pool their resources to buy a bottle of cheap fortified wine, their favorite libation, and share the contents with other Indians. Or one Indian, having cashed a welfare cheque, would hold out his handful of money to his friends for them to take whatever they needed; Indians assumed that they would share in the liquor, food, or housing of other Indians.

As for liquor, the practice of freely sharing was part of a tradition that also required freely accepting offered drink. For one Indian to refuse a proffered drink was regarded as tantamount to an insult and not the sort of gesture made with ease or comfort by the ordinarily passive, sober Indian. As a result, even an Indian with a built-in distaste for alcohol, one who realized there would be serious physical consequences to taking the drink, accepted it rather than give offense to a fellow Indian.

For North American reserve Indians, drinking to get drunk had become the chief and most favored form of recreation, akin to what attending football or hockey games was to the white. Prodded by investigating social scientists for explanation for their drinking, young Indians frequently replied that they drank "because there was nothing else to do." Having nothing else to do was a literal truism for thousands of Indians on scores of reserves, for days stretching into weeks, and weeks stretching into months. Even the most conservative government reports put the unemployment rate on Prairie reserves at upwards of seventy percent.

Drinking because there was nothing else to do was true not only of young reserve Indians of all ages. And drinking to get drunk, far from carrying with it the stigma which was attached to it in some areas of white society, became recognized among Indians as a desirable social objective. It was one in which the older children in the Indian families frequently joined, even though getting physically abused was sometimes the lot of the children in the violently concluding chapters of the drinking bouts. The smaller children reached the age of discretion when they learned to get out of sight when their parents were drinking.

Alcohol was the lubricant that made Indian social events worth attending. Getting drunk was an end in itself whenever Indians had money enough, a top priority when family allowance cheques, welfare cheques, or old age pension cheques arrived. And of course, in the urban setting of the Prairies, once the Indians became numerous, white leeches swarmed around the drinkers to part them from their money. As the dispatcher of a Winnipeg taxi company explained, in the autumn of 1978 when I phoned for the third time to complain about the non-arrival of a cab at the City Hall, "look mister its payday for the Indians today and I can't afford to send another cab anywhere near the north end. Every time I send one within half a mile of the City Hall I lose him for twenty-four hours to the Indians."

At the end of those twenty-four hours the taxi driver would have most of the proceeds from the Indians' welfare cheques that had not already gone to the government liquor stores. On the remote reserves it was often the air-taxi operators who cashed in on Indian welfare payments. In northern Manitoba in the winter of 1980 the Indians of the God's Lake Narrows reserve voted to end Prohibition on their reserve and permit liquor to be legally brought in. Behind that decision was a long siege of trouble with bootleggers flying in booze and selling it to the Indians for up to sixty dollars a bottle. After repeal the northern air taxis brought it in legally and sold it illegally for forty or fifty dollars a bottle. By the summer of 1981, the band was up to its ears in trouble. Drinking had increased, there was an increase in child neglect, serious crime was such a problem on weekends that the RCMP sent two constables in every Friday to assist the band policemen. In a long story on the situation on the northern reserves in the *Winnipeg Free Press* of 9 Sept. 1981, it was reported that leaders of the reserve were now beginning to agitate for another plebiscite in the hope of returning the reserve to dry status. Prohibition had not deterred the air taxi operators from flying in planes loaded with booze to be disposed of for profits ranging from $2,000 to $5,000 a trip. All that repeal had done was reduce the profits marginally while drastically increasing the amount of drinking on the reserve.

The concept of saving, of putting something aside for a rainy day, has been alien to North American Indian philosophy whether the Indians were Cree, Blackfoot, Navaho, Algonquins, Shoshone, or

Ojibway. In no other aspect of Indian life has it been more alien than in relation to alcohol. No bottle of fortified wine, the much favored Indian drink, was ever left unfinished and the drinking comes to an end only when both the supply of alcohol and the supply of money is exhausted. This aspect of Indian drinking was a direct result of the long period in which Indians were forbidden by law to possess or drink alcoholic beverages. Once the bottle was in hand, disposing of its contents quickly became a matter of urgent priority to avoid arrest for possessing it. So there was no sitting around nursing a drink as an encouragement to casual conversation. Curiously enough this drinking pattern survived among Prairie Indians well into the 1970s, long after there was any compelling legal reason for hasty consumption of evidence of illegality.

More often than not, Indians did their drinking on empty stomachs. That, coupled with gulp drinking, caused alcohol to have a much quicker impact on the vital organs and thus a quicker reaction than with white people. Whites would get drunk as quickly as Indians if they consumed their liquor in the same way. A hundred years of reserve dependency turned a warrior people into models of docility when sober. But passivity quickly passed with the ingestion of alcohol and Indians became explosively aggressive, particularly toward friends and members of their family circle. Among American as among Canadian Indians, crime increased with alcohol consumption, a fact obviously attributable to group drinking and group interaction.

Of all the factors which have caused distress to the Indians, group drinking undoubtedly heads the list. A white drunk, having seriously over-imbibed in a tavern, would ordinarily attract but little attention as he began weaving his way homeward down the street. Indeed, as long as he minded his own business and stayed out of trouble, his unsteady progress might have evoked only benign amusement on the part of a patrolling policeman.

Such was seldom the case with an Indian drinker because whether the locale was Regina, Calgary, or Cheyenne, Wyoming, there were only drinking Indians. It was this high-group-visibility that was the Indian's undoing. They would come to a halt, with a good deal of pushing and shoving and milling about, on a downtown street corner, probably with no clear destination in mind. Policemen who anticipated trouble were seldom disappointed, and when they moved in to break it up probably did so with a lot more vigor than would have been shown if the trouble had blown up unexpectedly.

During the late 1960s, almost for the first time in history, the term "police brutality" began to appear in the public prints of Prairie cities. Unquestionably, prejudice against Indians did develop within urban police forces. For many police officers, the only physical trouble they had was with Indians, because the arrests of Indians for drunken and disorderly behavior far outnumbered similar white arrests.

In a study of public drunkenness in Regina, completed in October 1980 by the Saskatchewan Alcoholism Commission, researchers did a detailed examination of the 3,368 cases of persons arrested for public drunkenness in Regina during 1977. The sampling of these files revealed that sixty-two percent of the arrestees were Indians, thirty-eight percent were white, even though the natives accounted for only fifteen percent of the city's population. The study concluded that part of the explanation for the disproportionate number of Indians arrested was their high visibility, the fact that they were transients in the city and had no access to private property in which to consume their booze. The study also noted that many of the arrests were second, third, and fourth offenders.

In all the Prairie cities arresting drunks was motivated mainly by a need to get them off the streets rather than for punitive reasons. The practice was to file them in the drunk tanks for the night and turn them loose in the morning when they had sobered up. The white drunks could then catch a bus and go to work or go home. But being turned loose in that way posed a major problem for reserve Indians. Their home could be twenty-five or thirty miles away and they had no way of getting there. So they went looking for a lift home from other Indians in the only place they could expect to find them — in the local beer parlors. Ten hours later they might expect to be booked into the drunk tank for another night, along with their friends. When this happened three or four days running, a short jail sentence for the offenders became mandatory.

After years of struggling with this revolving door, the attorney general of Alberta and the cities of Lethbridge and Fort McLeod pooled their resources and set up a special bus service for the exiters from the drunk tanks. Instead of turning the Indians out onto the streets on the morning-after they loaded them on the bus in each city and ran them back to the Blood and Piegan reserves where they lived.

The Saskatchewan study found that Indians were sent to jail oftener than white drunks. That fact led to charges of police discrimination and persecution of Indians. A more likely explanation was that Indians were being caught up in groups of repeaters that clogged the works of a system which allowed single drunks to slip through.

In this arresting process there is little question that Indians got knocked around, sometimes with what was in fact excessive brutality. But it was often the kind of excess brutality which drunks, whether Indians or white, brought on themselves. Regardless of the circumstances, however, the deteriorating relations between Indians and police came increasingly to public attention in Winnipeg, Regina, and Lethbridge as it did in the 1960s and early 1970s in Minneapolis, Baltimore, and Tucson, Arizona.

In no area were Indian-police relationships more abrasive than on the Canadian reserves themselves. The RCMP, which policed the reserves, were in a no-win situation. If they moved in to break up drunken disturbances, they antagonized everybody involved. If they failed to do so, and serious injury resulted, they were charged with neglect of duty. If they arrested a couple of over-intoxicated wayfarers sprawled by a roadside, they'd be criticized. If they left them there and harm came to them, the Mounties would be blamed.

By the middle 1970s drinking on the reserves, with its concomitant violence, had reached the stage where band chiefs were becoming alarmed. Unhappy with the way the RCMP were doing the job, they thought the substitution of Indian policemen might be more efficient. That was tried on a number of reserves, but the untrained Indians seldom lasted long in the job. For them merely to take the job ostracized them from their friends and neighbors because no drinking Indian loved any policeman. Ultimately in Alberta the solicitor general and some band councils got together and worked out a rough and ready system for providing the reserves with native cops. Agents of the provincial government selected a dozen likely prospects and sent them off to Regina to be specially trained in police work by the RCMP. After ten weeks of intensive instruction they were returned to the reserves to take over most of the law enforcement chores.

The RCMP itself also became concerned with the image of the force and worked out an elaborate program to indoctrinate its entire force with the need for sensitivity to Indian susceptibilities. It set up a special cross-cultural indoctrination course and made it compulsory for all recruits and encouraged its regular constabulary to take it.

Designed to familiarize policemen with cultural differences, values, conflicts, and prejudices, the course was a total immersion study of Prairie social history, with heavy emphasis on the problems of Indian and immigrant minorities in Prairie multi-racial society.

In addition to the indoctrination of its staff, the RCMP adopted a policy of recruiting native constables to serve on its regular force. In recognition of the deficiences of Indian education, Indians were permitted to enter the force with lower educational standards than other recruits. They were assigned to the regular force as special constables and if they served with satisfaction for three years, and upgraded their educational level, they would shed their "special constable" patches and become regular Mounties. Assigning these constables to duties in the vicinity of the reserves was expected substantially to improve relationships between the Mounties and the Indians.

As long as having liquor on the reserves is permitted, the challenge facing the tribal policemen will be a formidable one, and the cross-cultural pull on the Indian constables themselves will be severe. Recognizing that fact, and alarmed over the impact of alcohol on the reserve residents, many reserve leaders like those at God's Lake Narrows are having second thoughts about living on "wet" reserves. Indeed, many have convinced their followers to change their minds and restore Prohibition. In Manitoba, seven of the forty-two reserves that voted "wet" have changed their minds and gone back to "dry" status; in Saskatchewan five out of thirty-seven did the same; and seven out of twenty-seven reserves in Alberta.

Aside altogether from alcohol, the Indians in an urban environment have had all the worst of it. Curiously enough it has been the Indians most highly publicized virtue that has been at the root of much of his trouble. That, until alcohol intruded upon it too, was the strength of Indian familial ties. The nuclear Indian family extended almost to infinity, and the Indians looked after each other, individuals moving back and forth readily within the group. Before 1970 family ties were so strong that an Indian who had "made it" in urban white society might feel the pull of family so strongly that he or she would quit her job and move back to the reserve. Nothing militated so strongly against Indians seeking to become permanently established in Prairie cities as family ties. Nothing save alcohol caused so much white antagonism toward Indians to develop.

In getting established in a city the Indians perforce had to seek the cheapest housing accommodation available, and there was seldom any cheap accommodation in the booming Prairie cities. What was available was the near derelict housing in such run-down conditions that no other tenants could be found, housing vacated by the poorest of immigrant families as soon as they could afford better accommodation. Such housing was available in tenements in Winnipeg's near north side, Regina's near east side, Saskatoon's west side, and Calgary's near south-east area.

To the Indians migrating into this kind of accommodation, there was little difference from what was normal for them on the reserves. Indeed some of this slum housing, which at least had piped in water and electricity, was a substantial improvement from what they had 'enjoyed' on the reserve. This, as Edgar J. Dosman pointed out in his book, *Indians: The Urban Dilemma*, created two problems for the Indian tenant. The newcomers would soon find themselves playing host to bevies of non-paying guests, relatives from the reserve who simply took up permanent lodgings with them on moving into Saskatoon. The overcrowding imposed impossible strains on everybody, especially on the financial resources of the original tenant. Dosman cited the case of one young family head who had been through this routine several times before giving up and returning to his reserve. Later on, he made one more stab at making it in Saskatoon, took pains to keep his Saskatoon address secret from his reserve relatives, friends, and acquaintances. That did not work for long either: they tracked him down and moved in.

In their reserve hovels few Indians were ever exposed to the art of good housekeeping. Garbage, when it was eventually moved, was given the old heave-ho into the back yard. It did not take long for the point to be reached in the 1970s when Indians came to be regarded even by slum landlords as the absolute bottom-of-the-barrel tenants. Once the provinces had civil rights legislation on the statute books, Indians in the urban setting had good reason to complain about being discriminated against in rental housing. Telephone inquiries about vacancies produced pleasant-voiced descriptions of the advertised property, but when Indians turned up to rent it the owner or agent insisted the property was no longer available. There was obvious discrimination. But it was frequently discrimination against Indian over-crowding and Indian housekeeping more than discrimination against Indians per se.

In Calgary unscrupulous real estate agents were thus able to cast the reserve Indians in the role of "block-busters" in seeking to get control of blocks of old houses for redevelopment of the sites with modern apartment buildings. A Calgary business executive cited the case of a relative who owned two rooming houses in a downtown location. Several houses on either side had been acquired by a developer who planned to demolish them to make way for a high-rise apartment project. The owner of the two rooming houses was blocking the project by refusing to sell. Eventually the agent for the developer confronted the owner with this ultimatum: either sell the property at the last offering price or the agent would rent the houses on either side to Indians. The owner refused to sell and the developer's agent did as promised. It was not long before the houses that might have been comfortable abodes for six or seven people were home for twenty Indians.

The congesting of Indian dwellings coupled with the sub-marginal housekeeping might well have been tolerated had it not been for the fact that the Indian tenants were also drinkers. Similar hiving together of families took place in Prairie cities with the immigration of refugees including the boat people. It was not uncommon for an apartment owner to rent a suite to a refugee couple and find a dozen people bedded down in sleeping bags on the floor. The refugees encountered some deep-seated prejudice in the white communities. But liquor was not a problem and they found employment doing the kind of work white people spurned and were soon able to work themselves into housing that more nearly squared with white norms. Alcohol prevented the Indians from doing likewise.

By the mid 1970s the lamentable visibility of the drunken Indians on the downtown streets, and the tenancy problems created by their ingrained herd instincts, combined to do irreparable damage to the image of the Indians of the Prairies. To the white Canadians all Indians were drunken Indians. The tragic irony is that this epithet was becoming firmly attached just at the time when the Indians' self-image was beginning to improve, when Indian leaders were successfully encouraging their people to become prideful of themselves, their history, their culture, and their place in society. The native people were beginning to find places in education and were agitating for leadership openings for Indians in all phases of Indian life.

With the awakening of the Indians on the reserves to pridefulness in their "Indianness" there came a growing recognition of the fact that alcohol had become one of their pressing social problems, about which they as Indians would have to do something. It was when the

Indians themselves moved to grapple with their problem that they made everything worse. Their solution became the problem.

For most of the 1970s Kenora, Ontario, a resort town 125 miles east of Winnipeg, was Canada's prime example of everything that was wrong with Indian-white relationships. South of Kenora, on a dozen islands in and around the shores of the Lake of the Woods were half a dozen Indian bands scattered over twenty-four reserves. Many of these Indians had lived on reserves adjacent to Keewatin and Kenora prior to the war but had been shunted onto the newer reserves in an Indian Affairs land swap. It was a switch which many of the older Indians resented and this resentment was a factor in souring relationships before booze entered the picture.

The displaced Indians still regarded Kenora as home, and it remained the supply base for the 7,000 reserve Indians in the vicinity. As a tourist center it was also the base from which Indians served as guides for summer fishermen and autumn duck hunters. It was also the market for the blueberries, wild rice, and fish harvested in the Lake of the Woods watershed. With the opening of the taverns and liquor stores to the Indians Kenora also became the place where the Indians converted not only their harvests but their welfare cheques into potable alcohol. Many of them traveled to Kenora by canoe from their island reserves. Getting back to their reserves while under the influence exposed them to the imminent danger of drowning if the weather soured while they were on the water. Of the almost 200 Kenora area Indians who died violently in the 3½ years ending 30 June 1973, 42 were by drowning. In only 51 of the violent deaths was liquor not involved.

Unexpectedly high in the list of causes of death was exposure, mainly by Indians collapsing while drunk and freezing to death enroute to their homes. It was this factor that led in 1973 to the establishment of Indian night patrols to search the Kenora streets and environs for passed-out drunks and, when they were located, take them to a safe haven, the hospital emergency ward, or later to a detox center set up by the Addiction Research Foundation. The first haven was an unused church property the Indian leaders located and equipped with blankets. It became a place to which the drinkers could direct their feet instead of trying to make it home to their reserves and perishing on the way. The success of the Kenora haven led to the establishment of similar centers in Winnipeg and across the west. Coupled with the Salvation Army hostels they became, in the phrase of an official of the Alcoholism Foundation of Manitoba, "the solution that became part of the problem."

Without places providing shelter for the night, they would have been under some compulsion to go back to the reserves. Given the haven, they stayed in town and continued to drink for as long as liquor was available from other Indians, which, of course, was for as long as the other Indians had it or the money to buy it with. The haven thus became a magnet that attracted the over-imbibed Indians to remain in Kenora to renew their struggle with John Barleycorn on the morrow. So the Indians multiplied on the streets of the city and thus antagonized the white residents who blamed their visible presence for the decline in the tourist trade. That trade was falling off sharply in the 1970s but for reasons that had nothing to do with Indians, and a good deal to do with changing vacation patterns.

Across the Prairies, the Salvation Army centers and other havens also created a special problem for the sober, non-drinking, job hunting Indians. When an Indian applied for a job and gave his address as the Salvation Army hostel the prospective employer was apt to leap instantly to the conclusion that the applicant was just another drunken Indian or he would not have been living there. Application filed and forgotten.

What cannot be filed and forgotten is the Indian liquor problem itself; and it cannot be effectively treated because of the doubt that clouds the definition of Indian alcoholism. There is a body of theory that holds that Indian alcoholism is psychological addiction rather than physical addiction. In that view, Indians do not become fatally addicted the same way white people do. The incidence of death from cirrhosis of the liver is lower among Indians than among whites. Opponents of this theory simply say that in time the Indians will catch up when their binge drinking evolves into uninterrupted sieges of boozing.

Nobody yet knows the full extent to which alcohol is undermining the health of the Prairie Indians, neither the Indian Affairs branch, the alcoholism foundations, the medical profession, nor the law enforcement agencies. Nobody knows, even approximately, how many alcoholics there are either on the reserves or in the cities and towns. All any of these agencies or organizations ever see are the tips of the icebergs: the drunken Indians asleep on the benches in Winnipeg's downtown parks, panhandling Indians in downtown Regina and outside Calgary liquor stores, destitute Indians waiting on benches in welfare offices. Beneath was an iceberg of young

Indians taking to alcohol at earlier and earlier ages and dying at earlier and earlier ages. A placement officer of a child welfare agency is stung by criticism that she is placing Indian children in white foster homes. Under her iceberg are ever growing numbers of neglected, mistreated and abandoned children from broken Indian marriages for whom no Indian foster homes exist.

The Alcoholism Foundations of the provinces vie with the Department of Indian Affairs in expanding and extending their detoxification and treatment centers for Indian alcoholics. Every year the numbers of the treated grow along with the costs of treatment. And each year there are more alcoholics to treat than ever before. These are society's solutions for the Indian drinking crisis — medical services, welfare services, and havens for the afflicted. But if the severity of the problem continues to intensify, the solution simply will continue to be part of the problem.

CHAPTER NINE
ALCOHOLICS ANONYMOUS, A PRAIRIE GROWTH INDUSTRY

For the better part of 6,000 years mankind has been fooling around with potable alcohol in one form or another. For the better part of 5,900 years it did so without very much curiosity about what the physiological effects might be on the innards of the drinkers. True there were earnest injunctions in most of the world's religions against the overuse of alcohol. But these strictures were concerned only with the external aspects of over-consumption, with drunkenness, boorishness, and anti-social behavior. The public image of the drunkard was the morally flawed, staggering, panhandling skidrower. Or it was the shivvering, shaking, and bemused prisoner in the dock awaiting a mumbled "ten dollars or ten days" sentence for the drunken disorderliness that had culminated in a street brawl the previous night. This, in the main, was what the Anti-Saloon League and the Prohibition movement were concerned about.

This was an aspect, too, of which the advocates of liberalizing the drinking laws took cognizance. In their animadversions on the folly of restrictive liquor laws, there was always passing reference to the "small minority of drunkards and wastrels" who gave drinking a bad name. Strict treatment of such scum was socially justifiable. What was not to be tolerated was allowing the existence of a few hopeless, incurable drunkards to deprive the majority of mankind of the innocent enjoyment of beverage alcohol.

Such attitudes created an environment in which unruly drunks were treated as demi-criminals, subject to arrest on sight by patrolling policemen. First and second offenders might be released with pro forma reprimands by bored police magistrates, but when they eventually touched skid-row bottom in their slide from respectability and affluence they became, in criminal code parlance, "a loose idle and disorderly person, to wit: a vagrant". Only when they were laid low with delirium tremens in the drunk-tanks were they transferred to hospital emergency wards to be restored to sobriety, and to the streets. Between bouts with booze they were exhorted by family, friends, social reformers, clergymen, and law enforcers to mend their ways, be like other men, and stop their everlasting drinking to excess.

Completely unrecognized in those 5,900 years was the fact that the very chemical that was relaxing the nerves, sublimating inhibitions, elevating self-images and self-confidence, and replacing gloomy forebodings with warming euphoria was simultaneously attacking the central nervous system and the cortex of the brain, disrupting the functioning nerves of the eye and the inner ear, and distorting perceptions and judgment. As completely unrecognized by the medical profession was the fact that alcoholism was a disease that required treatment. Thus when a heavy-drinking sufferer from gastric ulcers was hospitalized for his ulcers no relationship between the drinking and the ulcers was assumed. The patient's stomach problem was treated and the patient was discharged with a casual, afterthought, warning that he really should do something to reduce his drinking.

The well of ignorance went even deeper. Also unrecognized was the fact that for every denizen of the skid-rows and the drunk-tanks of city jails there were perhaps fifty others whose families were being disrupted, whose future was being imperilled, whose job was being jeopardized, and whose friendship were being damaged irreparably by their compulsive drinking to excess. They ranged within the economic order from stockroom clerks and assembly line workers to plant managers, bank managers, and company directors. They included editors, doctors, lawyers, clergymen, housewives, politicians, and judges. These people, unlike the street drunks, came to the attention of the police only peripherally, through brushes with drunk-driving laws, for example. Even then they seldom encountered the interior of paddywagons or experienced the retching odor of the drunk-tanks. But they were by no means alien to delirium tremens or the interiors of hospital emergency wards.

It is another of history's ironic jests that it was a pair of just such compulsive upper-crust drunks who set the forces in motion which would ultimately profoundly modify alcohol's public image. They were William Wilson and Dr. Robert Smith who in April 1935 came together as total strangers in an Oxford Group, one-on-one therapy session. They were the "Bill W" and "Dr. Bob" whose encounter led to the formation of Alcoholics Anonymous whose promulgation of the disease theory of alcoholism aroused the interest of the medical profession and ultimately led to a vast expansion of scientific research into this hitherto neglected subject.

Perhaps giving credit for what followed to Wilson and Smith is putting it too strongly. Certainly neither man, nor both men combined, equalled the world-scale influence of Dr. E. M. Jellinek. While Wilson and Smith were struggling with the birth pains of AA, Jellinek was embarked on a crusade to arouse the scientific community to the opportunities which existed for scientific investigation of the effects of beverage alcohol — ethyl alcohol or ethanol — on the organs, tissues, and cells of the human body.

Hard upon his founding of the Yale Center for the Study of Alcohol, Jellinek brought out the first issue of the *Quarterly Journal of Studies on Alcohol* in 1939. The encouragement which Jellinek gave to scientific research was immense as his own interest expanded to embrace the whole world of alcoholism. That Jellinek and Alcoholics Anonymous arrived on the world scene contemporaneously meant they were able to build on each other.

The spread of Alcoholics Anonymous across the Prairies of western Canada has been one of the most important social developments of the post-war era. It was not so much that there was a wildfire spread. Its membership across the Prairies has never exceeded 10,000, but its members became persuasive lobbyers of governments to recognize alcoholism as a disease and divert money from liquor profits to provide treatment facilities for its victims.

Wilson was a New York stock-broker who had survived into his forties, though barely, despite an almost maniacal thirst. Smith was an Ohio doctor who was a seemingly incorrigible drunk long before the pair got universal acceptance for the word "alcoholic" as an acceptable euphemism for the word "drunkard." In their sober interludes, both men were card-carrying espousers of the "Oxford Group." Known originally as the Moral Rearmament Movement, founded by a Pennsylvania Dutch educator, Frank Buchman, this was a pious Christian sect of the 1930s dedicated to the search for salvation by achieving lives of individual perfection. Buchman's reception at Oxford proved to be so enthusiastic that his sect became known as the Oxford Group and as such spread from England to western Europe in the early 1930s and then back into the United States and up into Canada. Its articles of faith included dedication to such things as absolute honesty, absolute purity of mind, the conducting of ongoing self-audits for incipient character faults, and public confession of any harm done, followed by redressing the wrong.

The Oxford Group roots of Alcoholics Anonymous are clearly visible in such tenets as the public confession of misdeeds and misbehavior, the expiation of sins committed against others, therapy on a one-to-one basis. It was as a born again convert to the Oxford Group that Wilson was first able to interrupt his long ride on the drunkenness-to-sobriety-to-drunkenness merry-go-round. And like many fresh converts to a new religion he became a zealous missionary in the alcoholic haunts of New York where he sought to convert other drunks to sobriety through the Oxford Group.

Somewhere along Wilson's road to Damascus he was struck with the idea that drunks needed drunks. Alcoholics needed other alcoholics because as each alcoholic helped another to sobriety he reinforced his own commitment to sobriety. Certainly that had worked for Wilson whose commitment to helping others had speeded his own rehabilitation. Then, in April 1935, Wilson undertook an important business assignment to Toledo, Ohio, and the assignment blew up in his face. He was sorely tempted to reach for a bottle to drown his sorrows, as he had done so often in the past. Instead he reached out and found another drunk, fellow Oxford Grouper, Dr. Robert Smith. Wilson nursed Smith through his hangover, converted him to sobriety, and Alcoholics Anonymous was conceived.

Pre-Toledo, however, Wilson's success as a joint missionary for the Oxford Group and sobriety was decidely minimal. Time after time he was able to demonstrate that one drunk talking to another drunk about drinking could achieve sobriety for both. Unhappily the cures achieved were transitory and Wilson ultimately lost about as many converts as he gained. Something more than Oxford Groupism was clearly needed to commit Wilson's clients to lives of permanent sobriety. That something was supplied by Dr. William D. Silkworth, who had treated Wilson on many of his bouts with booze in the years before his conversion to the Oxford Group.

Preaching to alcoholics, Silkworth argued, would never work because down through the years it never had worked. Drunks could not be enticed, shoved, or forced into sobriety. They had to be convinced that drunkenness was a disease, a disease that for them was as incurable as cancer. It fitted, Silkworth postulated, rather well into a recently discovered disease category called allergies. People probably developed allergies toward alcohol as they developed allergies toward dust or dog hair. Nobody knew how or why, but it was clear that with such an allergy one could no longer drink alcohol without traumatic physical reaction.

It was these practical, meat-on-the-bones Silkworth arguments filtered through the spirituality of Wilson and Smith that transformed Oxford Groupism into Alcoholics Anonymous. It took four years to evolve, for its founders to develop their 12-steps program into a saleable doctrine. It was an evolution marked by slow proselytizing by Wilson in New York and Smith in Toledo on a one-to-one basis until they had small groups together. Then the small groups became larger groups, and the larger groups became cells that divided and multiplied. The groups in Toledo expanded to Cleveland, Chicago, and Minneapolis; and from New York to Philadelphia, Washington, and Los Angeles.

By 1941 AA had a couple of thousand members scattered across the United States when it came to the attention of the *Saturday Evening Post*. A laudatory article in that magazine by Jack Alexander precipitated a flood of inquiries from all across the United States and as far away as Toronto and Vancouver. For those who missed the *Post* article there came Charles Jackson's book, *The Lost Weekend*, which appeared in January 1944 and was immediately made into the Academy Award winning movie of 1945. The hero of Jackson's book was an out-of-control alcoholic, and as Ray Milland played the role in the movie, he shocked untold thousands of watchers into the recognition of their own station on the road from social drinking to acute alcoholism. After Alexander and Jackson cum Ray Milland, nothing could stop the mushrooming spread of Alcoholics Anonymous. But it was an organization like none that had ever gone before.

AA with its million-plus membership came to success by violating all the rules for putting any kind of an organization together. It had but a single entrance requirement, the admitting by the applicant that he was an alcoholic who had lost control of his drinking and desired to be cured. It was open to any race, creed, or color. It took no part as an organization in any other religious, political, cultural, or social activity. It permitted no member publicly to identify himself or anyone else with the organization. It required nothing of its members save a desire to be cured of the disease that afflicted them, and to help other alcoholics to achieve sobriety. The members were free to attend meetings or stay away as they liked, but at meetings they were expected to offer what assistance they could to any newcomer in their midst. They were also expected, but never compelled, to work with other alcoholics on a one-to-one basis. If they could afford to do so they were expected to make small contributions toward the cost of operating regional and national offices. No AA group was ever permitted to accept assistance of any kind from non-members, even in the form of charitable bequests.

There is little inherent in the Twelve Steps of Alcoholics Anonymous, either taken singularly or in total, to foreshadow the kind of impact the movement would have. Certainly nothing in the AA credo compares with the ringing "I believe" of the articles of faith of other religions. Instead, as a quick reading demonstrates, it is more of an exercise in sublime understatement.

THE TWELVE STEPS
OF ALCOHOLICS ANONYMOUS

1. We admitted we were powerless over alcohol — that our lives had become unmanageable.
2. Came to believe that a Power greater than ourselves could restore us to sanity.
3. Made a decision to turn our will and our lives over to the care of God as we understood him.
4. Made a searching and fearless moral inventory of ourselves.
5. Admitted to God, to ourselves and to another human being the exact nature of our wrongs.
6. Were entirely ready to have God remove all these defects of character.
7. Humbly asked Him to remove our shortcomings.
8. Made a list of all persons we had harmed, and became willing to make amends to them all.
9. Made direct amends to such people wherever possible, except when to do so would injure them or others.
10. Continued to take personal inventory and when we were wrong promptly admitted it.
11. Sought through prayer and meditation to improve our conscious contact with God, as we understood Him,

praying only for knowledge of His will for us and the
power to carry that out.

12. Having had a spiritual awakening as the result of these
steps, we tried to carry this message to alcoholics, and
to practice these principles in all our affairs.

What made Alcoholics Anonymous work was simply drunks
talking to drunks about drunkenness, repeating what they already
knew to be the truth. Alcoholism was a disease, an illness that could
never be cured, but like some other illnesses it could be arrested, if
the sufferer faced the facts and determined to do something about it.
What had to be done was recognize that they were simply allergic to
alcohol. Once a person had passed across the borderline between
heavy drinking and compulsive alcoholic drinking that person will
always remain an alcoholic. There can never be a return to social
drinking. Thereafter for an alcoholic "one drink is too many and
1,000 are never enough." So the concentrated effort of the alcoholic
must be on not taking the first drink, to live without doing so a day
at a time, an hour at a time, or a minute at a time. AA's twelve steps
was simply a will-assisting liturgy for a sufferer trying to resist the
temptaton to take the first drink. What made AA work was the
commonality of experience. What happened in Alcoholics Anonymous, in the felicitous phrase of Dr. David A. Stewart, was that the
"dynamics of fellowship" had free reign to demonstrate that
leaderless groups can accomplish wonders simply by purposefully
coming together.[1]

Alcoholics Anonymous, was no cure-all for alcoholism. The
religious overtones of its twelve steps credo repelled many prospective members. The atmosphere of its meetings was attractive to
gregarious types who were happiest and most at ease in group
situations; they were least attractive to introverted loners who
unfortunately seemed to bulk largest in the alcoholic population.
Nor was AA's medicine one which was either easy to take or usually
effective with the first dose. Par for making it with AA was usually
three or four falls from sobriety before the status of recovered
alcoholic was achieved. And that status seldom was achieved by
more than one in seven of the first-time meeting attenders.

Alcoholics Anonymous reached Toronto in 1942 but its entry into
western Canada was somewhat delayed. Indeed, it made little
headway in Toronto either because Canadians everywhere were
much too busy worrying about the Second World War to have much

time for worrying about drunks. There were exceptions, of course. In Toronto there was Dr. H. D. Archibald, a professional social worker who started a campaign to get the government to divert some of its liquor profits to establishing a treatment center for alcoholics. He was ultimately appointed research director for the Ontario Liquor Control Board and the first director of the Alcohol Research Foundation. Under Archibald it expanded to become the Alcohol and Drug Addiction Research Foundation and grew into Canada's most important center for scientific research into all manner of addiction, the Addictions Research Foundation.

Dr. Archibald's primary concern in the beginning was with the sociological effects of alcoholism. In Winnipeg, Dr. Alex Pincock had the same concerns plus the pressing daily problem created by alcoholics spilling out into the corridors of his psychiatric wing of the Winnipeg General Hospital. Alcoholics were one of Pincock's medical responsibilities. But when he tried to treat his alcoholic patients his success rate was hardly more impressive than Bill Wilson's had been in the pre-Toledo phase of his career.

When Pincock heard about the work being done in Minneapolis by Alcoholics Anonymous, he sent one of his assistants, Dr. Brian Bird, to the Minnesota city to investigate. Bird came back loaded with AA literature, including the book *Alcoholics Anonymous* which Wilson and Smith had written in 1937 to give their movement a name and get their organization into business. Pincock devoured the literature, gathered up four of his most difficult patients, and held the first AA meeting in western Canada in his office in the summer of 1944. Within a few months the group was solidly enough established to open a club room on Osborne Street.

Progress in Winnipeg, however, was painfully slow for the first few years. Providing care for the far-gone drunks during their preliminary sobering-up stage of recovery over-strained the re-sources of the membership. It often became almost a matter of an AA member sneaking a delirious brother into a hospital by the back door, so stringent was the hospital bed shortage, the aversion to alcoholics, and the total lack of specialized treatment centers. Nevertheless AA was an idea whose time had come. The one Winnipeg group became two and then suburban St. Boniface made it three. It spread to Minnedosa in southwestern Manitoba, to Brandon, and as far north as The Pas and Flin Flon. All the while Alex Pincock was agitating to get an alcoholic treatment center established by the Manitoba Government. That was a campaign that would take the better part of a decade to reach fruition.

As was the case in Manitoba, Alcoholics Anonymous came into Alberta from the United States — imported by an executive of a pre-Leduc oil company, Hudson's Bay Oil and Gas Co. Ltd. His name was Jack Johnson, and he strangely enough, was a life-long non-drinker. He read a summary of the Jack Alexander article in a magazine digest and sent off a request to New York for more information about AA, convinced that it could be something that one of his relatives could use. It was not, not at the moment anyway, but Johnson kept the AA material handy, passed it around to drunks of his acquaintance, and eventually was successful in 1945 in getting the first Calgary AA group organized. Though he was barred by the rules from being a full-fledged member of AA, Johnson nevertheless made a lifetime commitment to the organization and for thirty-five years was one of its most enthusiastic recruiters.

It was a member of a rare breed indeed, a Jewish alcoholic, who carried the AA gospel to Edmonton and Lethbridge. George Crystal was the owner of three Alberta hotels, the Corona in Edmonton, the York in Calgary, and the Marquis in Lethbridge. Having discovered AA in Vancouver, he became one of its most dedicated members. It was common experience of AA members everywhere to get frantic pleas for help from drunks just coming out of a delirium tremens or in fits of the uncontrollable shakes or immobilizing hangovers. The self-assumed task of the AA member was to lead the sufferer out of his travail and back to sobriety. Crystal always could find a room in one of his hotels in which to park a drunk until his overwhelmed central nervous system had time to recover. But he went a lot further than that. It has always been part of the AA credo that committed members must be able to look alcohol straight in the eye and not yield to temptation. Alcoholics must feel comfortable pouring drinks for others while not pouring for themselves. Crystal expressed his confidence in his fellow members of AA by giving them jobs as bartenders in his hotels, jokingly confessing to his associates in AA, "they make the best kind of bartenders — they don't drink up all the profits!"

In Alberta Alcoholics Anonymous was unique in having a member like George Crystal capable of providing an emergency treatment facility. Elsewhere there were the unreceptive hospital emergency wards and there was nothing else. What was needed, in the view of the recovered alcoholics, was government run emergency treatment facilities for alcoholics. That, in the context of the 1940s, was about as revolutionary an idea as anyone had voiced since Lenin had talked up the revolution in Russia. The idea of spending tax-payers' money on drunks got short shrift from the politicians. Nevertheless the AA members kept talking it up to their friendly politicians, focusing attention always on the money the government was making out of booze. The government was creating the problem, surely it had some responsibility for solving it.

One politician who listened was Dr. J. Donovan Ross in Alberta, a back bench supporter of the Social Credit Government, who agitated in the party caucus and in the legislature for a treatment center. But it was not until he became minister of health in the Manning cabinet that he was able to get anything done about it. In 1952 Ross was able to pry $100,000 out of the government with which to fund the Alberta Alcoholism Foundation. It joined with the attorney general's department in establishing the Belmont Rehabilitation Center near Edmonton under the direction of George Strachan. In the beginning Belmont was a combination jail-hospital, most of its inmates alcoholics convicted of minor misdemeanors who previously would have gone to jail.

In Manitoba it took even longer to move the government, despite Dr. Pincock's incessant prodding. It was not until after the Bracken Commission report in 1956 that Manitoba established its first foundation and treatment center. Saskatchewan established a Bureau of Alcoholism under the Department of Health in 1953. It established out-patient treatment centers in Regina and Saskatoon but it was not until 1968 that the Alcoholism Commission of Saskatchewan was set up to provide rehabilitation, educational and research programs on alcoholism.

Once in business the provincial agencies "growed like Topsy." Treatment centers were established throughout the three provinces and all the foundations became involved in educational projects, ranging from special programs for Indians to immersion courses for drunken drivers. For fiscal 1978-79, Alberta's commission operated on a $12,889,000 budget, Saskatchewan on $3,178,000, and Manitoba on $4,270,000. They began by allocating a few thousand dollars in the 1950s and twenty-five years later were high into the million dollar annual budgets, for full-fledged departments with hundreds of highly trained specialists. But despite their vast expenditures, no government was able to make the smallest dent on the problems they had created for themselves when government liquor control was superseded by government liquor merchandising.

By the time the Prairie governments were edging into the treatment field for alcoholism the Ontario Government had its Alcohol Research Foundation laying the basis for what would soon become one of the world's leading research institutions specializing in the problems of alcoholism. So successful did it become that none of the western governments saw any purpose in establishing duplicating research branches and all relied heavily on Ontario's research efforts.

And while all this was going on Alcoholics Anonymous was quietly spreading across western Canada as it was spreading across the United States and western Europe. A railway engineer from Broadview would encounter it in Brandon, take the idea home and re-export it to Regina. Traveling salesmen, who had operated on the assumption that drinking went with the territory, discovered AA and took it up as a sideline. Members of the medical profession, frustrated by their own inability to devise a successful treatment for chronic alcoholics, followed the Pincock precedent and referred their worst patients to AA. Concurrently, the American Medical Association was going through the formalities of elevating alcoholism to the category of registered diseases, a process that was only slightly less cumbersome and ritualistic than the canonizing of saints. Alcoholism gave the AMA a lot more definition trouble than many other diseases because trying precisely to define alcoholism was like trying to catch fog in a sieve. It was no wonder that formal recognition did not come until 1956.

Indentifying it as a disease raised a hundred questions beyond mere basic definitions, questions whose answers would be pursued interminably into the nooks and cranies of medical research. Why, fundamentally, did people drink to excess? Why could some people drink more than other people without visible effect? Why did various racial groups react differently from other groups to alcohol? Was a tendency toward alcoholism inherited or acquired? Was the tendency of alcoholism to run in families the product of home environment or genetics? Why could some people imbibe large quantities over long periods of time with impunity while others became alcoholics by consuming much smaller quantities in shorter intervals? Was alcoholism a disease of the mind or the body? Or both? What, indeed, was an alcoholic?

Alcoholics Anonymous settled for a simple, uncomplicated

definition of an alcoholic — someone with a liquor problem who could not give up drinking by will power alone. Dr. Jellinek once laconically described an alcoholic to a Canadian friend as "someone who drinks and has trouble." Later, in an interview with *Time*, he defined a potential alcoholic as "a man who gulps his drinks, sneaks a few on the side, worries about his drinking, stops talking about his drinking and has blackouts."[2] He later formalized it into what gained world acceptance as the Jellinek definition: Alcoholism is any use of alcoholic beverages which causes damage to the individual, to society, or to both.

World-wide during the late nineteenth and early twentieth centuries some documentation of experimental research on alcohol was accumulated. But until the repeal of Prohibition in the United States in 1933 most of it remained filed in the laboratories of the experimenters. Following repeal, the rapidly rising tide of drunkenness increased medical curiosity about the fundamental nature of alcoholism. What was there about this fascinating chemical that was capable of causing so many different and frequently contradictory reactions in different people? Tentative answers to the questions began appearing in the medical journals of two continents. In addition to Yale's *Quarterly Journal of Studies on Alcohol*, the *Journal of American Medical Association*, the *British Medical Journal*, and *Lancet* magazines were all making more space available for reports on studies of medical aspects of alcohol consumption.

In all this there was the usual duplication of effort that characterizes so much scientific research, coupled with similar volumes of inconclusive findings and contrary results. There were, of course, many cases where firmly founded judgments based upon seeming conclusive evidence were overturned later by more thorough research or with different approaches to the problem. An example of that was the linking of alcohol to cirrhosis of the liver, in experiments by Dr. D. A. Best, the co-discoverer of insulin, in 1949.

Dr. Best conducted extensive experiments with rats to determine the cause of the liver damage which was being noticed in alcoholics. He spiked his rats' water with alcohol and fed them a well-balanced diet, but was unable to identify any liver damage in the animals. It had been noted that in many alcoholics a serious loss of appetite accompanied increased consumption of alcohol. Coupling that fact with the results of his experiments Dr. Best concluded that the damage being caused to the liver of alcoholics was by dietary deficiences rather than by alcohol. One result of the Best paper was the adaption of vitamin therapy to the treatment of alcoholics. Another, because of the eminence of Dr. Best in the world of medical research, was somewhat to retard further experimentation in the field of liver damage. More than a decade would pass before two American experimenters, Dr. C. S. Lieber and Dr. L. M. DeCarli, were able to demonstrate an incontrovertible cause and effect relationship between alcohol and liver damage.[3]

The reason why the Americans got one result and Best another arose from the way in which the experiments were conducted. Dr. Best spiked his rats' drinking water with measured quantities of alcohol and fed them an adequate balanced diet. Dr. Lieber noticed that his rats seemed to be repelled by the taste of alcohol and tended to drink less water when it was mixed with alcohol. He suspected that in the Best experiments the rats had not actually ingested all the alcohol provided to them. He recast the experiment to get around their aversion to the taste. He put them on a nutritionally balanced liquid diet to which alcohol was added, and denied them solid food. In this experiment the damage caused to vital organs by ingestion of alcohol was conclusively demonstrated. These results were later confirmed by the same researchers in extensive experiments with monkeys.

Another false assumption about the impact of alcohol on body tissues was demolished in France where millions of Frenchmen were daylight-to-dark, cradle-to-grave imbibers of wine with their meals, and between meals. Yet the outward signs of alcoholic addiction, so apparent in Anglo-Saxon over-drinkers, were seldom seen in France. This spread the illusion that the French were living proof that one could imbibe unlimited quantities of wine without ill effect. In fact, careful study of French necrology statistics revealed that the French were the world's prime victims of cirrhosis of the liver which shortened the nation's life span. The effect of alcohol on vital organs came to light in the behavior of patients in French hospitals. Deprived of their normal daily alcohol intake on admittance to hospitals, patients exhibited all the usual withdrawal symptoms of acute alcoholism, up to and including delirium tremens and acute physical reactions.

By 1960 the research on alcohol had taken off in all directions. The psychiatrists, the sociologists, and the psychologists were all into it and the debate began to rage over whether alcoholism was a physical or a mental disease; or a sociological aberration rooted in poverty and a submarginal environment. It was left to Dr. Jellinek to spell out in his book. *The Disease Concept of Alcoholism,*[4] that everybody was right.

Jellinek's view of alcoholism was that it should be classed as a genus rather than as a species of disease. He described it as something like Hibiscus, a genus whose species ranged all the way from herbs and shrubs to trees. Some species of alcoholism could be considered a disease, some were only symptoms of a disease. Some were neither a disease nor symptoms but only a habit. And some were none of these. There were, Jellinek suspected, enough species of alcoholism to run through the nineteen letters of the Greek alphabet. He confined himself to the use of the first five letters to identify his species.

Alpha alcoholism he defined as a purely psychological and continuing dependence on the use of alcohol to relieve bodily or emotional pain. It does not lead to loss of control or inability to abstain, necessarily. It causes severe disturbances of personal relations, disrupts family life, causes absenteeism and decreased productivity at work. It may be accompanied by nutritional deficiences but no physical disturbances from withdrawal symptoms are suffered.

Jellinek's definition of an alpha alcoholic is almost a classic definition of a "problem drinker" though Jellinek boggled at the term and refused to use it in his book. Alpha was not, he said, a disease but it could develop into *gamma alcoholism*, which was, over a period ranging from three to fifteen years. On the other hand, the psychologically dependent alpha drinkers might continue their unabated drinking over twenty-five or thirty years without developing physical dependence on alcohol.

Beta alcoholism is very similar to alpha with complications, including damage to the central nervous system, gastritis, cirrhosis, all of which may occur without psychological dependence. The cause may be group heavy drinking, binge drinking, and nutritional deficiency. It causes acute family budgetary problems, absenteeism, inefficiency. It too may develop into gamma alcoholism, but is less likely to do so than alpha.

Gamma alcoholism includes many of the symptoms of both alpha and beta but is characterized by the acquisition of increased bodily tolerance for alcohol, adaptive cell metabolism, severe withdrawal symptoms, physical craving, and loss of physical control. Gamma is the predominant species and the one which Alcoholics Anonymous accepts.

Delta has all of the gamma symptoms plus an inability to abstain; but a gamma alcoholic does not go through the distressing psychological and social experiences of the others. It is the predominant species in France.

The *Epsilon* alcoholic is the periodic binge drinker. He can go on the wagon for three, six, or nine months, fall off, and return to abstinence full of remorse.

Anyone who qualified under any of these headings was conceded by Jellinek to be an alcoholic, though he felt neither alpha nor delta groups qualified as diseases from a strict medical viewpoint.

It will be noted that none of Jellinek's definitions promotes Silkworth's thesis of an allergic reaction to alcohol. In their laboratory experimenting, researchers were able to catalog an almost infinite number and variety of reaction of body cells to alcohol. A strictly scientifically defined allergic reaction was not one of them. Alcohol, ergo was not an allergen in the sense that rag weed, pollen, animal hair, household dust, feathers, etc. are allergens. So in his book Jellinek specifically ruled out the allergy concept of alcoholic disease, but he accepted it as a handy, even appropriate, word for Alcoholics Anonymous to use in their proselytizing. In less than fifty years the word allergy has traveled from the obscurity of laboratory science to common usage. And as far as common usage was concerned the way some human bodies react to alcohol defined "allergy" perfectly though that did violence to the scientific exactitude of Dr. Jellinek.

Though the word addiction has unsavory connotation, which caused its usage to diminish, some authorities have held that the use of that word best describes the disease. Thus R. Straus and R. G. McCarthy:

> An essential criterion of addiction is insatiability. It is this phenomenon — the persistent seeking of the unattainable in the fantasy world of alcohol — which distinguishes the alcohol addict. Alcohol addiction may be defined as a condition in which the drinking of alcohol beverages becomes persistent, uncontrollable, repetitive and progressive destruction of the psychological and social functioning of the individual.[5]

Though he was fulsome in his praise of the good that Alcoholics

Anonymous was doing, Jellinek viewed its general approach as overly simplistic. AA insisted that an imperative for membership was admission that one's drinking was out of control. But in one survey he did of 2,000 members of AA, Jellinek found that at least thirteen percent were Alpha types who never experienced loss of control. He thought it unlikely that any but a small percentage of Alphas would ever seek help from AA and that almost none of those with Beta alcoholism would do so. This was the group, he said, that turned up most often in general hospitals. Despite such quibbles, however, Jellinek was a firm supporter of the AA doctrine of solving the alcoholic's problem through total abstinence. And if the Alpha and Beta alcoholics did not fit into AA's definition of alcoholics they were nevertheless shunted in the direction of Alcoholics Anonymous by thousands of doctors in the United States and Canada, frequently to find solution to their problem through total abstention. Included among the professionals who used Alcoholics Anonymous were many psychiatrists and psychologists who might have been expected to be able to apply solutions of their own.

This practice did indeed produce an ironic situation. A disease is whatever the American Medical Association defines as a disease and the Canadian Medical Association accepts. It was under pressure from its state associations that the AMA added alcoholism to its roster of official diseases in 1956 and that made the treatment of it the monopoly of the medical profession. Laymen undertaking to treat alcoholics after 1956 could be subject to prosecution for practicing medicine without a license. Having the medical profession functioning as de facto recruiters for a lay organization certainly made Alcoholics Anonymous unique among quasi-medical fringe groups.

There was one very good reason for the medical profession's widespread support of AA. There was no other cure for any of the Jellinek classes of alcoholics, or for anyone else's definition of what it was. Not that any AA every claims that membership in the organization is a cure: it goes into what cancer patients call remission and will only remain dormant as long as the patient avoids liquor. As one researching doctor once put it — "an alcoholic is somebody who doesn't drink".

Over the years the search for a cure for alcoholism has given rise to a great deal of experimentation with what was called the revulsion or aversion treatment, feeding alcoholics pills which made them sick if they drank alcohol. The most notable of these was Antabuse or disulfiram. Administered by injection or by the mouth, it would keep an alcoholic off drinking for twenty-four hours by suppressing a craving for the stuff and making the patient sick if alcohol was imbibed. The treatment was effective in some cases for periods of three, six, or nine months, but in many cases the patients simply stopped taking the pills and went back to the bottle. With the development of new mood altering drugs, physicians began pre-scribing tranquilizers for their women patients with anxiety prob-lems in the hope of weaning them from using alcohol to ease their tensions. Unhappily, in thousands of these cases, single addictions to alcohol became double addictions to pills *and* alcohol. There was AA, and despite all the magic of modern science, nothing else.

It is clear, from the different types of alcoholics Jellinek was able to define by 1960, that alcoholism was a far more complicated disease than Wilson and Smith had ever suspected when they founded Alcoholics Anonymous. Obviously as Jellinek insisted, what would work for one type was unlikely to work for another. AA members have come to recognize and accept that fact and develop an almost cynical objectivity toward the backsliders who fall from sobriety. For every truly recovered alcoholic in AA perhaps four or five will have passed through the organization with only minimal effect. Contemplating a fellow-drunk's progress a recovered alco-holic may remark with a shrug "He's not ripe yet, I suppose. No point in worrying about him until he hits bottom and realizes for himself that he has hit bottom. Only then will he be capable of deciding whether he wants to live or die." Within that attitude is a sort of recognition of Jellinek's thesis, that the drop-out may be an alpha or a beta who, hence, will not be amendable to the AA treatment until he progresses as far as the gamma category.

Obviously Alcoholics Anonymous is not for everybody. But who is it for? Literally it is for hundreds of thousands of men and women to whom beverage alcohol has become an impossible addictive burden, a destructive agent to their minds, their bodies, their families, and their lives in society. How many? Nobody knows for sure. AA keeps no membership rosters, but it does keep track of the groups as they form and there are more than 100,000 AA groups in the United States and Canada. That would put the membership substantially above 1,000,000 and rising.

On the Prairies there were 650 groups in 1980 with just under 10,000 active members. Across Canada a reasonable guess would be that Alcoholics Anonymous has 50,000 members and that its membership is growing at the rate of about ten percent a year. And why shouldn't it grow, when the membership pool of alcoholics from which it draws is growing even faster? Asking the question in that form poses another: how many alcoholics is our society incubating each year? each month? every day? It is essential to get some kind of a handle on the numbers involved here in order to determine how far society can travel in its present direction before disaster strikes in the form of total social upheaval. Here again we must turn back to Dr. Jellinek, who was worrying about this very problem more than thirty years ago and came up with a formula for estimating the numbers of alcoholics in any given period.

Jellinek was convinced that the key to estimating the number of alcoholics in society lay in the medical records of persons suffering from liver complaints. Ultimately, if one drank enough alcohol over a long enough period, it damaged the liver. If the damage were sufficiently severe the result would be fatal. What had to be done was (a) determine the proportion of the adult population who drank; (b) identify the number of persons with liver complaints; (c) determine the number of death from cirrhosis of the liver; (d) determine the proportion of deaths attributable to alcohol. Given all this information an equation could be devised to enable an estimate to be made o the number of alcoholics in society.

Such an equation was devised by Jellinek and was applied in many areas of the United States during the next fifteen years after Jellinek circulated it in 1942. In 1955, Dr. R. E. Popham of the Alcoholic and Drug Addiction Research Foundation tested it out on Canadian statistics — an in-depth survey of alcoholics in a single Ontario county — and concluded that it worked reasonably well.

Twenty years later Dr. Wolfgang Schmidt and J. deLint, also members of the staff of the Addiction Research Foundation, reworked the Jellinek formula, mainly for Ontario but projected it across the whole country. Putting the two studies together yields the following table which illustrates the massive growth of alcoholism on the Prairies:

Estimated Number of Alcoholics by years

	1935	1945	1955	1965	1975
Manitoba	3,890	4,930	7,780	13,800	24,500
Saskatchewan	3,110	5,010	5,330	8,400	17,900
Alberta	2,720	5,270	9,120	15,200	37,300
TOTAL	9,720	15,210	22,230	37,400	79,700

Number of Alcoholics per 100,000 population over 20 years of age

Manitoba	910	980	1,470	2,400	3,800
Saskatchewan	600	980	990	1,600	3,200
Alberta	600	1,040	1,430	1,900	3,400

In the forty years between 1935 and 1975, Prairie population increased by 50% while the tabulation reveals that alcoholism increased by 700%. In Saskatchewan, where there was no increase in population, the increase in alcoholism was 400%. More revealing perhaps are the figures in the lower table, particularly those for the post-war period. Over the first, pre-Bracken-Commission-decade, the rate of increase in alcoholics per 100,000 adults was 30%. Between 1955 and 1965, the first decade of the cocktail-bar era, less a couple of years, the rate of growth rose 50%. In the next full decade of total liberalization of the liquor laws, the growth rate of alcoholism jumped to 75%.

If recourse is made to the sales figures in chapter seven page 109 it will be seen that the rate of growth of the alcoholic population did not keep pace with the rate of increase in sales. In the 1965-75 period gross sales for the three provinces rose by 175% compared with the 75% growth rate for alcoholics per 100,000 adults. The explanation for the different rate growth is simple. Alcoholism does not develop with the first drink, or the first hundred drinks of beverage alcohol. As Jellinek pointed out, it can take an alcoholic from three to fifteen years to move from mild social drinking to the late stages of gamma alcoholism. This only means that it takes time for the liver to become cirrhosic, and it takes even more time for patients to die from cirrhosis of the liver, and more Canadians are dying from cirrhosis of the liver than ever before. As long ago as 1976 Dr. Schmidt delivered a paper to the Canadian Foundation on Alcoholism and Drug Dependencies developing the conclusion that cirrhosis of the liver was the most rapidly increasing cause of death in Canada. In absolute numbers, of course, liver damage does not bulk large in the morbidity tables, accounting for around sixteen per thousand deaths in Canada, but here too the numbers are doubling every decade.

CHAPTER TEN
IF IT WERE A NEW DRUG, NO GOVERNMENT WOULD ALLOW IT

As Dr. Charles S. Lieber said, in a speech responding to his receipt of the First Research Society on Alcoholism Award for Scientific Excellence, the golden age of alcoholism research extended from 1964-65 to 1977-78.[1] In that dozen years, financial support was lavished on all manner of investigations into the effect of beverage alcohol (scientifically, ethyl alcohol or ethanol) on the vital organs of the body and functions of the brain, and into the relationship of alcohol to aberrant psychological and social behavior.

In the United States individual foundations vied with state and national institutions not only in funding research but in devising and instituting care and treatment programs for alcoholics. Western Europe and the United Kingdom were almost as involved and in no other place was the exercise more vigorously pursued than in the province of Ontario. The Ontario Alcohol Research Foundation, which in the beginning relied on the province's universities to carry on its scientific research, was evolving into the Addiction Research Foundation with its own extensive laboratory facilities. Its own scientists were postulating theories and pursuing them so assiduously that they would soon achieve world reputations in the scientific community.

By the half-way mark of Dr. Lieber's golden age, the Ontario Alcohol Research Foundation alone had funded almost one hundred experiments whose results merited publication in the journals of the scientific disciplines of the world. Its staff members produced papers for delivery to scientific conclaves of the United Kingdom, Canada, and the United States, promoting similar avenues of research. In addition the ARF staff undertook important statistical compilations that became the factual foundation for much alcoholism research.

During the same period, in the United States, thousands of experiments were being undertaken with rats, mice, guinea pigs, cats, rabbits, and humans. The result of these experiments poured out into the scientific journals and triggered more of the same.

Strangely enough, however, one of the most important discoveries to emerge from the golden age of alcohol research came not from any of the scientific laboratories but from the perked curiosity of a pediatric resident of the Seattle County Hospital in Washington State in 1968. The resident was Dr. Christy Ulleland whose curiosity was aroused by several newborn charges who were failing to thrive no matter what diet or treatment she prescribed. The babies had another thing in common — all three had been born both underweight and underheight for term. Dr. Ulleland began to wonder, in a mood of growing frustration, whether the trouble might lie in something the babies brought into the world with them at birth. She went pawing over the medical records of the mothers and discovered that all had been heavy drinkers, certifiable alcoholics, during their pregnancies. Could it be that whatever retarded their prenatal growth was still preventing them from achieving normal development? Dr. Ulleland expanded her medical record-probing to the back files of the hospital to see if any other alcoholic mothers had given birth to subnormal babies.

The search yielded twelve heavy drinking mothers and, sure enough, ten of them had underweight and underheight babies. That was at least prima facie evidence that there was a causal relationship between alcohol and the abnormal babies. Dr. Ulleland gathered her data into a scientific article and sent it off to the *Annals of the New York Academy of Science* which published it in 1972.[2]

In a process of doing her research Dr. Ulleland brought her problem babies to the attention of several senior members of the University of Washington medical staff. Three of them became actively interested in pursuing the connection between booze and subnormal offspring. They were Drs. Kenneth Jones and David W. Smith of the Dysmorphology (crippled children) Unit of the School of Medicine's Department of Pediatrics, and Dr. Ann Pytkowicz Streissguth of the School's Division of Child Psychiatry. Out of their research developed two articles that were published in the British medical journal, *Lancet*, in June and November, 1973.[3] In them the connection between alcoholism and deformed babies was positively identified and labelled the Fetal Alcohol Syndrome. The first *Lancet* article was introduced as follows:

> Eight unrelated children of three ethnic groups, all born to mothers who were chronic alcoholics, have a similar pattern of craniofacial, limb, and cardiovascular defects associated with prenatal-onset growth deficiency and development delay. . . .
> Eight children of alcoholic mothers were (first) brought together and evaluated at the same time by the same observers (K.J. and D.W.S.). Four of these children were recognized as having a similar pattern of altered growth and morphogenesis. Thereafter two other children were ascertained by the abnormal features in the first four patients while the remaining two affected children were ascertained because their mothers were chronically alcoholic.

In other words, four children were included because they all had the same physical characteristics, two others because they looked like the other four, and the children of two alcoholic mothers were included because of the mothers' alcoholism. The deficiencies of the children went far beyond Dr. Ulleland's underweight, underheight, and unthriftiness. In addition, the babies had small eye slits, flattened faces, absence of palm creasing, facial hair at birth. The commonest feature of fetal alcohol syndrome was mental retardation, accompanied by hyperactivity, irritability, tremulousness, and difficulty with sucking and feeding. The more severe the physical symptoms, the more severe the mental retardation; but as later research was to indicate, mental retardation, and other defects, were frequently detected in babies that did not exhibit the entire spectrum of physical symptoms.

The world-wide circulation of *Lancet* drew the international attention of the medical profession to the Jones and Smith *et al* identification of fetal deformity with acute alcoholism. This attention soon revealed that the Fetal Alcohol Syndrome was not the discovery of the American doctors after all. A team of French doctors in Lyon, headed by Dr. P. Lemoine, had studied the offspring of 127 alcoholic mothers, had come up with similar data and reached the same conclusion as Drs. Jones, Smith *et al*. The publication of their findings in a French medical journal in 1968 predated the *Lancet* articles by five years. But until the report by the American doctors nobody outside France seems to have read Dr. Lemoine's report.

Then all the historians in sight began to get into the act of reminding Jones, Smith *et al* that they had only been re-inventing the wheel.

Aristotle himself was quoted to the effect that "foolish, drunken or hare-brained women for the most part bring forth children like themselves." Carthage and Sparta were both reported to have had laws forbidding newly married couples drinking, to prevent conception during drinking which would result in deformed babies. In 1834 a select committee of the British House of Commons reported that infants born to alcoholic mothers sometimes had a starved, shrivelled, and imperfect look. In 1905, T. A. McNicholl published the results of a study of the effect of alcohol on school children of New York.[4] He found that of 6,624 children of drinking parents, 53% were dullards; among 13,523 children of abstainers only 10% were dullards.

If the relationship between the ingestion of alcohol and damage to the fetus was known for so long why did it take until 1973, or 1968, to get it formally recognized and identified? There are a number of explanations. The most obvious is that FAS babies do not exhibit grotesque abnormalities that are instantly attention-grabbing. The FAS babies, to ordinary eyes, are not so much deformed as just plain homely. It took the skilled fingers and practiced eyes of examining specialists to identify their dysfunctions. Indeed the major abnormality — mental retardation — was infinitely more difficult to identify than those which could be spotted at birth.

The wonder is that FAS was discovered at all. These babies might easily have passed unnoticed had two or three of them not happened together in young Doctor Ulleland's pediatric ward, and had she not been of the new breed of gynaecologist who was prepared to question some of her profession's respectable preconceptions. One of these was that the placenta protected the embryo-fetus from damage by chemicals and other substances ingested by the mother. Indeed, ornaments to her profession were on record as asserting that the fetus was specifically immune to alcohol. An eminent British-American geneticist, Dr. M. F. A. Montagu, Chairman of the Department of Anthropology at Rutgers University, wrote what could be called a "how-to-survive" manual for pregnant women in 1958. Entitled *Life before Birth* it was later published in paperback by The New American Library and sold thousands of copies. In a chapter on "Tobacco Smoke and Other Poisons," Montagu wrote:

Unexpectedly, alcohol in the form of beverages, even in

immoderate amounts, has no apparent effect on a child before birth. A mother who drinks heavily is not apt to be a good mother, but the reason is not that alcohol itself harms her child, but her everyday life style is likely to be unhealthy, untidy and unstable. Her nutrition is usually poor and this has a direct influence on her child's development. But it can now be stated categorically after hundreds of studies covering many years, that no matter how great the amount of alcohol taken by the mother neither the germ cell nor the development of the child will be affected ... An amount of alcohol in the blood that will kill the mother is not enough even to irritate the tissues of the child.

By coincidence, Dr. Montagu's book was reaching the paperback racks when the notorious thalidomide scandal was making headlines and rocking the medical profession and the pharmaceutical industry to their foundations. The pathetic appearance of the armless and arm-deformed babies sparked an urgent drive to isolate the cause for the deformities. In the process attention was focused as it had never been before on all manner of birth deformities and defects. And that attention stayed there long after thalidomide was no more. And because the research into FAS was a kind of lineal offshoot of the thalidomide scandal it may be useful at this point to recall the salient features of the earlier event.

The thalidomide story broke like a thunderclap over the medical profession of this continent when an American heart specialist, Dr. Helen Taussig, returned from Germany to deliver a speech to a medical convention in Baltimore on the epidemic of phocomelia that had broken out in Germany, the United Kingdom, Portugal, and Australia. Literally translated, phocomelia means "seal extremities," an abnormality in which babies are born without arms and with hands attached to shoulders like seal flippers. The babies ran the gamut from those otherwise normal, except for missing fingers, to those without hands, arms or feet. By the spring of 1962 there were over 6,000 cases of deformed children in Germany and the United Kingdom alone.

By the time that Dr. Taussig made her speech, and later published long illustrated articles in the *Journal of the American Medical Association*[5] and the *Scientific American*[6] the cause of the epidemic had been isolated. It was the tranquilizing drug "thalidomide", which had been prescribed widely as a treatment for morning sickness of pregnant women during the early stages of their pregnancy. Like all other drugs, thalidomide had been extensively tested on laboratory animals prior to being licensed for use on humans. The German and British tests, however, were not adjudged adequate by American officials and license had been refused there and delayed in Canada until April 1961.

Although the better part of a decade separated thalidomide babies and the Fetal Alcohol Syndrome the two must be regarded as episodes of a single process, a double-edged discovery that would revolutionize the science of gynaecology by uprooting concepts like that of Dr. Montagu that had survived for generations. Dr. Sumner J. Yaffe put it this way:

> Before 1961 most reports of drug effects on the fetus were concerned with the perinatal period, particularly with the effect of narcotics and analgesics on the fetus at the time of delivery. Thalidomide changed that and, if any positive action was derived from that disaster, it was that attention was focused on the possibility that other drugs less teratogenic than thalidomide had not yet been recognized as such. Until the thalidomide catastrophe there was not a great deal of interest in the subject and hence there had been little clinical research into the problem. We now know that any drug or chemical substance administered to the mother is able to penetrate the placenta to some extent unless it is destroyed or altered during passage. Placenta transport of maternal substances to the fetus and of fetal substances to the mother is established at about the 5th week of embryonic life. Foreign substances cross the placenta, primarily by simple passive diffusion, to establish an equilibrium between the maternal and fetal blood, with the rate of passage primarily dependent upon the concentration gradient. The "placental barrier" is a myth and the use of this term should be discontinued.
>
> Hence, administration of a drug to a pregnant woman presents a unique problem to the physician; not only must he consider maternal pharmacologic mechanisms, but also he must be constantly aware of the fetus as a potential recipient of the drug. When malformations observed in an infant at birth are apparently the result of drug administration during the first trimester the drug is considered to be a teratogen.[7]

All this should not be taken to imply that abnormalities of the fetus had been ignored by the profession. The identification of German measles as a cause of fetal deformity was well established. It was known that a massive dose of quinine could sometimes cause abortion, and when it did not left the fetus with hearing impairment. When abortions occurred to seemingly healthy mothers efforts were made to track down the substance which caused the abortion.

In order to put the thalidomide scandal into perspective it must be placed within the context of those times. It arrived on the scene just about as the era of the miracle drug was coming of age. The world seemed on the threshold of achieving a new freedom — freedom from disease and freedom from pain. First had come the sulfonamides from which the term "miracle" drugs had derived, because they were so effective against so many diseases. Then came penicillin and a profusion of antibiotics from ambomycin, alphabetically, through streptomycin to xanthocillin, along with a succession of newer drugs to replace the tarnished bromides and barbituates. Concurrently with all this, the age of affluence was dawning, along with the nailing of the right to universal medical care to the masthead.

A race, especially women, long accustomed to living with the minor aches and pains and worries to which the flesh was heir became accustomed to rushing to the doctor, the drug store, the medicine chest, or the liquor cabinet at the first signs of minor sniffles, pin-prick aches, or the onset of the blues. Then came the chemical revolution and the attitude of the medical profession changed. Dr. Yaffe described the situation perfectly when he wrote: "Most people in our contemporary society (as well as their physicians) seem to regard life as a drug deficient disease, to be cured or even endured only with the aid of innumerable medications."[8]

Inevitably with clinical experience serious side-effects became identified with the miracle drugs and their early glamor faded. The side-effects naturally reduced the number of ailments for which the drugs could be prescribed. The use of drugs that began life as general purpose pain killers became more and more confined to specific complaints. Naturally, as their miracle drugs became decreasingly miraculous the laboratories intensified their search for new miracle drugs to replace them. By the end of the 1950s thalidomide was emerging as just such a drug.

It was a perfect sleeping pill with two particular advantages[9] It allowed the swallowers to awaken the next morning without a hangover of any kind, and people could not commit suicide with it. Its manufacturers in Germany combined it with aspirin and other medicines and sold their concoctions as cures for migraine, influenza, chilblains and asthma. In liquid form it was also a popular pacifier for children. In some formulations it was available across the counters of the drug stores without prescription. In others prescriptions were needed. It was widely used in both forms in German hospitals, nursing homes and nurseries. Next to being prescribed as a sleeping pill, the drug's most popular use was a treatment for morning sickness of women in their first stages of pregnancy.

In the pre-marketing research on laboratory rats, thalidomide had no effect on limb development and was negative to the side effects of other drugs. Then came the thalidomide babies and the drug was retested on rats again and again. Once more all the results were negative. It was only when the research turned retrospective, to cataloging all the substances ingested by the mothers that thalidomide was identified beyond doubt as the cause of phocomelia. Establishing that fact was a scientific break-through in the history of biological science and opened new vistas for biological research. *For the first time it was demonstrated that specific organs could be damaged by specific chemicals ingested at a specific time.* It was the embryologist's precise time chain of organ growth that provided the conclusive proof.

A microscope can detect the first signs of limb development at ten days. It takes the form of a slight swelling where the shoulder will ultimately form. By the forty-second day, tiny limb buds can be seen by the naked eye when the embryo is scarcely an inch long.[10] Obviously the process of tissue differentiation and organogenesis (the formation of organs) takes place very soon after the onset of pregnancy, roughly between the twentieth and fiftieth day. By the end of the eighth week the organs are all pretty well in place and the embryo has become the fetus. By then the fetus is pretty well safe from structural changes although it can suffer any number of serious impairments to the organs that are in the early process of developing.

These facts became the foundation on which the case against thalidomide was based. The women who ingested thalidomide very early in pregnancy produced the babies with "seal hands". The women who took the drug in the later stages of pregnancy suffered no ill-effects and produced normal children. Legs form in the embryo somewhat later than arms. Some women produced babies that had defective legs as well as arms. What caused the drug to attack the limbs of the embryo and nothing else has not been determined. That was only one of the many mysteries that remained after the epidemic ended.

Another mystery was why thalidomide emerged from extensive testing on rats with a clean bill of health. Rats and mice are the work horses of biological testing laboratories. Hundreds of thousands are bred and sacrificed world wide every year in medical research into the possible effects of drugs and chemicals on the human body. Until thalidomide their reliability was taken for granted. That any drug could be species specific, to man in particular, was indeed a shock to medical science. But alcohol is not another such drug. Its effect on the cells and organs of rats and mice can be extrapolated to mankind with confidence.

One positive result of the thalidomide experience was to arouse laboratory interest in finding causes for the other, less spectacular, abnormalities that were turning up in the new-born in hospital delivery rooms and nurseries. This research encompasses not only how alcohol affects the organs and cells but how it affects the materials that dictate the shape and function of the cells and holds the cells together, or keeps them apart.

Fetal Alcohol Syndrome was at first a broad jump from the particular to the general. Thalidomide affected only the extremities and the phocomelia babies were born with their intelligence unimpaired. FAS babies were likely to be impaired in many ways. Even as Jones and Smith were making their first investigations they encountered new abnormalities. It was in the three additional babies they added to their original eight that they made perhaps the most important discovery of all — brain damage. Here in scientific terminology is their almost laconic description of that discovery:

> All three patients were judged to have a cardiac anomaly, further emphasising the frequency of this defect in the Fetal Alcohol Syndrome. Two of them had a cleft soft palate, a new observation in this disorder.
> The findings in the brain of patient 2, the first case of Fetal Alcohol Syndrome on whom a necropsy was performed, are of special relevance. There was serious disorientation of both neuronal and glial elements as well as incomplete development of the brain which must have started before 80 days'

gestation, judging from the absence of the corpus callosum. Some of the functional and structural abnormalities in this syndrome may relate to the types of aberration in brain morphogenesis observed in this patient. These secondary features include microcephaly, developmental delay, and fine-motor dysfunction, which showed itself in early infancy by tremulousness. Some of the joint anomalies could be related to neurological impairment of the fetus, including reduced movement.[11]

As word of the discovery of the Fetal Alcohol Syndrome spread slowly through the obstetrics-gynecology-pediatrics discipline, the interest in fetal abnormalities that had been aroused by the phocomelia epidemic increased. Patients turning up at prenatal clinics were more closely questioned about their drinking habits and smoking habits and much more detailed records were kept. A number of hospitals across the United States launched broadly based surveys of the relationships between drinking mothers and deformed babies. The largest of these earlier surveys was a joint exercise of the Boston City Hospital and the Boston University Medical School.[12]

This survey involved 559 maternity cases, heavy drinkers, moderate drinkers and abstainers — 52 heavies, 226 moderates, and 281 rare or abstainers. The result confirmed on a mass scale what the Jones-Smith team had discovered from its dozen patients: the heavy drinkers gave birth to babies with more fetal damage than did the moderate drinkers while the abstainers had the least damage of all. In the heavy drinking group, 32% had congenital anomalies, 62% had growth anomalies and 64% had functional disturbances. These figures compared with 15%, 22%, and 28% respectively for the moderate drinkers and 8%, 21%, and 29% for the abstainers. The Boston results differed from those of the original data of the Jones-Smith team in one important aspect. None of the babies in Boston emerged with the cranial-facial characteristics of FAS babies. Why not? And why did not all the fetuses of the heavy drinkers exhibit congenital anomalies instead of only 32% of them?

One answer may be that in the Boston study the pregnant women were all given vitamins with calcium and iron supplements. It may well have been that these extra elements may have diminished the impact of the alcohol on the cells of the various parts of the body. It is an established fact that alcoholics as a class tend to lapse into inadequate diets as the disease runs its course. The Boston experiment raised the possibility that dietary deficiencies may be a contributing factor in the Fetal Alcohol Syndrome.

Another answer may lie in the imponderables inherent in any definition of what constitutes a "heavy drinker." The Jones-Smith mothers were all certifiable alcoholics, to the extent that several had experienced delirium tremens while pregnant. The average intake of the Boston heavy drinkers was around four ounces of absolute alcohol, roughly five or six drinks. And none drank every day. That much booze would not have got the Jones-Smith mothers started. Obviously, it must have taken the kind of consumption that the Jones-Smith group experienced to produce the facial, head and body distortions that turned the FAS babies into recognizable types.

The distinctive facial and cranial malformations of the FAS babies represented the extreme impact of alcohol on the fetus. Before that stage was reached, damage was done progressively to a number of organs, damage which would intensify as alcohol consumption increased, but which might be arrested if consumption was abated.

By 1978 research had progressed to a point where it was possible to identify four types of teratogenic abnormalities directly traceable to alcohol: central nervous system dysfunctions; growth deficiencies; a characteristic cluster of facial abnormalities; and variable major and minor malformation. The latter included everything from cleft palate, deformed ears, and small teeth with faulty enamel, to eye, ear, mouth, and skeletal malformations, heart anomalies and infant hirsuitism.

The significance of the results lies in the fact that damage can be done to the fetus by alcohol even if consumption is only moderate. Left unanswered, of course, is how much or how little can cause damage? When is the human fetus most vulnerable to the impact of alcohol? during the first trimester of pregnancy like thalidomide? or during the second or the third. Are some organs, the brain for example, more susceptible to damage at one time rather than at another?

Of this there is not the slightest doubt: the human organ that is most susceptible to serious damage from alcohol is the human brain — in embryo, in fetus, in infancy, and in old age. Jones-Smith found brain damage in their examples. It was confirmed by many other experiments, notably by a team headed by Dr. S. K. Clarren, and reported in the *Journal of Pediatrics*.[13]

The team did microscopic examination of the brains of eleven who died prematurely or immediately after birth. Of the eleven, four exhibited similar malformations "stemming from errors in migration of neuronal and glial elements". Once the brain damage was encountered in the four babies the team checked back on the medical history of the mothers and found all four had been heavy binge drinkers during pregnancy. None of the other seven mothers were heavy drinkers though three did report consumption of alcohol at lower levels. The team was able to get a reading on the alcohol consumption because all the women had participated in a 1,500-woman survey of the drinking habits of pregnant women.

All four fetuses had suffered from severe structural damage to the brain. But only two of the four had developed the external features of Fetal Alcohol Syndrome babies. Prior to this study it was believed that microcephaly (small skull growth) caused the mental retardation encountered in FAS babies. This study indicated that in utero exposure to alcohol, particularly heavy exposure in binge drinking on the part of the mothers, could also cause structural brain damage, damage which would probably prove fatal when it did not cause severe mental retardation.

And what happens to the FAS babies once they are out of the research centers and into the world? Is it possible that through special diets and special training they may be able to make up for the growth they lost prenatally? Dr. Streissguth has been devoting much of her professional life to the pursuit of answers to that question and her prognosis is far from encouraging. In an article in the *American Journal of Orthopsychiatry*[14] in 1977 she reported follow-up data on FAS babies from a survey done in a dozen hospitals of twenty-three women who had been labelled chronic alcoholics. Two non-alcoholic controls for each mother were selected on the basis of matching race, age, education, economic status, and geographic location. Here are some of Dr. Streissguth's conclusions:

> Offspring of alcoholic mothers had a seventeen percent perinatal mortality rate, compared to two percent of the controls. One-third of the surviving offspring of alcoholic mothers had enough features listed on the medical record to be retrospectively classified as Fetal Alcohol Syndrome.
>
> The mean IQ of the offspring of alcoholic mothers was 81 at age seven, compared to 95 for matched controls. . . . It is important to remember that these children were mostly not children with the physical characteristics of Fetal Alcohol

Syndrome. Intellectual deficits were found in 44% of these children of alcoholic mothers, often even in the absence of the physical characteristics of the syndrome. . . .

1. Are these children not handicapped by the unpredictable environment provided by the alcoholic mother? Some of our most retarded subjects have been raised entirely in excellent foster homes; we believe the primary damage to the central nervous system occurs in utero. In one study we did find somewhat, but not significantly, lower IQ scores in children who had remained with their alcoholic mothers through the age of seven years. However, the number of subjects studied was very small and nothing was known about the circumstances of maternal absence in the child rearing. It may be that the critical variable is not whether the child remains with its natural mother, but whether the natural mother continues to drink.

Certainly the environment plays an ameliorating role in any child's development and the same is true for children with Fetal Alcohol Syndrome. On the other hand, we have known foster mothers to give up in despair because they could not significantly improve the intellectual attainment of children with Fetal Alcohol Syndrome. . . .

2. What about the role of specialized school settings, infant stimulation, etc.? We believe that each child should be given every opportunity to develop to his own fullest potential, and we encourage the best possible remedial experience for each child. . . . Hyperactivity is a frequent but not constant behavioral concomitant of Fetal Alcohol Syndrome. For such children, specialized educational placement is often essential if they are to learn to capacity.

3. What about the possibility that the children will catch up intellectually? Are they just slow starters who will outgrow their deficits? We find this unlikely but obviously the only way to be sure is to follow a sample of children through time and study how they turn out.

If beverage alcohol consumed by pregnant women in large doses causes brain damage and mental retardation, is alcohol therefore the primary cause of the growing number of mental retardants? Of course there was mental retardation long before the women took to drink the way they have in the last half of this century, but it is conceded to be the cause of enough mental retardation to justify the medical profession, with almost a single voice, to urge their pregnant patients to stop drinking. More, many of the advisers are now suggesting that women abandon both booze and cigarettes six months before they decide to become pregnant.

Until FAS, mental retardation had been blamed on many things, on German measles, on smoking, on the taking of drugs during pregnancy, upon genetic abnormalities. But in the research that followed the FAS discovery medical science zeroed in on something specific when it linked alcohol to mental retardation. As the scientists described it, the Fetal Alcohol Syndrome was at the far end of the spectrum of possible effects of alcohol on the fetus. Before that end was reached much other damage was caused.

One would have expected that such an important double-barrelled discovery would have captured the attention of any number of Prairie authorities. Certainly the liquor boards would have been expected to sit up and pay attention; and if not the liquor boards certainly the provincial governments who controlled them. If the products they were merchandising were in fact causing grievous bodily harm and mental retardation to the human embryo, was it not something demanding their attention? At least to the extent of funding a massive research campaign to find answers to the vexing questions the discoveries had raised?

And what about the medical profession, on whose lap the Fetal Alcohol Syndrome ultimately came to rest? For the Canadian Prairies, the Fetal Alcohol Syndrome was a non-event. The discovery had all the impact of a grasshopper hitting a windshield — it left a mark to which no one paid the slightest attention. The liquor boards went gaily about their purpose in life, selling more booze for more profit every month. More women were taking to the bottle, at an even younger age and drinking more every year. And the medical profession continued to function behind what might be called an informational iron curtain.

But how could your friendly neighborhood obstetrician be expected to become privy to the Fetal Alcoholic Syndrome? He was unlikely to be an avid reader of *Lancet*, or to subscribe to the American research journals which were getting onto it. The main obstacle to his keeping abreast of the march of science was time. When the average practitioner's appointments sheet was cleared for the day there was precious little time left for upgrading his knowledge of his craft through reading.

If there were such opportunities, what was there to read? Certainly the FAS discovery made no headlines in the Prairie newspapers to catch his eye. None of the magazines that cluttered his outer office carried a line on the subject. None of his own trade journals paid it more than passing attention. It was almost a year after the *Lancet* article before the *Journal of the Canadian Medical Association* acknowledged the discovery of FAS. It only did so then in the shape of a highly condensed summary as part of an editorial comment on alcohol, tobacco, and pregnancy. Noting on 20 April 1974 that recent studies had shown but a small difference in size between children of smoking and nonsmoking mothers, the editorial (vol. 110, p. 903) concluded: "Also the gap between the offspring of smokers and non-smokers is not widening over the years, so maybe we should not worry too much if mother smokes, whereas we should worry a lot if she is boozing heavily during her pregnancy."

How deeply worried this Canadian professional journal became may perhaps be judged by the fact that it was not until April 1979, five years later still that the journal carried an article from Dr. A. B. Morrison and Dr. M. O. Maykut of the Department of National Health and Welfare calling the attention of the profession to the Fetal Alcohol Syndrome. The article urged the physicians to acquaint patients of childbearing age with the hazards of excessive drinking. It also asked Canadian physicians to report cases of FAS coming to their attention. Aside from these references to FAS in 1974 and 1979 the Journal ignored the FAS discovery until its 15 July 1981 issue. The Ontario Addiction Research Foundation had sponsored a conference in Toronto on "Alcohol and the Fetus" to which were invited a number of outstanding American authorities on FAS. The meeting was held in April 1980, and fifteen months later the Journal published three of the conference papers.

In November 1974, the *Canadian Family Physician* carried a long article on the prevention of mental retardation. It was a summary of just about everything that was known about mental retardation to that time. It listed nine categories of causes of mental retardation, from rubella, chromosome defects, malnutrition, infection, and brain trauma to sensory impairment, blood incompatibility, single gene recessiveness, and toxic substances. In the latter it included drugs taken during pregnancy, lead poisoning from paint, smoking, and x-ray radiation. It did not mention the Fetal Alcohol Syndrome and the word alcohol did not appear anywhere in the article. This article appeared more than a year after the discovery of FAS.

Obviously, the Canadian medical profession cannot spend its waking hours thumbing through the research journals of the world. So vast is that literature that the *Journal of Studies on Alcohol*, for example, now devotes every second monthly issue exclusively to summarized extracts of research papers on alcohol published elsewhere.

But what made the Canadians' disregard for the discovery of FAS particularly unfortunate was that it came at a time when mental retardation was emerging from the family closets into the light of day in Canada. Until the Second World War, there was a widespread folk tendency to regard the appearance of a mental retardant as either an indication of God's wrath or of the mother having been horrendously frightened at a critical hour of her pregnancy. In either case the retardant had an impossible cross to bear. The most severely brain damaged were shunted off quietly to what was called in Manitoba "The Home for the Incurables" where they were filed and forgotten.

But by the 1950s parents of retarded children had begun to band together to seek the assistance of society in coping with their problem. The city schools set aside classrooms for the retarded; teachers with special skills for teaching "children with learning disabilities" began to make their appearance; techniques were devised for catching slow learners up with their peer groups; sheltered workshops for the retarded sprang up across the Prairies. By the onset of the 1970s there were even athletic contests for the mentally retarded.

There remained, however, despite spreading enlightenment, a hesitancy on the part of society to look reality in the eye. There was an almost universal reluctance to do a census of the mentally retarded in order to determine how many there were, of what category of severity, in order to come adequately to grips with the problem. In the late 1960s, however, several American researchers did some extrapolating from specially conducted surveys. They concluded that across the population as a whole there would be 27.4 children of all levels of retardation per 1,000 of the population. Of these, 3.7 per 1,000 would have IQs of below 50, making them severely retarded.

While there may be a number of factors present in American demographic statistics that are inapplicable in Canada, there has been a tendency in studies of Canadian mental health to use them anyway. The assumption is that conceding that 2.74% of the population is retarded provides as useful a ballpark figure as could be obtained by an exhaustive census taking. So if the American figures are applied to the Prairie provinces, where there were 70,145 live births in 1979, it would mean that there were 1,922 retarded babies born to Prairie mothers that year.

Of those abnormal babies, how many owe their abnormality to the alcohol ingested by their mothers? There is no answer to that question because while newly born babies are monitored for a number of things, alcoholic damage is not one of them. This is a particularly serious omission because the full measure of the damage may not be done at the hour of the baby's birth. High levels of alcohol reaching the fetus during the first trimester of pregnancy will cause central nervous system dysfunction. But it is during the third trimester *and for the first six months of life* that the worst brain damage is done by a heavy drinking mother.[15]

The first six to twelve months after birth is the critical period when rapid brain growth leads to the maximum brain volume. It is during this period that the vital neurons of the brain are produced and their functional interconnections established. Experiments with rats fed alcohol during their earliest lactating period resulted in their suffering a nineteen percent drop in brain weight despite the fact that their body weight equalled that of their litter mates. Thus if the drinking pattern of the human mothers were identified at birth, and successful steps were taken to prevent the babies from being adversely affected by their mothers' milk, some degree of mental retardation might well be avoided.

But the birth of mentally retarded babies is only one aspect of the problem. This is something that is externally identifiable as the babies emerge into childhood. It may also be that babies are carrying within their bodies organs whose serious impairment passes unidentified but which will become health impairing in later life. Thalidomide drew attention to the importance of the time element in dictating how drugs can affect certain specific areas of the anatomy. Experiments with ethanol and rats have carried this knowledge a great deal further.[16]

For example, pregnant rats were fed heavy shots of alcohol during certain specified periods of gestation. During the eleven to thirteen day period the brain weight of the fetus was not reduced but the heart, kidney, and liver weights were reduced by twenty, thirty-nine and twenty-two percent respectively. Other fetuses exposed to ethanol during a fourteen to sixteen day period showed decreases in brain, heart, kidney, and liver weights of ten, twenty-two, twenty-four, and seventeen percent. The clear implication is that pregnant women who get moderately stoned on New Year's Eve may avoid giving birth to a baby with brain damage, or any of the outward symptoms of FAS, but may have a baby with less than perfectly functioning heart, kidney, and or liver.

What all this adds up to is that the discovery of FAS has added a new dimension to all the other problems arising from the massive increase that has occurred in consumption of alcohol over the last twenty years on the Prairies. Excessive drinking not only has become a critical problem for increasing numbers of men, women, and children. It has become a threat to future generations, to generations yet unborn.

And it goes even further than that. Research that has flowed from the FAS discovery has postulated that there are hereditary and familial implications in alcoholism. In a recent study entitled "Familial Incidence of Alcoholism," Dr. N. S. Cotton concluded with these paragraphs:

> Studies conducted over the last four decades have shown that, on the average, almost one-third of any sample of alcoholics will have had at least one parent who was an alcoholic. Lucero et al found that if one member of a family is an alcoholic, 82% of the time there is at least one other alcoholic in the family.
>
> In every study of the families of alcoholics and non-alcoholics, the incidence of alcoholism was higher in the families of alcoholics. Alcoholics were more than six times more likely than nonpsychiatric patients and more than two times more likely than psychiatric patients to report parental alcoholism. Thus, a high rate of parental alcoholism is not merely a general characteristic of a disturbed population but a specific characteristic of a sample of alcoholics. While these data support the widely held view that alcoholism can be a familial disease, it is important to point out that they are not sufficient to allow the finding of a hereditary or an environmental etiology of alcoholism.
>
> Alcoholism was more prevalent in male than in female relatives of alcoholics, in the families of women alcoholics than of men alcoholics and in near than in distant relatives. In addition, these studies indicate that alcoholism occurs

more frequently than does mental illness in the families of alcoholics. Depressive and psychopathological features, the only excesses of mental illness observed, were consistently secondary to rates of alcoholism.

Although the data in these family histories cannot identify the mechanism mediating between alcoholism and a family history of alcoholism, some of the literature uses family histories to support the position that alcoholism is genetically, as opposed to socially, transmitted in families.[17]

The children of heavy drinking women run the danger of suffering serious physical and mental damage in the womb. But if, by some process as yet undiscovered, they manage to emerge intact from that experience, have they acquired an addiction to alcohol that will only show up when they begin their journey through puberty?

One reason why answers to these and similar questions are impossible to obtain stems from the reluctance of the medical profession to embark on some fundamental research. Two of the three Prairie governments are now monitoring FAS, after a fashion. Someone in each government is keeping track of the number of cases that have been identified. Thus Alberta has got some thirty cases listed. Saskatchewan has ninety, but Manitoba has not established a registry. In most of these cases in Alberta and Saskatchewan, the mothers tend to be native women. It is also noted that native women seem to be more addicted to binge drinking than other women, and it is the monumental binges that produce full-fledged, recognizable FAS babies.

But if alcohol is the primary cause of the increase of mental retardation within society, that fact should be established so counter-measures may be devised. One method of doing so is by retrospective surveys of pregnancies. When brain damage is determined an exhaustive probing of the mother's memory could be undertaken to identify the substances that were ingested which caused damage, when and in what quantities. In November 1981, the Government of Alberta sponsored a conference on the prevention of mental retardation. Retrospective assessment was not on the agenda. An attending physician who was questioned about it dismissed the idea as impractical. He said:

> You can't go back a year after and expect a woman to remember what she was drinking and how much during her

first trimester, or her last. Besides a mother of a retarded child has a heavy enough cross to bear without me going digging into her pregnancy and giving her a monumental guilt complex that will torment her for the rest of her life.[18]

It is a dilemma.

But the German doctors did retrospective assessments of hundreds and hundreds of pregnancies, believing no doubt that the urgency to isolate the cause of phocomelia far outweighed passing threats to the mothers' peace of mind. It was only this vigorously prosecuted investigation that did solve the problem. And once the solution was found instant action was taken to prevent any possible recurrence. In Canada, during the half year the thalidomide drugs were licensed for use, a total of 114 phocomelia babies were born, of whom only 74 survived, 35 of them severely damaged. On the universally accepted principle that one more preventable phocomelia baby was too many, the government outlawed thalidomide. The ongoing production of 2,000 mentally retarded babies a year on the Prairies alone, and rising, is seemingly an insufficient motivation for government action on the alcohol front.

The threat beverage alcohol abuse holds for the newborn is of course of vital social concern on its own account. It is made doubly so by the physical damage it is doing to the bodies of the adult alcohol abusers themselves. The extent of that damage was recently documented by a study of 5,000 autopsies performed on alcoholics at the University of Southern California Medical Center for Los Angeles County.[19] Identified in the study was acute and chronic liver disease, pancreatitis, hematological abnormalities, muscle damage, and damage to the nervous, digestive, endocrine, and skeletal systems. The most common pathological change in alcoholics was fibrous formation within the liver, pancreas, myocardium, and skeletal muscle. The only organs of the body which were impervious to alcohol damage were the ear and the joints. Alcohol was capable of damaging, directly or indirectly, every other human organ.

The entire situation was superbly summarized in a single sentence by Dr. R. E. Kendall in the British Medical Journal when he wrote, "if ethanol were a newly synthesized substance the Committee on Safety of Medicine would certainly not allow it to be administered to human beings."[20]

CHAPTER ELEVEN

SO WHAT DO YOU SUGGEST?

Where do we go from here?

Here is a point in both time and place where excessive consumption of alcoholic beverages has become so disruptive a force that it imperils social tranquillity and becomes a menace to the health of the people. Most urban police chiefs will testify that they could reduce their force by a third if it were not for booze-related crime. There is hardly a hospital whose emergency ward is not under siege from alcoholics on its threshold. At least half the divorces being granted in increasing numbers are related to excessive drinking. It is also blamed for the increasing numbers of battered wives turning up at shelters and crisis centers.

Here is also across Canada because whatever is true of the consequences of excessive alcohol consumption on the Prairies is also true in every other region of the country, and indeed for the whole western world. Consider these statements:

The statistical evidence of the last 25 years . . . suggests that the ill effects of alcohol are reaching levels which can no longer be ignored by society. There are believed to be at least 300,000 alcoholics [in our country] . . . and that figure takes no account of the immense amount of harm done to families in divorce, violence and related illness, and to attempted suicide. Admissions to psychiatric hospitals related to alcoholism have increased by a factor of 25, offenses connected with drunkenness have doubled in the last two decades. The annual cost to society of drunken driving alone is put at $250,000,000. In fact there has been a rise in all alcohol related indices which have been measured, and

problems which were once the prerogatives of middle-aged
men are being increasingly encountered in the young and in
women. . . .

Such statements might reasonably be expected to turn up in the
annual reports of Prairie police commissions, departments of health,
or alcoholism foundations. No one would be surprised to find them
in reports of similar bodies in any Canadian province or in any
American state. They are in fact from the *British Medical Journal* for
10 February 1981, from its leading editorial which called for
immediate government action to solve the alcoholism crisis in the
United Kingdom. That such a crisis exists will come as a surprise to
Canadian opinion molders who have always regarded the British
Isles as a bastion of people who can "handle their liquor" and whose
public houses system was a model which Canada might well adopt.
Recourse to the scientific journals on alcohol, moreover, will quickly
reveal that the alcohol problem which Canadians share with the
British is shared equally with the Americans, the French, the
Spaniards, the east Germans, the Finns, and the Hungarians. Indeed
the only areas where alcoholism is not a problem seem to be China,
the Moslem countries, and the so-called developing countries of
Africa and South America.

There is little doubt that alcoholism is particularly acute and
increasingly serious in western civilization. Does that indicate that
there is something in the way in which western civilization is
evolving that is driving people to drink? Are the stresses and strains
of industrial capitalism proving too much for the denizens of
contemporary society? Dr. Jellinek thought so as early as 1946 when
he told *Time Magazine:* "Alcoholism is the source of much human
misery, but fundamentally human misery is the source of al-
coholim."[1] Dr. Noel Herschfield, a noted Alberta internalist, in a
1979 speech paraphrased Jellinek this way: "Alcoholism is not a
disease, society is the disease."[2]

Wherever we look, across the Prairies, across Canada, across the
United States, across Europe, there has been a spectacular growth in
the consumption of alcohol over the last ten years, over the last
twenty years, over the last thirty years. In the 1970 to 1980 decade,
the per capita consumption of alcohol on the Prairies rose from 1.9
gallons of absolute alcohol per year to 2.6 gallons.[3] That increase of
approximately forty percent is probably par for the rest of the
drinking world as well. In Canada as a whole the result was an

increase in the number of alcoholics within the population from 300,000 to 650,000.[4] It is obvious from these figures that the numbers of alcoholics being produced rise with per capita consumption, but at a faster rate.

Will the increase in per capita consumption in the 1980s match the rate of increase of the 1970s? Probably. One of the features of the developing drinking pattern of the 1970s was the entry of teenagers into the drinking force. That has increased the number of drinkers substantially although the per capita consumption of teenagers will not approach that of their elders, in the beginning.[5] But once a taste for the stuff has been acquired consumption is bound to increase so that by the time the current fifteen year-olds reach twenty-one they will undoubtedly be drinking more than twenty-one year-olds did when twenty-one was the minimum legal drinking age. As a result, the production of alcoholics is bound to accelerate because the earlier a person starts to drink the greater is the risk of becoming an alcoholic. The growing number of teenagers already being identified with alcohol problems emphasizes the seriousness of the hazard to them.

From all this, one reaction to the question — where do we go from here? — must be: if alcohol consumption increases during the next twenty years at the same rate that it increased during the last twenty years the society that we know is headed for disaster. What then can be done to save the situation, to reverse the trend and head off the disaster? Until there is a revolutionary change in public attitudes, in the mass public mind, the answer must be: little or nothing.

The consumption of alcohol, as previously noted, has become as basic to western lifestyle as the consumption of cigarettes, the consumption of sugar, the consumption of salt. It is recognized everywhere as an enhancement of the occasion, whether the occasion is a campaign of seduction, the completion of a business deal, the attendance at an athletic contest, or merely watching television. It is as much an essential preliminary to the entry into a relationship as the lighting of cigarettes. And it is regarded as an inalienable human right which any group of politicians will try to abridge at its peril. The politicians themselves have recognized that fact by their steady stripping away of restrictions, in a process, moreover, that has proceeded over the past twenty years without a word of discouragement from voices of dissent in the temperance wilderness.

One impediment in the way of any reversal or even minor

deviation in political attitudes toward beverage alcohol is the fact that most politicians are drinkers themselves, some of them apprenticing alcoholics. Certainly it is a rare occasion when a political celebration of any kind, from a civic election victory party to a testimonial dinner for a retiring senator, is completed without the booze being cracked open. Some bubbly and beer usually will suffice for the former but the latter calls for the "good stuff." There will be cocktails and highballs before dinner, wine of vintage with the meal and the speeches, liqueurs with the post-prandial deal making. Even service club luncheon chairmen have fallen victim to the suspicion that without a no-host bar attendance will diminish, perhaps fatally. So deeply embedded has the notion of "doing alcohol" become in our society that the chairmen's fears are probably well-grounded.

The depth of that embeddedness can perhaps be illustrated by the way in which the women of Alberta celebrated the fiftieth anniversary of the Privy Council decision in the famous "persons" case of 1928-29. That case was taken, after the Supreme Court of Canada had ruled women were not persons and therefore ineligible for appointment to the Canadian Senate, to the British Privy Council by five famous Alberta women and it ended the political discrimination against women in Canada. The women were Judge Emily Murphy, author Nellie McClung and Louise McKinney, both former members of the Alberta Legislature, Irene Parlby, only woman member of the Alberta cabinet, and Henrietta Edwards.

The local council of women in Calgary decided to celebrate the fiftieth anniversary of that victory with a gala dinner in Calgary on 18 October 1979. They sold more than 700 tickets, filling the largest ballroom in the city. Flanking the entrances to the ballroom were a series of stand-up bars in front of which the women were stacked five deep waiting to purchase their cocktails, highballs, and other alcoholic esoteria.

The heroic five, whose memory was being honored, were among the most dedicated prohibitionists the country ever produced! All had played major roles in the crusades to ban the bars in 1915 and 1916 and to outlaw them again in 1920.

Even if the country were faced with a crisis of alcoholism far greater than anything experienced in 1980, it is difficult to envision an affirmative vote for prohibition in any provincial referendum. Certainly there is no politician anywhere on the horizon who would be willing to be found dead being identified with a Prohibition campaign, even with a campaign forcefully to reduce alcohol consumption to manageable proportions.

The fundamental problem facing society is that drinking has become so cradle-to-the-grave popular, so overwhelmingly accepted in so many ultra-visible human activities that it will take a behavioral revolution in human attitudes to set back the alcoholic clock. The trouble is wherever the ill effects of alcohol abuse are identified it is always only a minority of the drinking population that is involved. The full Fetal Alcohol Syndrome affects only a minority of the children born to mothers who drink to excess; but nobody can even guess how many babies carry hidden scars from prenatal contact with alcohol by way of moderate drinking mothers. Drinkers who drive their cars with too much alcohol in their blood never account for more than a minor proportion of the (a) drinkers or (b) cars on the road.

Millions of Canadians have come to enjoy a drink with their meals without any damage. Certainly the opening of restaurants to the service of liquor has immensely improved the quality of the food and the service all across Canada. Thus any actions that are taken to reduce the consumption of alcohol are bound to arouse cries of protest from all the casual drinkers, gourmet eaters and restaurateurs across the country. What right, they will demand, does society have to penalize the unoffending and harmless majority for the sins of a small minority of the population?

A legitimate objection, surely. But in the aggregate the minorities are not all that insignificant. When all the alcoholics, and the four or five additional family members they each put upon; the FAS babies and the many times as many lesser brain damaged and retarded children; all the victims of the highway slaughter by drunken drivers; all the thousands of victims of alcohol-fractured families; all the victims of alcohol-related criminal activities; all the sufferers from terminal heart and liver diseases; when all these are added together it is not such an insignificant minority any more.

Despite the power of all the vested interests, the seemingly insuperable political sloth coupled with what seems to be substantial public commitment to booze, public attitudes do change, political pendulums do swing, ethical and moral antenna do become sensitized to danger signals. And this frequently happens while no one is looking, particularly the politicians whose thinking frequently follows rather than leads public opinion. As the 1980s approached signs began to appear that some serious rethinking was taking place about the wisdom of allowing the ever rising tide of alcohol consumption to continue unchecked.

Prairie governments were becoming aware that a problem existed and that there was a need to awaken the public, and particularly the younger generation, to the dangers of alcohol abuse. Saskatchewan in 1979 had a comprehensive publicity program in place utilizing the television, print media, and the high school systems. Manitoba and Alberta followed in 1981 with amply budgeted campaigns preaching restraint and moderation. The vulnerability of all such "educational" efforts was they tended to flounder on the shoals of an adult lifestyle that personified self-indulgence and lack of restraint. If that was not problem enough, they are undermined further by the superbly crafted beer advertising on television in Alberta and Manitoba and in the eye-catching and colorful liquor advertising in the newspapers and magazines. The beer advertising emphasizes the macho male image coupled with ecstatic distaff reaction to freshly poured suds; the whiskey, rum, and vodka advertising focuses on the elegant and success-orientated lifestyles of the hard liquor consumers.

Teenagers growing up in homes where boozing in some form is a fact of life are naturally far more impressed by example than by precept. Until the adult population starts to show signs of understanding the hazards inherent in their own behavior, propagandizing the school children will likely remain an exercise in futility.

The advocacy of educational programs directed toward the children begs all kinds of questions. Children growing up in alcoholic homes go through the most intensive in-service educational programs on the hazards of beverage alcohol. Yet statistics have demonstrated that there is a pronounced tendency of alcoholic parents to raise alcoholic children. Is it humanly possible, given the reality of peer pressure and environmental influence, plus inherited characteristics, to devise an effective educational course for sub-teens and junior teens?

Is the proposal to launch "educational campaigns" simply another symptom of governmental predilection for trying to solve problems by throwing money at them? That, to a substantial extent is what has happened to the alcoholism problem itself. Governments began by diverting modest sums from their liquor profits to succor the victims of alcohol over-indulgence. They hired a few people, set up treatment centers, and counselling agencies. As years passed they expanded the agencies and the activities of the agencies and sent missionaries out into the communities to "educate the public." Then the government set up quasi-independent provincial foundations with multi-million dollar annual budgets and expanded treatment facilities with staffs running into the hundreds.

And nothing is ever enough. The problem has got completely out of hand. The alcoholics multiply by geometric progression. About the best that can be said for this, what might be called, "concerned humanitarianism run riot" is that they, the practicing alcoholics, have never had it so good on their lubricated slide to oblivion!

What is required before anything else is attempted is nothing short of a reordering of the public mind toward beverage alcohol, the reversal of the sixty-year consuming trend that began with the repeal of Prohibition in 1923-24. A return to Prohibition is an obvious impossibility. Nevertheless, a reversal of the upward trend in per capita consumption might be possible, given only a slight change in public attitude. Perhaps that change could be achieved if the educational campaigns being mounted by governments were accompanied by some tightening of the liquor regulations to emphasize the seriousness of the message they were conveying.

For twenty years all change has been toward liberalization. Perhaps some back-tracking might have a salutary effect, particularly inasmuch as the back-tracking might be carried out with a minimum of inconvenience to the drinkers. The amount of cutting back that is possible may be gauged from some figures. Prior to the arrival of the cocktail bars, the Prairie cities all got by with a handful of liquor stores and a dozen or so beer parlors. In 1981 Calgary had 666 licensed premises dispensing liquor by the glass, Edmonton had 644, Winnipeg had 486, Regina had 176, and Saskatoon has 179.[6] The gross sales to these establishments is immense. In Alberta their purchases accounted for more than a quarter of the Liquor Board's $517,000,000 in annual sales. When it is considered that the boozoriums sell the liquor they buy from the Board at a 400% markup it is clear that the value of the gross sales of the liquor retailers exceeds that of the government monopoly.

Would it be practical for the Prairie governments as a first step to declare a moratorium on liquor licenses? The proliferation of outlets has reached the point where a drinker is seldom more than a two-minute walk from a drink in the downtown cores, or more than a five-minute drive away elsewhere in the cities. A hundred fewer outlets would hardly be noticed.

Two other measures might accompany the enforced attrition.

Business hours might be restricted as they are for the English public houses which are required to close from 2:00 P.M. to 6:00 P.M. Alberta once required its beer parlors to shut down during the supper hour, a move that had a salutary effect on the street drunkenness later at night. The hiatus forced the drinkers to go home for supper because there was nothing else to do. Once home they tended to stay there. In Manitoba the beer parlors are still required to close for the supper hour, but as beer is still available in the lounges, often only a minute's walk away, the restriction seems to have little effect.

By itself the afternoon shutdown of the entire beverage trade would not solve the alcohol abuse problem. It might not even make much of a dint in it. But it would come as a sort of warning shot to call the attention of the drinkers to the fact that beverage alcohol in any of its guises was not soda pop that could be drunk with impunity.

Along with these changes could come a dilution of the absolute alcohol content of all liquor and beer and the removal of all fortified wine from the market. The brewers and the beer drinkers might jointly protest that Canadian beer drinkers demand strong beer, that they dislike the taste of "weak American beer." Alcohol content, as any brew master will testify, has nothing to do with the taste of beer. Public taste can be varied by eradication of one taste and the substitution of another.

Concurrently with the changed regulations of the urban outlets could come the restoration of the minimum drinking age to twenty or twenty-one years. It is now conceded by most students of the problem that the lowering of the drinking age to eighteen in 1970 was an unmitigated disaster. For one thing, it brought the big-for-their-age fourteen to sixteen year-olds into the drinking scene, and particularly the sixteen-year-old girl friends of the eighteen year-olds. The impact on highway traffic accidents has been horrendous.[7] Teenage drinking has became an unexpected and vexing problem for many high school administrators. In a recent poll taken by the Government of Manitoba of the public's attitude toward drinking there was one area in which the public realized a problem existed and wanted something done about it. That was the drinking age. Saskatchewan and Ontario have already raised the age to nineteen years, and it was done without noticeable public protest. Most of the American states have changed their minds. Michigan, for example, raised the minimum back up to twenty-one years. Some states have a different minimum age for access to beer than for hard liquor.

Only eleven American states permit eighteen-year-olds access to all types of liquor.

The slaughter of the innocents on our highways by drunken drivers now exceeds the anticipated death tolls of small scale wars. The difference is that even small scale wars arouse the vital concerns of governments and peoples alike while drunken driving casualties are regarded almost as a social norm. Drinking and driving has in fact become a social norm. It has done so because the justice system permits it, even encourages it, by its cavalier attitude toward liquor offenders. A society that was serious about stamping out the drunken driving slaughter would not permit enforcement officials to fudge the charge-laying process to enable repeaters to be tried as first offenders. It would not allow magistrates discretionary power when the license-cancelling requirements of the law were involved, or where jailing for repeaters was involved.

Being drunk while committing an offense would be treated as an additional offense, just as in some jurisdictions carrying a gun while committing a robbery compounds the penalty. In some provinces convicted drunken drivers are required to attend lectures on highway safety as part of their penalty. A better idea might be to suspend a thirty-day jail sentence on condition the offenders place themselves on thirty, sixty, ninety day disulforam treatment regimen. Marketed under the trade name of Antabuse, etc., disulfiram brings on paroxysms of vomiting if a single drink of alcohol is taken within twenty-four hours. The offender would have to report daily to a central office for his pill, as parolees are often required to report to police stations. Perhaps, after a month on this pill, the offender might have experienced a non-alcoholic lifestyle that would encourage him to adopt it permanently. The odds, of course, are against it; but at very least it would keep convicted drivers from committing another offense for the term of the sentence.

If the authorities ever became serious about enforcing the law against drunken driving and were looking for a deterrent, they need hardly look further than publicity. Fifty years ago, when jail sentences were mandatory for drunken driving convictions, it was the inviolate rule of both Winnipeg newspapers that the names of all jailed drunken drivers had to be published. The drunks feared the publicity more than the jail and frequently exerted extreme pressure in vain efforts to keep their names out of print. The fear of going to jail may not have acted as much of a deterrent, but the certainty of the publicity certainly did. Today it would probably take a full page of a newspaper to list the names and addresses of all the fine payers for liquor offenses in a month.

Reduction in the number of boozoriums and restrictions of drinking hours would help to focus attention on a seldom discussed aspect of alcoholic addiction. Physical addiction to alcohol is in part the result of steadily yielding to temptation. Alcoholic progression begins when the once in a while drinker becomes a regular imbiber of a cocktail at lunch, then two cocktails at lunch, then a couple more after work and a couple before dinner, and a couple more instead of dinner. By the time it is recognized that a habit has been formed, building up the will-power required to break the habit is difficult enough when drink is hard to get. It is infinitely more difficult when the temptee must run the gauntlet of liquor outlets between his workplace and his bus, and between his bus stop and his home; when there are handy outlets that will enable him to convert worktime coffee breaks into double-Scotch breaks. The ubiquitous bars of the turn of the century were recognized as wellsprings of temptation both by the Ban-the-Bar crusaders and by the drinkers themselves.

The litany — "It's those cursed bars" — was painfully familiar to wives, clergymen, and social workers in the pre-war era. The widespread recognition of the potency of temptation put the muscle in the Ban-the-Bar crusade that brought in Prohibition. It was to get away from temptation that even brought many problem drinkers to the Northwest Territories before the turn of the century. It was to provide drinkers with a haven from alcohol temptation that led to the promotion of the city of Saskatoon as a bone-dry metropolis at the turn of the century.

Such measures as the foregoing might be useful as steps to begin the softening up of public opinion to a point where it might be willing to face the facts. But these measures alone would be far from effective in bringing about a decline in drinking. One has only to look at the United Kingdom, where public house licenses and hours are restricted, to discover the British are no better off than any one else. In fact it was in Britain that the medical profession recently launched a vigorous campaign to persuade the government to take drastic action further to limit consumption of alcohol in all its forms.

One of the leaders was Dr. R. E. Kendall, a professor of psychiatry at the University of Edinburgh. He developed his ideas in a series of lectures and published them in an article in the *British Medical Journal* for February 1979. His thesis was that the medical profession should make a wholesale retreat from the disease concept of alcoholism with the aim of forcing the government to search for a political solution by way of restrictive regulations on the sale of alcohol. He argued that the disease concept had forced the medical profession to assume responsibility for a health problem for which *the doctors had no medical solution.* As Dr. Kendall saw the situation, the disease concept has become everyone's official dogma, with medical organizations, alcoholics themselves and well meaning do-gooders all urging governments to accept the concept and act on its implications. Alcoholics must not be blamed or punished; they are sick people and therefore entitled to all the rights and privileges enjoyed under national health insurance schemes; doctors must accept them as patients before they reach the stage of delirium tremens, dementia, or cirrhosis of the liver; and governments must provide facilities for treatment and rehabilitation.

But one solution is about as effectual or ineffectual as another: some alcoholics do achieve remissions, but society produces alcoholics at a much faster rate than the medical profession and all the caring facilities are capable of drying them out, as Dr. Kendall demonstrates from the statistics. For example, in Scotland in 1956 there were 732 admissions to hospital for alcoholism and alcoholic psychosis; in 1966 there were 2,755 admissions; and in 1976 the number was 4,388. That was a five-fold increase in twenty years. By 1976 there were twice as many men being admitted to psychiatric hospitals for alcoholism as for any other cause.

Dr. Kendall challenged basic assumptions which had led the medical profession

> to try to identify the psychological or metabolic abnormality that prevents [alcoholics] from drinking normally and safely like other people. At present neither of these assumptions appears to be justified. Evidence that alcoholics differ from other people except in the amount they drink remains scanty and inconclusive. Medical treatment seems to be largely ineffective, and the number of alcoholics needing treatment is rising so fast that it is difficult to envisage any therapeutic facilities, medical or otherwise, coping effectively with them. There is good evidence, on the other hand, that people become dependent on alcohol in the same way as they

become dependent on heroin — by drinking more than a critical amount for a sufficiently long time — and that the number of people drinking more than this critical amount is largely determined by the average consumption of the population as a whole.

Here Dr. Kendall was relying on the work of Dr. S. Lederman, the French scientist and Dr. Jan deLint, senior scientist of the Ontario Addiction Research Foundation. Dr. Lederman did an exhaustive statistical analysis in 1956 into the relationship between general consumption rates and acute alcoholism and developed the controversial "Lederman hypothesis" that if per capita consumption over a given period increased by fifty percent the increase in the number of alcoholics would approach one hundred percent. Dr. deLint in 1975 did a survey of the liquor consumption of twenty-five industrial countries and found that consumption had increased substantially in twenty-four during the 1960s and that the increase in consumption was accompanied by a matching increase in alcoholism.[8]

Why this world-wide increase in the consumption of alcohol? For the same reason there was such an increase in the Prairie Provinces during the cocktail bar era — rapidly improving economic circumstances of the populace, inflation of wages and salaries, and a reduction of governmental restrictions making for greater availability.

Dr. Kendall's statistics for Scotland roughly parallel those for the Prairies found on page 112 of chapter seven. In Scotland between 1950 and 1976, the amount of time a manual laborer had to work to pay for a pint of beer dropped forty-eight percent, from twenty-three minutes to 12 minutes. The time required to pay for a bottle of whiskey dropped sixty-eight percent from six hours to two. The definitions may not be precisely the same, and the time frame is somewhat different, but the comparisons on the Prairies are roughly the same — a drop from five hours in 1956 to an hour and a half in 1976 for whiskey, and from nine minutes to three minutes for a bottle of beer. The figures would suggest that the trend may be arrested and eventually reversed if the price ratio is restored to where it was before the problem reached epidemic proportions.

Following the development of the Kendall thesis and a great deal of public discussion in the United Kingdom, the Royal College of Physicians set up a commission to make a thorough inquiry into the alcoholic problem. In March 1980 the commission released its report. Its recommendations included: drastically reducing the number of places where alcoholic beverages are sold; a national ban on all beverage advertising except in the places where it is sold; increased excise taxes on alcohol to the point where the price of a bottle of Scotch is triple the prevailing price of ten dollars.[9]

The uproar which would result in England if the Government ever tried to ban liquor advertising may well be imagined. But it would not be a patch on the chorus of vituperation that would erupt at similar action in Canada from the magazine publishers, newspaper owners, and the radio and television industry. The newspapers could easily absorb the loss of their liquor lineage but, as previously noted, it would destroy the magazine business. Nevertheless several Canadian provinces are in the process of demonstrating that partial bans on advertising have little inhibiting impact on the public thirst. British Columbia and Saskatchewan ban all liquor advertising; Manitoba has a partial ban. But the advertising still comes flooding into Manitoba and British Columbia on cable television and in national Canadian and American magazines and newspapers.

The demand for the British Government to take action on the alcoholism crisis has been taken up vigorously by several British medical journals. But like governments everywhere the British Government seems always to have more important crises than alcohol to wrestle with. It is not simply a matter of reluctance to deal with a question that will cost governments electoral support. Vested interests have become so entrenched that beverage alcohol has become seemingly invulnerable to assault or persuasion. France is a perfect example.

Several studies by French doctors had called attention to the serious cirrhosis problem of that country, where half the hospital beds were occupied by alcoholics and half the health costs of the nation were attributed to alcohol. But as a third of the French population depended on the grape for their livelihood, it was almost impossible to move any government to action.[10] In Britain, the loyalty of the citizenry to the pub style of leisure runs so deeply through the fabric of society that any government will meddle with it at their peril, regardless of the burgeoning gloom of the medical profession.

The vigor with which the British medical profession has been pushing their temperance proposals caught the attention of the Canadian Medical Association. At the CMA convention in 1981 it had a full debate on alcoholism in which it heard its Chairman of the

Council of Health Care, Dr. W. R. Ghent, declare that "alcohol has undoubtedly caused more real problems and human grief than any other drug that has ever afflicted mankind." In the end the convention fled for the hills with a resolution calling on Ottawa to appoint a Royal Commission to study the problem. Such an appointment should effectively dispose of the question for the 1980s at least.

Curiously enough, if the Canadian physicians had kept up with their reading they might have discovered that a Canadian colleague had anticipated the British study on the relationship of price to consumption by twenty years and reached the same conclusions. The study "Death by Liver Cirrhosis and the Price of Beverage Alcohol" was done by Dr. John R. Seeley of the Addiction Research Foundation and appeared in the *CMA Journal* of 24 December 1960. It was a superbly crafted study and it came at the time when cirrhosis of the liver was only beginning to attract the serious attention of the Canadian profession. That can be seen from the apologetic, almost timid, tone with which Seeley introduced his paper:

Any condition that causes death may well be of interest to physicians, no matter how relatively rare the prevalence. More particularly might they be interested if, simultaneously, prevalence were rising while measures, perhaps quite simple, to reduce these death rates appeared to be available. If, in addition, the measures suggested did not add to the workload of the already overburdened physician, they might well be as welcome as mosquito abatement in relation to yellow fever.

Liver cirrhosis as a cause of death may well be in this category. Its contribution to mortality is small, though not exactly trivial, in modern Western nations. In Canada, in the last 50 or 60 years we have seen rates as low as 5.2 per 100,000 adults and as high as 11.4. Deaths so attributed have also ranged from about one-quarter of one per cent to about two-thirds of one per cent of all mortality. Such mortality is roughly comparable with suicide, or leukemia.

If we restrict interest to the years 1921-56 for which the data are relatively reliable, we get an impression of a rather dramatic rise in the proportion of the general mortality attributed to liver cirrhosis — and this at a time when nutritional deficiencies (which are commonly thought to be a contributing cause) have been widely and steadily diminishing. The average annual increase in the relative rate has been about 4% of each preceding year.

Some forms of liver cirrhosis, and more particularly some cirrhosis of sufficient severity to be a cause of death, has long been widely spoken of as a "complication of alcoholism."

Given the fact, however, of a strong association between liver cirrhosis deaths and "alcoholism prevalence", we might well ask how close the association is between the death rate from cirrhosis and the consumption of beverage alcohol.

If, moreover, that association should prove to be close and positive, then an interest in economics or public health will prompt us to enquire further as to the dependence of alcohol consumption on the price of alcohol. It is into these two aspects that this paper is, more narrowly, to enquire.

In the body of this book statistics resort mainly to gross and net sales in dollars and volumes. Dr. Seeley's arithmetic was much more precisely detailed: he buried himself in the raw statistics and refined them down to their essence. He converted all the beverages into imperial gallons of absolute alcohol, showed the price as a percentage of the average adult's annual personal disposable income, and computed the average adult (over fifteen years) annual consumption in gallons of absolute alcohol. As the following table from his paper demonstrates, when prices rose consumption declined, when prices declined consumption rose. It was as perfect an example as could be drawn of the Adam Smith law of supply and demand working exactly as the classical economists insisted it had to work. But that was not the way cirrhosis of the liver worked. The drinkers who despite wartime rationing and all the trouble of getting possession of the stuff, used their rising wartime incomes to increase their consumption, and lapsed into alcoholism, were fifteen years later in the cirrhosis wards. The liver death rates did nothing but rise, regardless of price fluctuations.

The Addiction Research Foundation in 1978 found the relationships set forth by Dr. Seeley still applicable. By 1974 the price was down a further fifty percent from 1956, consumption was up fifty percent, and deaths from cirrhosis of the liver were up seventy-five percent. The striking, long-term consistency that Dr. Seeley discovered did not lead him to engrave any conclusions on

Canada — Average Standard Relative Price of Alcohol, Average Consumption of Alcohol and Average Adult Death Rate By Liver Cirrhosis*

Year	Price of alcohol†	Consumption of alcohol‡	Un-standardized liver cirrhosis death rates§	Year	Price of alcohol†	Consumption of alcohol‡	Un-standardized liver cirrhosis death rates§
1926	.047	.62	—	1942	.034	.91	72.60
1927	.049	.62	—	1943	.035	.98	71.10
1928	.037	.77	—	1944	.039	.82	69.13
1929	.041	.85	—	1945	.037	.94	72.31
1930	.042	.87	—	1946	.035	1.20	76.38
1931	.046	.76	—	1947	.033	1.33	79.09
1932	.049	.65	—	1948	.028	1.46	83.09
1933	.065	.46	—	1949	.030	1.41	87.78
1934	.065	.46	—	1950	.028	1.44	88.59
1935	.052	.56	64.34	1951	.025	1.47	87.90
1936	.049	.63	65.17	1952	.025	1.46	91.30
1937	.046	.67	64.86	1953	.028	1.44	96.33
1938	.044	.74	68.38	1954	.028	1.46	98.28
1939	.044	.70	69.94	1955	.026	1.39	100.30
1940	.040	.74	67.08	1956	.024	1.51	107.99
1941	.037	.82	68.55				

* The primary data upon which all rates shown in the table were based are to be found in *Statistics of Alcohol Use and Alcoholism in Canada, 1871-1956*. All liver cirrhosis death rates were corrected to allow for the effects of the Sixth Revision of the International Lists of Diseases and Causes of Death.
† Average price of an imperial gallon of absolute alcohol, shown as a fraction of average adult annual disposable personal income.
‡ Average consumption per "adult" (person 15 years of age or older) in imperial gallons of absolute alcohol.
§ Deaths attributed to liver cirrhosis, per 1,000,000 "adults" (person 20 years of age and over); centred two-year moving average.

stone, but it did lead him to a number of interesting speculations. What would happen, he wondered, if the government boosted the price of all beverage alcohol by twenty or thirty percent over an extended period of say three years? How much would it reduce consumption and the death rate from cirrhosis? And how much would it increase the liquor profits of the governments? Dr. Seeley presented the politicians with a proposal that was almost ideal from every angle. Raising the prices as he suggested would give them a chance to improve the public health while simultaneously increasing the flow of revenue into government coffers.

The Manitoba Ministerial Advisory Committee on Liquor Control, in its 1981 report,[11] examined the way in which the retail price of a bottle of Canadian rye was constructed:

Cost of liquor	$1.49
Freight	.10
Excise taxes	1.87
Federal Sales Tax 12%	.41
Commission mark-up	4.04
Prov. Sales Tax 10%	.79
Retail Price	$8.70

If the price were doubled — and thus raised to a point where it absorbed no more of the average Canadian's income than it had done twenty-five years ago — the components would be:

Cost of liquor	$ 1.49*
Freight	.10*
Excise taxes	1.87*
Federal Sales Tax	.41*
Commission mark-up	11.95
Prov. Sales Tax	1.58
Total	$17.40
* No change	

Supposing the commission had sold 1,000,000 bottles of rye at $8.70, the province's income from profit and sales tax would have been $4,830,000. But if it sold only 500,000 bottles at double the price its take would be $5,975,000. If it chose the course suggested by the Royal College of Physicians and tripled the selling price to $26.10, and consumption was reduced by 66%, the income of the province would be almost $7,000,000.

But the question posed by Dr. Seeley in 1960 — how big an increase in price would be required to halt the rise in consumption? — is still afloat in limbo. Nobody paid any attention to his proposal, then or since. Until some government screws up enough courage to test the waters of public opinion and public taste there is no way of knowing. Of this there is probably little doubt, the heavy drinkers, the six-pack a day beer drinkers and the four or five highballs a day liquor drinkers, will hardly be affected. They are in the process of building cirrhotic livers, are physically or mentally addicted, and, if a financial crunch comes with the increased cost, they will find some other expenditures to reduce. They always do.

For the rest of the population there is some doubt as to what the reaction would be. The Addiction Research Foundation recently conducted a rather extensive survey of public opinion.[12] There were 1,078 interviewees in the 1,484 Ontario households surveyed in 104 areas. The interviews lasted approximately an hour and a total of 800 interviews were used in the final processing of the answers.

The interviewees "were put in the picture" as far as the seriousness of the alcoholism problem was concerned and their own drinking habits canvassed. They were asked what their attitudes were toward present price levels and what they would be if the prices of all alcoholic beverages were raised to a level that would reduce the numbers of alcoholics in the next generation by half. The drinkers were asked if they would reduce their own consumption, how much more they would be willing to pay?

Of the 800 respondents, eighty-five percent of the sample said they were drinkers, half had a drink at least once a week, and eleven percent drank every day. About half the respondents were satisfied with present prices while the other half, mainly middle-aged and heavy drinkers, felt prices were already too high. Nevertheless, most drinkers (sixty-eight percent) expressed a willingness to pay more for alcoholic beverages if the long-term result were a decrease in the prevalence of alcoholism. About half those willing to pay more were willing to pay one or two dollars more a bottle or for a case of beer. Of the drinkers who answered, 60% agreed their own consumption would not be affected by increased prices, 31.5% said they would reduce their consumption, and 7.5% said they would stop drinking.

The researchers concluded that a substantial segment of the population would support any government which used increased prices to reduce alcoholism and that the number might be increased by a "sophisticated educational program."

One of the difficulties with public opinion polls about beverage alcohol is with definitions. The person who turns up in one poll as a drinker may be defined as an abstainer in another. In the Manitoba

Ministerial Advisory Committee 1981 report, drinkers are defined as people who have had at least one drink in the past year. That definition is also used in some of the studies done in the United States, but such definitions surely make mincemeat of rational defining of drinking people. A person who has a drink "at least once a year" is far more abstainer than drinker. A more logical and useful set of definitions was developed by Callahan, Cissin, and Crossley from their nationwide American survey in 1969.[13] They broke the population into five categories:

Abstainers:	do not drink as much as once a year or not at all	32%
Infrequent:	drinkers drink at least once a year but not as much as once a month	15%
Light drinkers:	drink at least once a month but typically no more than one or two drinks each time	28%
Moderate drinkers:	drink at least once a month but typically no more than three or four drinks on a single occasion	13%
Heavy drinkers:	drink every day with at least five or six drinks, or more on occasion	12%

A re-examination of the ARF figures in light of these classifications leads to some interesting speculations. In the ARF survey eighty-five percent were categorized as drinkers and fifteen percent as non-drinkers. Of the eighty-five percent who drank, thirty-two percent would oppose any increase in price to combat alcoholism. That percentage coincides with the total of the medium and heavy drinking groups of the American classification. A logical assumption would be that it was the once-a-week-and-less group who agreed to the price increase and the medium to heavy groups who did not. If the fifteen percent abstaining portion of the population is added to the approvers of price increases then there would be a solid seventy-three percent of the population for whom price increases would be acceptable. And that makes sense for what difference would a price increase, even a substantial price increase, mean to people whose drinking amounted to no more than a drink or two a month.

The Addiction Research Foundation has produced several monographs on increased alcohol consumption. Dr. Wolfgang Schmidt and Robert Popham, jointly, and Dr. R. G. Smart have advanced arguments for the reversal of the liberalization of liquor laws and both papers have argued strongly that retail liquor prices be tied to the inflating price structure. Studies of conditions in Holland, Finland, and Denmark have all identified the striking increase in consumption that has accompanied the steady reduction of liquor prices in terms of spendable income of the populations.[14] The policies advocated by the British medical profession are being echoed all across the European Common market in modified form.

The Manitoba Ministerial Advisory Committee recognized that a relationship existed between price and consumption and recommended that the Manitoba government tie its liquor prices to the Consumers Price Index. That index has of course lagged behind the growth in spendable family income, and in 1982 the policy comes too late. However, if the tying of the booze prices to the consumer index were done retroactively to 1970 when the drinking age limit was lowered it would raise the 1982 price of a bottle of liquor or a case of beer to around twelve dollars.

Such an increase would undoubtedly set off a roar of protest from the serious drinkers. But would it have a serious effect on consumptions? The odds are overwhelmingly against it because that twelve-dollar bottle would be less than the equivalent of an hour's work for skilled tradesmen in the Prairie cities, less than an hour's work, even, for many of the unskilled workers of civic engineering departments. To put the prices at a level where they would become equal impedimenta to consumption that prices were before the Second World War would require increases to around sixty dollars a bottle for liquor and perhaps fifty dollars a case for beer. Anyone who seriously advocated establishing such a price level would be laughed off the block.

But while the laughter dies away it might be instructive to have the concerned physicians, criminologists, sociologists, and biologists calculate what the ultimate human cost will be from not doing exactly that.

NOTES

Chapter One
EVERYBODY KNOWS THE TROUBLE WE SEE

1. W. E. Heitland, *The Roman Republic* (2 vols., Cambridge, 1923), Vol. 2, pp. 202 - 229.
2. *Journal of Studies on Alcohol* 39 (1978): 1887-94.

Chapter Two
PROHIBITION: THE FACTS AND THE MYTHOLOGY

1. *Booze*, (Toronto: Macmillan Co. of Canada, 1972), p. 89 et seq.
2. *The Autobiography of Lincoln Steffens*, (New York, Harcourt Brace, 1931).
3. Jess Carr, *The Second Oldest Profession.* (New York: Prentice Hall, 1972).
4. *English Social History* (London: Longman's, 1942), pp. 341-342.
5. Ruth E. Spence. *Prohibition in Canada* (Toronto: Dominion Alliance, 1919).

Chapter Three
BACK TO THE BOTTLE, RELUCTANTLY

1. Robert Craig Brown and Ramsay Cook. *Canada 1896-1921: A Nation Transformed* (Toronto: McClelland & Stewart, 1974), p. 294.

Chapter Nine
ALCOHOLICS ANONYMOUS, A PRAIRIE GROWTH INDUSTRY

1. *Quarterly Journal of Studies on Alcohol* (June 1955): 251.
2. *Current Biography* (New York: H. W. Wilson, 1947), p. 335.
3. *Journal of Clinical Investigation* 44 (1965): 1009, 1021.
4. New Haven College University Press, 1960.
5. *Quart. Jour. of Studies on Alcohol* 12, (1951): 601.

Chapter Ten
IF IT WERE A NEW DRUG, NO GOVERNMENT WOULD ALLOW IT

1. *Alcoholism Clinical and Experimental Research* 5, #1 (Jan. 1981): 1.
2. Vol. 197: 167.
3. (9 June): 1267; (3 Nov.): 999.
4. *Quarterly Journal on Inebriety* 27 (1905): 113.
5. (30 June 1962): 80.
6. (August 1962): 29.
7. *Canadian Medical Association Journal* 122 (22 Mar. 1975): 728.
8. Ibid.
9. Dr. Helen B. Taussig, "A Study of the German Outbreak of Phocomelia," *JAMA* (30 June 1962): 1109.
10. Dr. Helen B. Taussig, "The Thalidomide Syndrome," *Scientific American* (August 1962): 32.
11. *Lancet* (3 Nov. 1973): 1001.
12. F. A. Seixas. *Journal of Studies on Alcohol* 39 (6 June 1978): 982.
13. *Journal of Pediatrics* 92 (Jan. 1978): 64.
14. 47 #3 (July 1977): 422.
15. Dr. M. J. Ashley, *CMA Journal.*
16. Dr. G. I. Henderson *et al. Alcoholism: Clinical and Experimental Research* 3 #2 (April 1979): 99-105.
17. *Journal of Studies on Alcohol* 40, #1 (Jan. 1979): 111.
18. Conversations with the author.
19. Dr. H. A. Edmondson. "Pathology of Alcoholism," *American Journal of Clinical Pathology* 74 (1980): 725-742.
20. (10 Feb., 1979): 371.

Chapter Eleven
SO WHAT DO YOU SUGGEST?

1. *Current Biography* (1947), p. 335.
2. Speech to B'Nai Brith Jan. 1979. Calgary.
3. *Special Report on Alcohol Statistics*, Health and Welfare Canada, 1981, p. 4.
4. Ibid., p. 14.
5. Ibid., p. 5.
6. Gov't Liquor Boards statistics.
7. *Journal of Studies on Alcohol* 1974-5-6; *Report of Advisory Committee on Alcohol Control*, Manitoba, 1981, pp. 163-180.
8. J. deLint, *British Journal of Addiction* (1975): 3.
9. U. P. I. report in the *Calgary Herald*, 21 Mar. 1980: B15.

10. Jellinek, E. M. *Bracken Commission Report* (1955), pp. 201-206.

11. p. 161.

12. Goodstadt, Smart, Gilles. *Journal of Studies on Alcohol* 9 (1978): 1630.

13. Don E. Beauchamp, *International Journal of the Addictions* 11, #1 (1976): 41-52.

14. A. J. Van-den-Lempel "Alcoholic Taxation and Consumption Problems," *Journal of Studies on Alcohol*, abs. 613, 42 #4 (1981): 237.

INDEX

Addiction, 153, 186-87. *See also* Alcoholism

Advertising. *See* Liquor advertising

Alaska Highway, 78, 79

Alberta, 4, 9, 16, 20, 23, 25-26, 32, 37, 39, 40, 52, 59, 62, 65, 78, 80-81, 82, 87, 90, 101, 107, 108

Alberta Liquor Control Commission, 41-43, 49, 61, 68, 70, 97-99

Albertan, The, 43

Alcohol and the Fetus conference, 170

Alcohol consumption: and aggression, 8; and Indians, 17, 18, 19; and teenagers and under thirties, 2, 3, 5, 6, 9, 11, 103, 109-11, 178-83; and the over thirties, 9, 11; and women, 54-55, 88, 89-90, 95, 97, 99, 100, 107, 108-09, 110; city and country compared, 3; effect of cocktails, 54-55, 56-57; effect of fortified wines, 109; effect of population, 66, 109; effect of unopened bottle regulation, 83; in American colonies, 17; increases with availability, 67, 109, 111, 187; increases with low cost, 190-95; increasing statistics, 12, 177, 195; in cocktail bar era, 7, 108-09, 110; in the Depression, 68, 71; in Manitoba, 104; in Prohibition, 76; in Second World War, 76-92 *passim;* medical effects of, 10, 104-05; psychological effects of, 104-05; related to crime, 7, 73; religious attitudes to, 16-17; "social," 56-57, 178-80; social effects of, 8, 9, 12, 16

Alcoholics, 102, 107; in Canada, 177-78; Indian, 135-36; in Manitoba, 103; on Prairies, 10, 154-55. *See also* Alcoholism and Alcoholics Anonymous

Alcoholics Anonymous, 76, 137-55; on Prairies, 139, 143, 144, 147, 153-54; Twelve Steps, 142

Alcoholism, 103, 106; allergy concept of, 140-41, 151; and Indians, 122, 135-36; and stress, 177; as addiction, 151-52, 185; disease concept of, 103, 107, 138, 141, 142, 143, 147, 150-52, 186; drug treatment for, 152-53, 184; education, 181-82; Alcoholism Foundation of Alberta, 107, 146; Alcoholism Foundation of Manitoba, 6; genetic factor in, 11, 173-74, 181; indirect effects of, 10; in France, 106; in U.K., 177, 185-86; medical effects of, 10-11, 13, 16, 137, 138, 139, 148, 156, 175; psychological addiction, 135, 150, 154; related to general consumption rates, 187; social effects of, 16; statistics, 155, 177-78; teenage, 5; treatment centers, 103, 107, 134-35, 136, 144, 146-47, 181, 186

Alexander, Jack, 141, 145

American Journal of Orthopsychiatry, 167

American Medical Association, 147, 152; Journal of, 148, 160

Annabella Street, Winnipeg, 47, 51

Annals of the New York Academy of Science, 157

Antabuse (disulfiram), 152-53, 184
Anti-Saloon League, 137
Archibald, Dr. H. D., 144

Bacchanalia: history of, 1-2, 7; revisited
in Prairie Canada, 1-2, 5, 7, 9, 12
Ban-the-Bars crusade, 24, 30, 76, 185
Bars, closing of, 25-26
Battered children, 8, 12; wives, 10, 12,
176
Beer: alcoholic content of, 182; sales,
109, 112
Beer by the glass campaign, 39, 40, 53,
63, 73, 109
Beer parlors, 43, 44, 45, 46, 51, 53, 57,
88, 183; in Alberta, 57, 59; in
Manitoba, 57; in Saskatchewan, 59;
women barred from, 88, 89, 107
Belmont Rehabilitation Center, 146
Bennett, R. B., 52
Best, Dr. D. A., 148-49
Beynon, Frances, 31
Bird, Dr. Brian, 144
Bishop of Regina (R.C.), 25
Bland, Salem, 32, 33
Blatchford Airport, Edmonton, 80
Bonifaces, 21
Bootlegging, 15, 34, 37, 38, 39, 118,
127; in Alberta, 52-53; in Manitoba,
46-53 passim, 57. See also Prohibition
Boyle, J. R., 38, 39
Bracken, Premier John, 40, 63, 101
Bracken Commission, 101-12, 146
Brandon, 123, 144
British Columbia, 11, 25-26, 28, 29, 62
British Commonwealth Air Training
Scheme, 77-78, 80, 86
British Medical Journal, 148, 175, 177,
186
British North America (BNA) Act, 18,
20, 25
Bronfman, Harry, 27-28, 36, 70
Brown, R. C., 32
Brownlee, John, W. F., 52, 53, 59, 108
Buchman, Frank, 139

Calgary, 2-3, 5, 9, 20, 21, 42, 44, 45, 54,
79, 81, 110, 123, 132-33, 135, 145,
179, 182
Calgary Herald, 2, 25, 93, 97, 98, 100
Campbell, Premier Douglas, 100, 108
Canada Temperance Act (Scott Act),
18
Canadian Family Physician, 170
Canadian Foundation on Alcoholism
and Drug Dependencies, 155
Canadian Medical Association, 152,
188; Journal of, 170, 189
Capone, Al, 60
Carr, Jess, 16
Children in care, 10
China, 177
Cigarette smoking, 95, 110, 165, 170
Cirrhosis, 10, 11, 135, 148-49, 154, 155,
188, 189-91
Clarren, Dr. S. K., 166
Clear Lake National Park, 3
Cocktail bars, 96, 97, 99, 100, 106, 107,
108, 114
Cocktails, 54-55, 56-57
Cook, Ramsay, 32
Cotton, Dr. N. S., 173
Coulter, Garnet, 100
Crerar, Hon. T. A., 32
Crowsnest Pass, 38, 42
Crystal, George, 145

DeCarli, Dr. L. M., 149
deLint, J., 154, 187
Depression, The, 32, 55, 67-75 passim,
88, 94
Dinning, R. J., 43, 61, 64
Disease Concept of Alcoholism, The, 150
Distillation, 16
Divorce, 8, 12, 176
Dosman, Edgar J., 132
Drinking age, 5, 82, 98, 109, 110, 111,
178, 183, 195; in Alberta, 98; in
Saskatchewan, 5, 111, 183; in
Ontario, 183; in U.S., 183-84
Drunken and disorderly behavior, 12,
14, 16, 21, 26, 74, 87, 137-38
Drunken driving, 6, 9, 184-85;
fatalities, 111, 180, 184

Dunkin Act, 18
Dunning, C. A., 61, 63

Economic change. *See* Social and
    economic change
Edmonton, 20, 42, 44, 45, 48, 79, 80,
    89, 110, 145, 182
Edmonton Journal, 25, 43
Edwards, Henrietta, 179
Emerson, Dr. Haver, 104
English pubs, 34, 89, 183, 188
Estevan, 6

Fetal Alcohol Syndrome (FAS), 10-11,
    157-75, 180
First World War, 12, 20, 89
Foremost, Alberta, 42
Fort McLeod, 122, 129
France, alcohol consumption in, 98,
    106, 149, 188
Franchise for women, 25, 29
French Canada, 18

Gagnon, Joe, 50-51
Gangsters, 60
Ghent, Dr. W. R., 189
Gibson, Lorne, 8
Gin: history of, 17
Gordon, C. W., 32
Government liquor monopolies, 29, 33,
    39, 41, 93, 95, 99. *See also* Liquor
    commissions
Greenfield, Herbert, 63

Haag, Dr. H. B., 104
Heaney, E. J., 103
Henders, R. C., 32
Herschfield, Dr. Noel, 177
Holland, 17
Hospital admissions, 7, 103, 138, 144,
    176, 188
Hotels, 21-23; bars in, 21-23;
    ownership and the breweries, 108

Immigration, 20-21, 62
Indian Act, 116-18; and the Bands, 118;
    and the provinces, 117, 118

Indian Affairs, Department of, 120-21,
    122, 134, 135, 136
Indian Conditions: A Survey, 122
Indians: and alcohol, 102, 116-36, 174;
    and alcoholic treatment centers,
    134-35, 136; and biological effects of
    alcohol, 116; and cultural influences,
    124-25, 126, 128, 131; and education,
    123; and the law, 23-24, 127, 128-31;
    and medical effects of alcohol,
    117-18, 122, 134, 135, 136; and social
    effects of alcohol, 133-34, 136; and
    welfare, 121, 122, 126, 127, 135;
    income, 119-21, 122; in Alberta, 123,
    129, 131; in Manitoba, 123, 127, 131;
    in Saskatchewan, 127, 131;
    population, 119; 121; urban
    movement, 118-20, 121, 123, 124,
    125, 127, 131-33, 135. *See also*
    Alcoholism
Indians: The Urban Dilemma, 132
Influenza epidemic, 32
International Institute for Research on
    the Problems of Alcohol, 106
Interprovincial shipments of liquor. *See*
    under Liquor sales
Ivens, William, 32, 33

Jackson, Charles, 141
Jellinek, Dr. E. M., 102, 106, 107, 139,
    148, 150-51, 152, 153, 154, 155, 177
Johnson, Jack, 145
Johnson, Stuart D., 8
Johnson, Walter, 51
Jones, Dr. Kenneth, 157, 158, 164, 165,
    166
Journal of Pediatrics, 166
Journal of Studies on Alcohol, 171
Juba, Stephen, 93, 100
Jubinville, Monseigneur, 54

Kalispell, Montana, 3
Keewatin, 134
Kendall, Dr. R. E., 175, 185-87
Kennedy, Edward (journalist), 88
Kenora, Ontario, 122, 134, 135
Kitchen, A. J., 103

Lancet, 148, 157, 158, 170
Laurier, Sir Wilfrid, 20
Lawlessness, 2-4, 5, 6, 12, 73, 176
LeDain Commission, 110
Lederman, Dr. S., 187
Lemoine, Dr. P., 158
Lethbridge, 42, 48, 107, 122, 123, 129, 130, 145
Le'Heureux, Dr. Paul, 101, 106, 109
Lieber, Dr. C. S., 149, 156
Life Before Birth, 159
Linden, Rick, 8
Liquor advertising, 112-15, 188; Prairie Provinces compared, 112-13, 181
Liquor commissions, 40, 42, 43, 61, 62-63, 64, 68, 74-75, 114. *See also* under provincial titles and Government liquor monopolies
Liquor permits, 40, 41, 42, 43, 44, 57-58, 65-67, 68, 80-81, 84, 85, 86, 87
Liquor prices, 56, 91-92, 112, 187, 190-95; related to consumption, 190-95
Liquor rationing, 78, 81-82, 85, 86, 87
Liquor regulations, 80-92, 95-101, 106, 107, 108, 137, 182, 185, 186, 188, 195
Liquor sales: economic influences on, 67, 110-11; increase with availability, 67, 109, 111, 187, 190-95; in cocktail bar era, 108-09, 114; in Depression, 68-69, 70-71, 72-73; in Manitoba, 104; in Second World War, 85-87; interprovincial shipments, 25-27, 35, 37-38; mail order, 25-28, 35; on prescription, 36, 37, 41; post Second World War, 91; profits from, 62-63, 64, 65, 85, 115; related to population, 66, 109; restrictions, 40-41, 81-82, 85. *See also* Beer sales and Wine sales
Liquor stores, 40-43 *passim*, 46, 47, 55, 64, 80, 112, 114-15
The Lost Weekend, 141
Lougheed, Dr. Morley, 103
Louis XIV, 18
Loyal Temperance Legion, 34, 55

McCarthy, R. G., 151
McClung, Nellie, 31, 33, 179

McCrae, Clifford, 101
Macdonald Hotel, Edmonton, 44
McDowell, Jack, 93, 100
McKinney, Louise, 31, 179
McNaughton, Violet, 31
McNicholl, T. A., 159
Mail order liquor sales. *See under* Liquor sales
Manitoba, 3, 9, 16, 19, 20, 25, 32, 37, 39, 40-41, 48, 55, 65, 66, 74, 81, 82, 83, 87, 91, 99, 103-04, 108
Manitoba Alcoholism Foundation, 196
Manitoba Committee on Alcoholism, 103
Manitoba Free Press, 29
Manitoba Liquor Control Commission, 42, 48, 49, 61, 68, 70, 100, 103-04
Manitoba Ministerial Advisory Committee on Liquor Control, 192, 194, 195
Manning, E. C., 99, 107, 146
Marijuana, 4, 8-9, 110, 111
Marital breakdown, 103. *See also* Divorce
Maritimes, 11, 14, 19
Marlborough Hotel, Winnipeg, 102
Massachusetts Society for the Suppression of Intemperance, 17-18
Maybank, Ralph, 103
Mayflower, 17
Maykut, Dr. M. O., 170
Mental retardation, 170-72, 174. *See also* Fetal Alcohol Syndrome
Milland, Ray, 141
Mills, Robert (Assistant RCMP Commissioner), 3
Minnedosa, Manitoba, 144
Moderation Leagues, 28, 29, 33-35, 37, 38, 39, 46, 51, 59, 73
Montagu, Dr. M. F. A., 159, 160, 161
Moose Jaw, 47, 51, 54
Moose Mountain National Park, 3
Moral Rearmament Movement. *See* Oxford Group
Morals, 4, 110
Mormon religion, 38, 107
Morrison, Dr. A. B., 170
Moslem experience, 16-17, 106, 177

Murder, 9
Murphy, Emily, 31, 179

North West Mounted Police, 19
Northwest Territories, 19, 185
Northwest Territories Act, 19
Nova Scotia, 11
Numbers, problem of, 3-4, 6

Ontario, 11, 19, 25-26, 117, 154, 193
Ontario Addiction Research
    Foundation (ARF), 11, 134, 135, 144,
    147, 154, 156, 157, 170, 187, 189,
    190, 193, 194-95
Ontario Alcohol Research Foundation.
    See Ontario Addiction Research
    Foundation
Ontario Liquor Control Board, 144
Orgies, 1-2
Ottawa, 27, 110, 123
Oxford Group (formerly Moral
    Rearmament Movement), 139-40,
    141

Parlby, Irene, 31, 179
Parties, 2, 4, 5
Payday drunks, 21-23
Permissive society, 4, 110
Persons case, 179
Phocomelia. See Thalidomide
Pincock, Dr. T. Alex, 103, 109, 144,
    146, 147
Plebiscites, 14, 27, 28, 46, 59, 91, 102,
    106, 107, 127; of 1898, 20; of
    1915-16, 25; of October 1920, 15,
    27-28, 35, 39; of 1923, 15, 33, 35, 39,
    40, 42, 46; of 1924, 15, 33, 39, 46, 63;
    of June 1927 (Manitoba), 51, 53, 57;
    of 1934 (Saskatchewan), 57, 59; of
    October 1956 (Manitoba), 106
Pledge cards, 23
Police, 2-4, 5, 16, 176. See also Royal
    Canadian Mounted Police
Popham, Dr. R. E., 154, 195
Prescription sales. See under Liquor
    sales
Progressive Party, 32
Prohibition, 12, 14-31 passim; alcohol

consumption in, 26, 37; bootlegging
    in, 14, 26, 46-47, 48, 53, 63, 73, 95,
    127; Canadian (1916-23), 12, 14-29
    passim, 185, 179-80; contrasted with
    U.S., 14-15, 19, 26, 60, 73-74, 95-97,
    102, 127; crime statistics, 12, 14; in
    Europe, 17; in State of Maine, 18,
    19; in Northwest Territories, 19;
    social effects, 14-15
Prostitution, 47, 48, 51

Quarterly Journal of Studies on Alcohol,
    139, 148
Quebec, 11, 20

Rape, 6-7, 8; cases in Winnipeg, 8
Regina, 4, 20, 21, 89, 122, 123, 130,
    135, 182
Riley, Harold, 101
Riots, 2-3, 5
Roblin, Sir Rodmond, 31
Roosevelt, Franklin D., 74
Ross, Dr. J. Donovan, 107, 146
Rothstein, Nathan, 103
Royal Alexandria Hospital, Edmonton,
    7
Royal Canadian Mounted Police, 37,
    110, 127-31
Royal College of Physicians, 187

St. Boniface, 50, 51, 54, 144
St. James, Manitoba, 95
Salvation Army, 103, 122, 134, 135
Saskatchewan, 5, 10, 14, 16, 20, 25-26,
    36, 39, 40, 41, 65, 74, 80-81, 82, 87,
    101, 107, 108, 121
Saskatchewan Alcoholism
    Commission, 129, 146
Saskatchewan Indians Federated
    College, 123
Saskatchewan Liquor Commission, 30,
    61, 70
Saskatoon, 123, 132, 182, 185
Saturday Evening Post, 141
Schmidt, Dr. Wolfgang, 154, 155, 195
Scientific American, 160
Scotland, 187
Scott, Premier Walter, 25, 31, 32

Scott Act, *See* Canada Temperance Act
Seattle County Hospital, Washington, 157
Second Oldest Profession, The, 16
Second World War, The, 75-89
Seeley, Dr. John R., 189-91, 192
Sentencing, 6-7, 9, 50, 137, 184
Sherman, Hon. L. R., 6
Silkworth, Dr. William D., 140-41, 151
Smart, Dr. R. G., 195
Smith, A. E., 32, 33
Smith, Alfred E., 74
Smith, Dr. David W., 157, 158, 164, 165, 166
Smith, Dr. Robert, 139, 140, 141, 153
Social & economic change, 7, 12, 20-21, 30, 53-54, 84, 93-94, 96, 110, 111, 187
Social distress, 31, 32
Social reform movements, 31-32
Soldiers: effect on Prohibition plebiscites, 15, 29, 34; effect on liquor trade in Second World War, 76-80, 82-83; returning to the depression, 32
Stewart, Dr. David A., 143
Strachan, George, 146
Straus, R., 151
Streissguth, Dr. Ann Pytkowicz, 157, 167-68

Taussig, Dr. Helen, 160
Teenage drinking. *See under* Alcohol consumption and Alcoholism
Temperance and Moral Reform Society (Alberta), 23
Temperance movements, 17-18, 19, 26, 31, 73. *See also* Ban-the-Bars crusade and Women's Christian Temperance Union
Thalidomide, 160-64
Thatcher, Premier Ross, 121
Thomas, Lillian, 31
Toledo, Ohio, 140, 141
Toronto, 96
Trades union movement, 33, 55, 94
Traffic offenses, 6, 9, 11, 183. *See also* Drunken driving

"Treating," 23
Treatment centers, alcoholism. *See* Alcoholism

Ulleland, Dr. Christy, 157, 158, 159
Unemployment, 7, 32, 55, 67, 71, 84
Union Government Movement, 32
United Church of Canada, 33
United Farmers of Alberta, 24, 33, 39, 63; of Manitoba, 24; of Saskatchewan, 24
United States, 14-19 *passim,* 26, 59-60, 73-74, 110, 117, 183-84

Victoria Day, 3
Violence, 7-8, 12
Volstead Act, 27

Waddell, Dr. J. A., 104
War brides, 89
War Measures Act, 26, 32
Watson, M. S., 103
Waugh, W. D., 61
Welfare costs, 9, 16, 94, 121, 122
White, Jennie, 31
Whiteford, Jean, 101
Willard, Frances, 19
Wilson, William, 139, 140, 141, 144, 153
Wine sales, 109; and Indians, 128; removal of fortified wines, 183
Winnipeg, 5, 7, 20, 21, 31, 42, 46, 47, 49, 50, 51, 54, 55, 72, 88, 93, 99-100, 102, 110, 123, 130, 135, 144, 182, 184
Winnipeg Free Press, 127
Winnipeg Grain Exchange, 33, 48
Women and alcohol. *See under* Alcoholic consumption
Women in work force, 94-95, 110, 111
Women's Christian Temperance Union (WCTU), 19, 24, 28, 34, 81, 102, 103
Women's suffrage, 31. *See also* Franchise for women
Wood, Henry Wise, 33
Woodsworth, J. S, 32, 33

Yaffe, Dr. Sumner J., 161, 162
Yale Center for the Study of Alcohol, 102, 139
Yorkton, Saskatchewan, 4, 27-28, 70

ABOUT THE AUTHOR

James H. Gray was born in Whitemouth, Manitoba, in 1906. When he was fifteen, he was forced to drop out of the Winnipeg school system to help support his family. He worked at a variety of jobs until the effects of the depression added his name to the numbers on the unemployment relief rolls. During the early thirties he wrote articles on a freelance basis. In 1935 he joined the staff of the *Winnipeg Free Press*, thereby launching his career as a reporter. In later years he assumed the editorship of *Farm and Ranch Review*, and from 1958 until 1963 he directed the public relations department of Home Oil Co. in Calgary.

Retirement allowed James Gray the opportunity to pursue his interest in western Canadian social history. His impressive list of publications stands as testimony to the success of his efforts. His books include *The Winter Years*, 1966; *Men Against the Desert*, 1967; *The Boy from Winnipeg*, 1970; *Red Lights on the Prairies*, 1971; *Booze*, 1972; *The Roar of the Twenties*, 1975; *Troublemaker*, 1978; and *Boomtime*, 1979.